APPLE™ BASIC:
DATA FILE PROGRAMMING

More than a million people have learned to program, use, and enjoy microcomputers with Wiley paperback guides. Look for them all at your favorite bookshop or computer store:

BASIC, 2nd ed., Albrecht, Finkel, & Brown
BASIC for Home Computers, Albrecht, Finkel, & Brown
TRS-80 BASIC, Albrecht, Inman, & Zamora
More TRS-80 BASIC, Inman, Zamora, & Albrecht
ATARI BASIC, Albrecht, Finkel, & Brown
Data File Programming in BASIC, Finkel & Brown
Data File Programming for the Apple Computer, Finkel & Brown
ATARI Sound & Graphics, Moore, Lower, & Albrecht
Using CP/M, Fernandez & Ashley
Introduction to 8080/8085 Assembly Language Programming, Fernandez & Ashley
8080/Z80 Assembly Language, Miller
Personal Computing, McGlynn
Why Do You Need a Personal Computer? Leventhal & Stafford
Problem-Solving on the TRS-80 Pocket Computer, Inman & Conlan
Using Programmable Calculators for Business, Hohenstein
How to Buy the Right Small Business Computer System, Smolin
The TRS-80 Means Business, Lewis
ANS COBOL, 2nd ed., Ashley
Structured COBOL, Ashley
FORTRAN IV, 2nd ed., Friedmann, Greenberg, & Hoffberg
Job Control Language, Ashley & Fernandez
Background Math for a Computer World, 2nd ed., Ashley
Flowcharting, Stern
Introduction to Data Professing, 2nd ed., Harris

APPLE™ BASIC: DATA FILE PROGRAMMING

LEROY FINKEL
San Carlos High School

and

JERALD R. BROWN
Educational Consultant

1807 · 1982
175 YEARS OF PUBLISHING

John Wiley & Sons, Inc.

New York • Chichester • Brisbane • Toronto • Singapore

Publisher: Judy V. Wilson
Editor: Dianne Littwin
Composition and Make-up: Trotta Composition

Library of Congress Cataloging in Publication Data

Finkel, LeRoy.
    Apple BASIC, data file programming.

    (Wiley self-teaching guides)
    Includes index.
    1. Basic (Computer-program language) 2. Apple
computer—Programming. I. Brown, Jerald, 1940-
II. Title. III. Series: Self-teaching guide.
QA76.73.B3F52   001.64'24   81-13100
ISBN 0-471-09157-X

Printed in the United States of America

82 83 10 9 8 7 6 5 4 3 2 1

How To Use This Book

When you use the self-instruction format in this book, you will be actively involved in learning data file programming in APPLESOFT BASIC. Most of the material is presented in sections called frames, each of which teaches you something new or provides practice. Each frame also gives you questions to answer or asks you to write a program or program segment.

You will learn best if you actually write out the answers and try the programs on your APPLE II computer (with at least one disk drive). The questions are carefully designed to call your attention to important points in the examples and explanations and to help apply what is being explained or demonstrated.

Each chapter begins with a list of objectives — what you will be able to do after completing that chapter. At the end of each chapter is a self-test to provide valuable practice.

The self-test can be used as a review of the material covered in the chapter. You can test yourself immediately after reading the chapter. Or you can read a chapter, take a break, and save the self-test as a review before you begin the next chapter. At the end of the book is a final self-test to assess your overall understanding of data file programming.

This book is designed to be used with an APPLE computer close at hand. What you learn will be theoretical only until you actually sit down at a computer and apply your knowledge "hands-on." We strongly recommend that you and this book get together with a computer! Learning data file programming in BASIC will be easier and clearer if you have regular access to a computer so you can try the examples and exercises, make your own modifications, and invent programs for your own purposes. You are now ready to teach yourself to use data files in BASIC.

Preface

This text will teach you to program data files in APPLESOFT BASIC. As a prerequisite to its use, you should have already completed an introductory course or book in BASIC programming and be able to read program listings and write simple programs: This is not a book for the absolute novice in BASIC. You should already be comfortable writing your own programs that use statements including string variables, string functions, and arrays. We do start the book with a review of statements that you already know, though we cover them in more depth and show you new ways to use them.

The book is designed for use by readers who have little or no experience using data files in BASIC (or elsewhere, for that matter). We take you slowly and carefully through experiences that "teach by doing." You will be asked to complete many programs and program segments. By doing so, you will learn the essentials and a lot more. If you already have data file experience, you can use this book to learn about data files in more depth.

The particular data files explained in this text are for APPLESOFT BASIC. Data files in other versions of BASIC will be similar, but not identical, to those taught in this book.* You will find this book most useful when used in conjunction with the reference manual for your computer system.

Data files are used to store quantities of information that you may want to use now and later; for example, mailing addresses, numeric or statistical information, or tax and bookkeeping data. The examples presented in this book will help you use files for home applications, for home business applications, and for your small business or profession. When you have completed this book, you will be able to write your own programs, modify programs purchased from commercial sources, and adapt programs using data files that you find in magazines and other sources.

*For programming data files in TRS-80 BASIC, MICROSOFT BASIC-80, and Northstar BASIC, read our other book, *Data File Programming in BASIC,* Finkel, LeRoy and Brown, Jerald R., John Wiley & Sons, Inc., Self-Teaching Guide, N.Y., 1981.

Contents

CHAPTER ONE

Writing **BASIC Programs for Clarity, Readability, and Logic**

Objectives: When you have completed this chapter you will be able to:

1. describe how a program can be written using a top-to-bottom format.
2. write an introductory module using REMARK statements.
3. describe seven rules to write programs that save memory space.

INTRODUCTION

This text will teach you to use data files in APPLESOFT BASIC. You should have already completed an introductory course or book in BASIC programming, and be able to read program listings and write simple programs. This is not a book for the absolute novice in BASIC, but is for those who have never used data files in BASIC (or elsewhere, for that matter). The particular data files explained in this text are for the APPLE II computer and the BASIC languages found on it.

Data files in other versions of BASIC and for other computers will be similar, but not identical, to those in this book. (If you are using a computer other than the APPLE II, you may want to read *Data Files Programming in BASIC,* available at your local computer store or bookstore.) You will find this text most useful when used in conjunction with the APPLE II reference manuals and the Disk Operating System (DOS) Manual: It is not a substitute for your careful reading of the APPLE II DOS Manual, though the workings of sequential and random access files are explained here in far more depth and with more examples.

Since it is assumed you have some knowledge of programming in BASIC and have practiced by writing small programs, the next step is for you to begin thinking about program organization and clarity. Because data file programs can become fairly large and complex, the inevitable debugging process — making the program actually work — can be proportionately complex. Therefore, this chapter is important to you because it provides some program organization methods to help make your future programming easier.

THE BASIC LANGUAGE

The computer language called BASIC was developed at Dartmouth College in the early 1960s. It was intended for use by people with little or no previous computer experience who were not necessarily adept at mathematics. The original language syntax included only those functions that a beginner would need. As other colleges, computer manufacturers, and institutions began to adopt BASIC, they added embellishments to meet their own needs. Soon BASIC grew in syntax to what various sources called Extended BASIC, Expanded BASIC, SUPERBASIC, XBASIC, BASIC PLUS, and so on. Finally, in 1978 an industry standard was developed for BASIC, but that standard was for only a "minimal BASIC," as defined by the American National Standards Institute (ANSI). Despite the ANSI standard, today we have a plethora of different BASIC languages, most of which "look alike," but each with its own special characteristics and quirks.

In the microcomputer field, the most widely used versions of BASIC were developed by the Microsoft Company and are generally referred to as MICROSOFT BASICs. These BASICs are available on a variety of microcomputers but, unfortunately, the language is implemented differently on each computer system. The APPLE version of MICROSOFT BASIC is called APPLESOFT.

The programs and runs shown in this text were actually performed on an APPLE II and an APPLE II PLUS computer using Disk Operating System (DOS) 3.3. (They will work in DOS 3.2, as well.) We wrote all of our programs using APPLESOFT BASIC. To use the programs in INTEGER BASIC, you will have to make the usual APPLESOFT to INTEGER modifications described in your reference manual. The file commands described in this text may be used in APPLESOFT or INTEGER BASIC. For INTEGER BASIC you may have to modify the file input and output statements, as described in your DOS Manual.

Where possible, we use BASIC language features that are common to all versions of BASIC, regardless of manufacturer. We do not attempt to show off all of the bells and whistles found in APPLESOFT BASIC, but rather to present easy-to-understand programs that will be readily adaptable to a variety of computers.

THE BASIC LANGUAGE YOU SHOULD USE

Conservative Programming

Since you will now be writing longer and more complex programs, *you should adopt conservative programming techniques so that errors will be easier to isolate and locate.* (Yes, you will still make errors. We all do!) This means that you should NOT use all the fanciest features available in APPLESOFT BASIC until you have tested the features to be sure they work the way you think they work. Even then, you still might decide against using the fancy features, many of which relate to printing or graphic output and do not work the same on other computers. Some are special functions that simply do not exist on other computers. Leave them out of your programs unless you feel you must include them. *The more conservative your programming techniques, the less chance there is of running into a software "glitch."*

This chapter discusses a program format that, in itself, is a conservative programming technique.

One reason for conservative programming is that your programs will be more portable or transportable to other computers. "Why should I care about portability?" you ask. Perhaps the most important reason is that you will want to trade programs with friends. But do all of your friends have a computer IDENTICAL to yours? Unless they do, they will probably be unable to use your programs without modifying them. Conservative programming techniques will minimize the number of changes required.

Portability is also important for your own convenience. The computer you use or own today may not be the one you will use one year from now; you may replace or enhance your system. In order to use today's programs on tomorrow's computer be conservative in your programming.

> Use conservative programming to:
> - Isolate and locate errors more easily.
> - Avoid software "glitch."
> - Enhance portability.

WRITING READABLE PROGRAMS

Look at the sample programs throughout this book and you will see that they are easy to read and understand because the programs and the individual statements are written in simple, straight-line BASIC code without fancy methodology or language syntax. It is as if the statements are written with the READER rather than the computer in mind.

Writing readable BASIC programs requires thinking ahead, planning your program in a logical flow, and using a few special formats that make the program listing easier to the eye. If you plan to program for a living, you may find yourself bound by your employer's programming style. However, if you program for pleasure, adding readable style to your programs will make them that much easier to debug or change later, not to mention the pride inherent in trading a clean, readable program to someone else.

A readable programming style provides its own documentation. Such self-documentation is not only pleasing to the eye, it provides the reader/user with sufficient information to understand exactly how the program works. This style is not as precise as "structured programming," though we have borrowed features usually promoted by structured programming enthusiasts. *Our format organizes programs in MODULES, each module containing one major function or program activity.* We also include techniques long accepted as good programming, but for some reason forgotten in recent years. Most of our suggestions do NOT save memory space or speed up the program run. Rather, readability is our primary concern, at the expense of memory space. Later in this chapter, we will present some procedures to shorten and speed up your programs. Modular style programs will usually be better running programs and will effectively communicate your thought processes to a reader.

THE TOP-TO-BOTTOM ORGANIZATION

When planning your program, think in terms of major program functions. These might include some or all of the functions from this list:

```
DATA ENTRY
DATA ANALYSIS
COMPUTATION
FILE UPDATE
EDITING
REPORT GENERATION
```

Using our modular process, divide your program into modules, each containing one of these functions. Your program should flow from module one to module two and continue to the next higher numbered module. *This "top-to-bottom organization" makes your program easy to follow.* Program modules might be broken up into smaller "blocks," each containing one procedure or computation. The size or scope of a program block within a module is determined by the programmer and the task to be accomplished. Block style will vary from person to person, and perhaps from program to program.

```
USE A MODULAR FORMAT AND TOP-TO-BOTTOM APPROACH
```

REMARK Statements

Separate program modules and blocks from each other using REMARK statements or nearly blank program lines. In general, programs designed for readability make liberal use of REMARK statements, but don't be overzealous. A nearly blank program line can be created by typing a line number followed by a colon (150:). A line number followed by REM (150 REM) can also be used.

```
100   REM     DATA ENTRY MODULE
110   REM **** READ DATA FROM DATA STATEMENTS 9000-9090
120
130   REM
200   REM     COMPUTATION MODULE
210   REM ARK
```

(Note: Your Apple computer will split the word REMARK into two words, as shown in line 210. Because this looks awkward, we encourage use of the word REM in place of the complete word.)

Begin each program module, block, or subroutine with an explanatory REM statement (line 100 and 110) and end it with a nearly blank line (line 120) or blank REM statement (line 130) indicating the end of the section.

Consistency in your use of REMs enhances readability. Use either REM or the nearly blank line with a colon, but be consistent. Some writers use the asterisks (****) shown in line 110 to set off REM statements containing actual remarks from blank REM statements; others use spaces four to six places after the REM before they add a comment (line 200). Both formats effectively separate REM statements from BASIC code.

You can place remarks on the same line as BASIC code using multiple statement lines, but be sure your REM is the LAST statement on the line. Such "on-line" remarks can be used to explain what a particular statement is doing. A common practice is to leave considerable space between an on-line remark and the BASIC code, as shown below.

```
220  LET C(X) = C(X) + U: REM ***COUNT UNITS IN C ARRAY

240  LET T(X) = T(X) + C(X): REM ***INCREASE TOTALS ARRAY
```

Using REMs to explain what the program is doing is desirable, but don't overuse it. (LET C = A + B does not require a REM or explanation!) REM should add information, not merely state an obvious step.

Like everything else said in these first chapters, there will be exceptions to what we say here. Keep in mind that we are trying to get you to think through your programming techniques and formats a little more than you are probably accustomed to doing. Thus, our suggested "rules" are just that — suggestions to which there will be exceptions.

GOTO STATEMENTS

Perhaps the most controversial statement in the BASIC language is the unconditional GOTO statement. Its use and abuse causes more controversy than any other statement. Purists say you would NEVER use an unconditional GOTO statement such as GOTO 100. A more realistic approach suggests that all GOTOs and GOSUBs go DOWN the page to a line number larger than the line number where the GOTO or GOSUB appears. This is consistent with the "top-to-bottom" program organization. This same approach—down the page—also applies to using IF. . .THEN statements (there will be obvious exceptions to this rule).

```
140   GOTO 210
150   IF X < Y THEN 800
160   GOSUB 8000
```

A final suggestion: A GOTO, GOSUB, or IF. . .THEN should not go to a statement containing *only* a REM. If you or the next user of your program run short of memory space you will delete extra REM statements. This, in turn, requires you to change all of your GOTO line numbers, so plan ahead first. Some BASICs do not even allow a program to branch to a statement starting with REM.

Bad	Good

```
      Bad                          Good

150   GOTO 300              150   GOTO 300

300   REM      DATA ENTRY   299   REM      DATA ENTRY
310   INPUT "ENTER NAME:";N$ 300   INPUT "ENTER NAME:";N$
```

A FORMAT FOR THE INTRODUCTORY MODULE

The first module of BASIC code (lines 100 through 199 or 1000 through 1999) should contain a brief description of the program, user instructions when needed, a list of all variables used, and the initialization of constants, variables, and arrays.

The very first program statement should be a REM statement containing the program name. Carefully choose a name that tells the reader what the program does, not just a randomly selected name. After the program's name comes the author's or programmer's name and the date. For the benefit of someone else who may like to use your program, include a REM describing the computer system and/or software system used when writing the program. Whenever the program is altered or updated, the opening remarks should reflect the change.

```
100   REM      PAYROLL SUBSYSTEM
110   REM      COPYRIGHT CONSUMER PROGRAMMING CORP. 9/82
120   REM
130   REM      HP 2000 BASIC
140   REM      MODIFIED FOR APPLESOFT BASIC BY J. BROWN
150   REM      ON APPLE II, 48K
```

Follow these remarks with a brief explanation of what the program does, contained either in REM statements or in PRINT statements. Next add user instructions. For some programs you might offer the user the choice of having instructions printed or not. If instructions are long, place the request for instructions in the introductory module and the actual printed instructions in a subroutine toward the end of your program. That way, the long instructions will not be listed each time you LIST your program.

```
170   REM      THIS PROGRAM WILL COMPUTE PAY AND PRODUCE PRINTED PAYROLL
180   REM      REGISTER USING DATA ENTERED BY OPERATOR
190   REM
200   INPUT "DO YOU NEED INSTRUCTIONS?";R$
210   IF R$ = "YES" THEN  GOSUB 800
220   REM
```

Follow the description/instructions with a series of statements to identify the variables, string variables, arrays, constants, and files used in the program. Again, these statements communicate information to a READER, making it that much easier for you or someone else to modify the program later. We usually complete this section AFTER we have completed the program so we don't forget to include anything.

Assign a variable name to all "constants" used. Even though a constant will not change during the run of the program, a constant may change values between runs. By assigning it a variable name, you make it that much easier to change the value;

that is, by merely changing one statement in the program. It is a good idea to jot down notes while writing the program so important details do not slip your mind or escape notice. When the program has been written and tested (debugged), go back through it, bring your notes up-to-date, and polish the descriptions in the REMs.

```
220  REM     VARIABLES USED
230  REM       G=GROSS PAY
240  REM       N=NET PAY
250  REM       T1=FEDERAL INCOME TAX
260  REM       T2=STATE INCOME TAX
270  REM       F=SOC.SEC.TAX
280  REM       D=DISABILITY (SDI) TAX
290  REM       X,Y,Z=FOR-NEXT LOOP CONTROL VARIABLE
300  REM       H(X)=HOURS ARRAY
310  REM       N$=EMPLOYEE NAME (20 CHAR)
320  REM       PN$=EMPLOYEE NO. (5 CHAR)
330  REM
340  REM     CONSTANTS
350  LET FR = .0613: REM    SOC.SEC. RATE
360  LET DR = .01: REM    SDI RATE
370  REM
380  REM     FILES USED
390  REM       ITM=FEDL. TAX MASTER FILE
400  REM       STM=STATE TAX MASTER FILE
410  REM
```

(Notice the method used to indicate string length in lines 310 and 320.)
(Notice the use of on-line remarks in lines 350 and 360.)

The final part of the introductory module is the initialization section. In this section, dimension the size of all single and double arrays and all string arrays, even though DIMENSION is not required by your computer. This is valuable information for a reader. Any variables that need to be initialized to zero should be done here for clear communication, even though your computer initializes all variables to zero automatically. This section also includes any user-defined functions *before* they are used in the program.

```
410  REM     INITIALIZE
420  :
430  DIM H(7),R(10,13),N$(30)
440  :
450  REM
```

THE MODULES THAT FOLLOW THE INTRODUCTION

The remainder of your program consists of major function modules and subroutines (and DATA statements, when they are used). Remember to separate each module from others by a blank line REM statement and a remark identifying the module. These modules can be further divided into user-defined program blocks, each separated by a blank line REM statement.

A typical second module would be for data entry. Data can be operator-entered from the keyboard or entered directly from DATA statements, a file, or some other device. Chapter 3 discusses in detail how to write data entry routines with extensive error-checking procedures to ensure the accuracy and integrity of each data item entering the computer.

For now, we suggest that you write data entry routines so that even a completely inexperienced operator would have no trouble entering data to your program. This means the operator should ALWAYS be prompted as to what to enter and provided with an example when necessary.

```
240 INPUT "ENTER TODAY'S DATE (MM/DD/YY)";D$
```

If data are entered from DATA statements, place the DATA statements near the end of your program (some suggest even past the END statement) using REM statements to clearly identify the type of data and the order of placement of items within the DATA statements.

```
9400  REM    DATA FOR CORRECT ANSWER ARRAY IN QUESTION NUMBER ORDER.
9410  REM    10 ANSWERS, MULT.CHOICE 1-5
9420  :
9430  DATA   4,5,1,3,2,1,1,4,4,5
9440  :
9450  REM    RESPONDENTS ANSWERS TO QUIZ
9460  REM    DATA STATEMENT FORMAT:
9470  REM    RESP. ID # FOLLOWED BY 10 RESPONSES TO QUIZ QUESTIONS
9480  :
9490  DATA   17642, 4,5,1,3,2,2,1,4,4,4
9500  DATA   98126, 3,5,2,3,2,1,5,4,5,2
9560  :
```

You can think of DATA statements as comprising a separate program module. The "inbetween" program modules might do computations, data handling, file reading and writing, and report writing. Modular programming style dictates that all printing and report generation, except error messages, be done in one program module labeled as such. This limits the use of PRINT statements to one easy-to-find location within your program. (There might be more than one print module.) This makes it that much easier for you to make subsequent changes on reports when paper forms change or new reports are designed. In the print module your program should NOT perform any computations except trivial ones. Make important computations BEFORE the program executes the print module(s). This may require greater use of variables and/or arrays to "hold" data pending report printing, but your programs will be much cleaner and easier to debug, since everything will be easy to find in its own "right" place.

SUBROUTINES

Program control flows smoothly from one module to the next. A well-designed module has *one* entry point at its beginning and *one* exit point at its end. The exception to this is a mid-module exit to a subroutine.

```
290  :
300  REM     COMPUTATION MODULE
310  :
320  LET T = (V * X) / Q
330  LET T9 = T9 + T
340  GOSUB 800
350  :
360  REM     REPORT PRINTING MODULE
370  :
```

A subroutine exit from a module always RETURNs to the next statement in the module. The use of subroutines is desirable provided you don't overdo it. Some program stylists recommend that the entire main program consist of nothing but GOSUB statements "calling up" a series of subroutines located later in the program. Such a technique is probably guilty of overkill. Strive for a happy medium between the two extremes of no subroutines and nothing but subroutines.

Technically, you need use a subroutine only to avoid duplicating the same program statements in two or more places in your program. A subroutine should be called from MORE than one place in your program. Otherwise, why use a formal subroutine? Program stylists now agree that subroutines enhance readability and clarity and can be used at the convenience of the programmer (you!). However, again the caution — don't overdo it. Use subroutines to enhance the flow and readability of your program. Stylists also agree that subroutines should be clearly identified using REM statements and set off from other program sections with blank REM statements. Program stylists disagree, however, on where to place the subroutines. There are two schools of thought. Placement of subroutines can be either immediately past the end of the module that calls the subroutine or in one common module toward the end of the program.

EITHER

```
300   REM      COMPUTATION MODULE
310   :
320   :
330   GOSUB 410
340   GOSUB 460

          :
          :
          :

400   REM      NUMBER CONVERSION SUBROUTINE
410   :

          :
          :

450   REM      COMPUTATION SUBROUTINE
460   :
          :
```

OR

```
330   GOSUB 810
340   GOSUB 910

          :
          :
          :

800   REM      NUMBER CONVERSION SUBROUTINE
810   :

          :
          :

900   REM      COMPUTATION SUBROUTINE
910   :
          :
```

JUST FOR LOOKS

You can do a host of things to your programs to enhance looks and clarity. These techniques are generally called "prettyprinting." Your Apple computer automatically performs many "prettyprinting" activities. All statement lines are evenly spaced. Extra spaces are added to BASIC statements to enhance readability of your program, even if you type the statements with no spaces at all. In fact, extra spaces that you typed accidentally—or on purpose—may be deleted automatically by your Apple computer.

Spacing

One way to make your programs look nice is to use line numbers of equal length throughout the program. If your program is small, use line numbers 100 through 999. If long, start the program at 1000 and continue to 9999. When your program is listed, it will be aligned neatly. It also improves the appearance if the entire program is incremented by steps of ten. Without a resequence command this is virtually impossible to do. A partial solution is to enter statements in sequence increments of ten when you first enter your program. When you have completed the program, even with changes, MOST of the program will still be in increments of ten. Learn how to use the RENUMBER program that is provided on your Apple System Master diskette. The RENUMBER INSTRUCTION PROGRAM will teach you how to renumber programs and program parts in "prettyprinting."

Other Techniques To Enhance Looks and Readability

You can do still more to make your program clearer to you and another reader. These few ideas are the "finishing touches."

Using the LET statement, even when unnecessary, enhances readability. The absence of LET can be confusing, especially in a multiple-statement line.

CONFUSING

```
260 X = Y:C = X * Y: IF X = N THEN X = C
```

BETTER

```
140  LET X = 0:Y = 0:C = 0
```

BEST

```
260  LET X = Y: LET C = X * Y: IF N = X THEN  LET X = C
```

Arrange BASIC statements so that they read smoothly from left to right, just as the readers' eyes flow across the paper. This includes placing A before B and 1 before 2. Some stylists recommend that in IF. . .THEN statements, you place the least varying variable last, as shown in lines 270 and 300 below.

```
150   READ A,B,C
        ⋮

260   FOR X = 1 TO 8
270   IF M(X) < > N THEN 290
280   LET M(X) = N
290   NEXT X
300   IF D$ = "STOP" THEN 999
```

If your typed statement is long, it is probably confusing, especially if it is a mathematical equation. Break it into two or more pieces so it is easy to read. Read the statements aloud to test their readability.

CONFUSING

```
250   LET T = (N * 3.75) + ((N - 40) * 3.25) + ((N - 60) / 3) / ((D * N) * A)
```

CLEARER

```
250   LET T = (N * 3.75) + ((N - 40) * 3.25)
260   LET T = T + ((N - 60) / 3) / ((D * N) * A)
```

UNDOING IT ALL TO SAVE SPACE AND SPEED UP RUN TIME

After reading all these rules and ways to enhance readability, you are probably wondering how you will remember them all. Chances are you won't, but we hope we have at least sensitized you to the need for writing clear, readable programs. You will adopt your own typing style based on some of these techniques, plus others that you devise for convenience.

Nearly every technique illustrated in this chapter uses what some would consider to be unnecessary memory space. You may in fact find that your computer memory is filled before you have completely entered your program. When this happens, either rethink your entire problem-solving technique or look for ways to save memory space by making changes to your program. A well-written, readable program takes up more memory space than a poorly written, less readable program. Thus, to save memory space, you may have to undo some of the things you did to enhance readability.

To save large numbers of memory "bytes:"

1. Use multiple statements per line.
2. Delete all REM statements beginning with the introductory module.

For further space saving:

1. Use one-letter variable names.
2. Delete unnecessary parentheses.
3. Reuse variables when possible (normally a terrible technique).
4. Dimension arrays sparingly.
5. Use GOTO, not GOSUB, for a routine accessed from only one place in a program.

If you are concerned about the speed of your program run, you can use some techniques to shave microseconds, even seconds, off the run time. Some of these overlap with the space-saving techniques.

1. Delete all REMs and/or move the introductory module to the end.
2. Use multi-statement lines.
3. Use variables rather than constants (as recommended earlier).
4. Define the most commonly used variables first.
5. Place subroutines before the main program.
6. Use FOR NEXT loops whenever possible.
7. Remove extra parentheses.
8. Limit the use of GOSUBs.

Remember, these techniques may speed up your run, but they are generally considered to be bad programming techniques and contrary to nearly everything said in this chapter.

To save space and lessen distraction we have not followed ALL the rules suggested in this chapter in the rest of this book. However, you will still find our programs easy to read and self-documenting.

CHAPTER 1 SELF–TEST

1. Will a useful program written in BASIC on one computer system also RUN on a different brand of computer that uses BASIC? Why or why not?

_____

_____

_____

2. How can you be most certain that a program you write will also run on another person's computer?

_____

_____

_____

3. What is meant by the portability of a computer program?

_____

_____

_____

4. Name at least three types of information to include in REM statements in a program's introductory module.

    _____

    _____

    _____

5. Describe the "top-to-bottom format" for organizing programs.

    _____

    _____

    _____

    _____

6. When branching statements such as GOTO and GOSUB are used, what statements should not be branched to and why?

    _____

    _____

    _____

7. Define "initializing."

    _____

    _____

    _____

8. What is the most important reason for designating a segment of a program as a subroutine accessed by GOSUB?

    _____

    _____

    _____

9. When writing a self-documenting, easy to read program, what sacrifices are made?

    _____

    _____

10. In a multiple statement line with three statements, the first being a REM statement, how many statements will be executed?

    _____

    _____

Answer Key

1. The program might not run on a different brand of computer, because different computers use different versions of BASIC.

2. Use conservative programming techniques and the least fancy statements in your version of BASIC.

3. Portability means that the program is likely to run on many computers with few or no modifications.

4. Variables used and what they stand for, files used, descriptive name for program, description of program if necessary, author of program, last revision of program, version of BASIC and/or system used. (any three answers)

5. To the extent possible, the program is written so that it begins execution at the smallest line number and procedes toward the largest, with a minimum of confusing branching within the program.

6. REM statements, in case they are removed from a program to save computer memory space.

7. The first time in a program that value(s) are assigned to variables or elements in an array (often means assignment of zeros); DIMENSIONING where needed.

8. The segment would otherwise have to be repeated because it is used more than once in executing the program.

9. Amount of memory used and possibly speed of program execution.

10. None. The computer goes on to the next line numbered statement if it sees that the first statement in the line is a REM.

CHAPTER TWO

An Important Review of BASIC Statements

Objectives: To review important aspects of BASIC. When you finish this chapter, you will be able to write BASIC statements using: LET, READ, DATA, INPUT, IF. . .THEN, FOR NEXT. GOSUB, RETURN, ON. . .GOTO, LEN, ASC, MID$, LEFT$, RIGHT$, and ONERR. .GOTO.

INTRODUCTION

We assume you have used BASIC to write programs and that you can read and understand a listing of a BASIC program (are you BASICly literate?); this information serves as a review. Many of the programming techniques in this and the next chapter will be used over and over again in programming data files. Even masters at programming in BASIC should give the material a quick run through. This is important information and skill to have under your belt so that you can give your fullest attention to learning file-handling BASIC statements and techniques in Chapter 4.

VARIABLE NAMES

In early versions of BASIC, the names you could choose for a variable were limited to one letter, or one letter and one number only. A, A1, Z7, Z∅, B$, and B1$ were all acceptable variable names: while AA, A25, SALARY, or NAME$ were unacceptable to the computer. In contrast, APPLESOFT BASIC and other new dialects of BASIC permit the use of multi-letter variable names. The unacceptable variable names mentiones above are all acceptable in APPLESOFT BASIC, as are NETPAY, GUESS, OLDNAME$, and many others you may think of. The temptation to use long variable names may be overwhelming, but beware! APPLESOFT *BASIC recognizes and identifies the variable using only the first two letters of the variable name.* Thus, the variables SALES and SALARY are not really two variables, but rather *one* – SA. PAYMENT and PAYROLL are also really the same variable – PA – in APPLESOFT BASIC. Be extremely cautious selecting variable names to avoid unusual errors that are hard to detect. Also note that longer variable names take up more computer memory space, which may become a problem as the programs you write become longer and more complex.

Another limitation when using long variable names is that you cannot use a combination of letters that are also used for a BASIC statement, command, or function. A Reserved Word List in your reference manual tells you which words cannot be a part of a long variable name. Examples are:

> FOR, DATA, NOT, LIST, PRINT, DIM, IF, THEN

Use of simple variable names (A, T1, Y$) precludes having to debug a program when the problem is a reserved word accidentally used (embedded) in a long variable name. Notice in our examples, that even with simple variables we have selected names that are more likely to be remembered and make sense to someone reading the program. We encourage you to do the same. Use T for total, T9 for grand total, S for salary, N$ for name, etc.

The letters O and I are poor variable names since they are easily confused with the number $\emptyset$ (zero), the number 1 (one), or the lower case letter l (el). Some experienced programmers reserve a few variables and use them the same way in all programs they write. X, Y, and Z are popular as control variables in FOR NEXT loops. K and C are popular for counting in statements like LET C = C + 1.

Variables, also called variable names or labels, identify for the computer a particular place in its memory where information is stored. The information may be numeric (a value) or alphanumeric (a string, discussed more fully later). A value or string is first stored by an assignment statement (LET, READ, INPUT), and subsequent references to the variable tell the computer to use the value or string assigned to (and identified by) that variable. Assignment statements are included in this review of BASIC.

(a)   Give two reasons for using simple variable names such as A, X3, and Y$.

_____

_____

_____

_____

_____

_____

_____

– – – – – – – – – – – – – – – –

(a)   1. Conserves computer memory space.
      2. No reserved words are accidentally embedded in the variable.
      3. Portability of programs between different versions of BASIC.
          (any two answers)

String Variables

The rules for constructing names for string variables are the same as for numeric
variables, except that a string variable always has a dollar sign ($) as its last character.
A is a numeric variable, whereas A$ is a string variable. A string is one or more letters,
symbols, or numbers that can be used as information in a BASIC program. Strings
are stored in the computer's memory with an assignment statement such as LET B$ =
"EXAMPLE OF A STRING." The string variable B$ acts as a label in the computer's
memory for the place where the string assigned to B$ is stored. A reference to B$
elsewhere in the program automatically tells the computer to use the string assigned
to B$. The string assigned to a string variable is often referred to as the "value" of
the string variable.

    String variables act much like numeric variables and can generally be manipulated
just like numeric variables. The crucial difference is that you cannot use string
variables in arithmetic expressions and calculations, even if numeric information is
assigned to the string variable. For example, LET F$ = "8.99" does not let you use
F$ in numeric calculations, even though the string is comprised of numbers.

    String variables and the strings assigned to them take up space in your computer's
memory. You can visualize this as a box or compartment that contains alphanumeric
information identified by a string variable. For example, the assignment statement
LET N$ = "ALPHA PRODUCTS COMPANY" can be thought of as creating a storage
compartment in the computer's memory like this:

N$	ALPHA PRODUCTS COMPANY

           ↑   ↑

   the string variable   the string

Remember that a string assigned to a string variable in this way has the string enclosed
in **quotation marks**. Only the information between the quotation marks comprises
the string; the quotes themselves are not part of the string.

    Many, if not most, business and personal applications of data files make much
greater use of alphanumeric data (strings) than numeric data (numbers or values), so
we are taking this opportunity to reinforce and extend your understanding of the use
of string variables. Notice the word "alphanumeric." This term comes from the data
processing industry and refers to data that may consist of alphabetic characters, numeric
characters, and/or special characters. For example, the product identification number
FC1372 appearing in a catalog is alphanumeric data consisting of two alphabetic
characters followed by four numeric characters. An address or hyphenated phone
number is also alphanumeric data. To use and store such information in BASIC,
assign it to a string variable (LET P$ = "FC1372") because a simple numeric variable
would not accept the two alphabetic characters. If an identification number is mostly

numeric, but includes a hyphen, asterisk, or even a space (e.g., 84992*, where the "*" denotes a special location, price, etc.), then it too requires the use of a string variable.

One string variable can have from zero to 255 characters, including all spaces, punctuation, and special characters. A string with no characters (zero characters) is called a *null string* or empty string. An assignment statement for a null string would be: 10 LET Z$ = "" . (There is no space between the two sets of quotation marks.)

There is a crucial difference between the *maximum* length of a string (255 characters) and its *actual* length. The actual length is the number of alphanumeric characters presently assigned to the string variable and stored in the computer's memory. Remember, spaces count as characters. Consider the lengths of the following strings assigned to string variables.

N$	ALPHA PRODUCTS

Actual length: Fourteen characters

C$	MENLO PARK, CA. 94025

Actual length: Twenty-one characters
                (includes comma, period, and spaces)

Now you do this one:

A$	161 DAWN ST. SUITE 3

(a)   What is the maximum length for a string assigned to A$?

_____

(b)   What is the actual length of the string shown as assigned to A$ above?

_____

— — — — — — — — — — — — — — — — — —

(a)   255 characters
(b)   Twenty characters

Since APPLE SOFT BASIC automatically assumes that a string variable can be assigned a string with up to 255 characters, there is no need to DIMENSION string variables. However, we recommend that you show a person using your program what the string size (maximum *actual* size) is for all string variables listed in the program. Do this by including REM statements in the introductory module, as shown:

```
140   REM   STRING VARIABLES
150   REM     N$=CUSTOMER NAME(20)
160   REM     A$=CUST.STREET ADDRESS(25)
170   REM     C$=CUST.CITY(15),STATE(2),ZIP(5)
180   REM     C$ HAS 26 CHAR. TOTAL INCLUDING SPACES
190   :
```

(a)   How many characters are contained in a null string assigned to a string variable?

_____

(b)   In the actual length of a string, how many characters does a space use?

_____

_ _ _ _ _ _ _ _ _ _ _ _ _ _ _ _

(a)   zero (none)
(b)   one

As noted earlier, you can *assign a string to a string variable using the LET statement*. Remember to place the string inside quotation marks, or the computer will reject the statement; it will tell you that an error has been made. Example:

```
240   LET N$ = "TYPE A POSITIVE"
```

Almost all versions of BASIC allow omitting the word LET from an assignment statement. For this reason, LET statements are sometimes called *direct assignment statements* to distinguish them from INPUT and READ assignment statements. A variable (numeric or string) followed by an equal sign (=) implies LET to BASIC; thus, the "implied LET" direct assignment statement can save a bit of typing and a little memory space. We generally include LET for clarity in reading a program listing. This statement:

```
240 N$ = "TYPE A POSITIVE"
```

means the same in BASIC as the example before this paragraph.

READ-DATA ASSIGNMENT STATEMENTS

DATA statements are like data files in that they hold data to be assigned to variables and are then used in a program. The difference is that a DATA statement holds data that can be used only by the program in which the DATA statement appears, whereas a data file can be created and the data used by a variety of different programs, since it is separate from the program itself. This will be explained in greater detail later.

The READ statement, which must have one or more DATA statements in the same program to READ from, is an assignment statement. One or more data items from a DATA statement are assigned to one or more variables by a READ statement.

```
10   READ A
20   DATA   15,  76.5,  1892,  -999
```

The statement READ A assigns a numeric value from the DATA statement to variable A.

```
10   READ A,B
20   DATA   15,  76.5,  1892,  -999
```

The statement READ A, B assigns two consecutive values from the DATA statement; the first to variable A, the second to B.

A program can also use the READ and DATA statements to assign strings to string variables. A DATA statement can contain strings as data items, and these strings are assigned to string variables by a READ statement using the same procedure as for reading numeric values.

```
220   READ A$,B$,C$
        :
        :
910   DATA   BLUE,  GREEN,  GOLD
```

In APPLESOFT BASIC, the individual string items in the DATA statement do not have to be enclosed in quotation marks *unless* the string data idem includes a comma, semicolon, or one or more leading spaces (blank spaces that are to be included and considered part of the string). In the latter cases, enclose the string data item in quotation marks, just as for a LET direct assignment statement. Any trailing spaces left between a string data item and the comma separating it from the next item in the same data statement are accepted as part of the string and duly assigned to the string variable. Note that the actual length of such a data item includes these trailing spaces, even though they seem invisible.

In the following example, quotation marks are necessary around each data item because a comma is part of the string data items themselves.

```
220   READ N$
        :
        :
910   DATA   "BROWN, JERALD R.",  "FINKEL, LEROY P."
```

Try this test program to see how the "trailing space" rule works on your APPLE.

```
220   READ N$,A$
230   PRINT N$;A$
910   DATA TEST    ,    ITEMS


]RUN
TEST    ITEMS
```

There should be only three spaces between the words TEST and ITEMS because the leading spaces before items are not included, while the trailing spaces after TEST and before the comma are included. Now change line 910 as shown below and RUN the program segment again.

```
910   DATA  "TEST    "," ITEMS"
```

(a)   How many spaces should now appear between the strings when the program is

RUN? _____

– – – – – – – – – – – – – – – –

(a)   six spaces

The computer uses an internal "pointer" system to keep track of items in a DATA statement that are "used up" or already assigned to variables in a program RUN. When executing READ-DATA statements, each time a data item is read and assigned to a variable the internal pointer advances one position in the DATA statement to the next data item. If the pointer is pointed at alphanumeric data (a string) and the READ statement is looking for numeric information to assign to a numeric variable, the program will terminate in an error condition. For example:

```
210   READ A
910   DATA  ALPHA,NUMERIC
```

An error condition would result from executing this program segment because the statement READ A is "looking" for numeric data to assign to the numeric variable A, but the pointer is pointing at alphanumeric information.

What will happen if this program is RUN?

```
210   READ A$,B$
220   PRINT A$;B$
910   DATA  17926, NUMERIC
```

(a)   Will the program RUN without an error condition? _____

(b)   What will be assigned to A$ and why? _____

_ _ _ _ _ _ _ _ _ _ _ _ _ _ _ _

(a) Yes
(b) A$ = 17926, since a number can be assigned as a string to a string variable (but
     not vice versa)

UNDERSTANDING INPUT,
AN IMPORTANT ASSIGNMENT STATEMENT

You can enter numeric or alphanumeric information to be assigned to a numeric
variable or a string variable using the INPUT statement. When using INPUT statements,
make certain that the data entry person using your program at a computer terminal
knows exactly what kind of information to enter for assignment to a variable by the
INPUT statement. To do so, *you* must fully understand how INPUT works in
APPLESOFT.

The INPUT statement should always include a prompting string (a message that
appears on the printer or display screen) to tell the user exactly what sort of information is to be entered. A typical format for an INPUT statement is:

```
160  INPUT "ENTER YOUR NAME, FIRST NAME THEN LAST:";N$
```

An INPUT statement without a prompting message (the part enclosed by quotes)
causes the computer to print or display a question mark; the computer then waits for
a response from the keyboard. There is nothing more frustrating to a computer user
than an INPUT question mark with no hint as to what sort of response is requested.
Always use a prompting string in an INPUT statement. If necessary, use PRINT
statements preceding the INPUT statement to explain to the user what information
to enter.

Another source of user frustration is the funny responses the computer can make
when incorrect data are entered. Consider the following example:

```
360  INPUT "ENTER PRODUCT NUMBER AND QUANTITY:";N,Q


]RUN
ENTER PRODUCT NUMBER AND QUANTITY:137
??
```

The user entered the number 137 after the prompting message and then pressed the
RETURN key. The computer responded with a double question mark (??), indicating
that more data were expected. Notice that the INPUT statement had two variables
to assign values to but only one value (137) was entered. An inexperienced user
would not know that.

RUN the same program segment again and enter three items of data.

```
]RUN
ENTER PRODUCT NUMBER AND QUANTITY:137,12,164
?EXTRA IGNORED
```

This general error message doesn't provide any help to the user since it doesn't pinpoint the problem. To make matters worse, the computer may accept incorrect data and assign it to the INPUT variables! Consider this example!

```
110   INPUT "ENTER TWO VALUES:";A,B
120   PRINT A,B

]RUN
ENTER TWO VALUES:3
??
?REENTER
ENTER TWO VALUES:
?REENTER
ENTER TWO VALUES:
```

USER ENTERS ONE VALUE ONLY AND PRESSES RETURN.
USER ENTERS NO VALUE AND PRESSES RETURN.
IT'S BACK LOOKING FOR A VALUE FOR 'A' AGAIN!

The same error conditions and input problems can occur in string data with an additional peculiarity. Consider the following program segment:

```
180   INPUT "ENTER CUSTOMER NUMBER AND NAME:";C,N$
190   PRINT C,N$

]RUN
ENTER CUSTOMER NUMBER AND NAME:13726
??
13726
```

Here the user entered the customer number (13726) and pressed RETURN, and the number was duly assigned to variable C. But when the ?? appeared, indicating that the computer expected yet another entry, the user pressed the RETURN key again without making another entry. While the computer wanted a second entry to assign to N$, it accepted "nothing" as an entry; that is, it accepted a null string and assigned it to N$. If we changed the INPUT variables to C$ and N$ (instead of C and N$), the computer would accept null strings for assignment to both string variables. In that case, the computer interprets two presses on the RETURN key as meaning that it should assign null strings to both variables.

Our insistence on the importance of understanding INPUT should now be hitting home. So what do you do for the accidental null string entry and the other eccentricities of the INPUT statement.

Two programming techniques can help eliminate errors. First, ask the user to enter only *one* value or string per INPUT statement, period! This makes data entry (and data checking, as we will discuss in the next chapter) nice and clean. For example:

```
RUN
ENTER CUSTOMER NUMBER:137
ENTER CUSTOMER NAME:BISHOP BROTHERS
ENTER PRODUCT NUMBER:18625
ENTER QUANTITY ORDERED:106
```

Second, to have *all* input entries, whether string or numeric, assigned to string variables. This eliminates error messages for numeric variables that cannot accept alphanumeric information for assignment. In the next chapter you will learn to test for null strings (no entry made) and appropriately advise the user with explicit messages as to the proper entry to be made. Numbers (numeric values) assigned to string variables can be converted from strings to numeric values for arithmetic operations using the VAL function. If Q$ = 106 (a string), then VAL(Q$) converts 106 to a numeric value that can be assigned to a numeric variable and/or used directly as a numeric value in a BASIC expression. VAL is discussed in the next chapter.

(a)   Write an INPUT statement that will result in the following RUN:

```
RUN
ENTER YOUR HOME ADDRESS:
```

_____

_____

_____

— — — — — — — — — — — — — — —

(a)   100 INPUT "ENTER YOUR HOME ADDRESS:";A$ (Your line number and string variable may be different.)

CONCATENATION

Strings can be joined to form longer strings; a process called *concatenation*. Strings are concatenated in BASIC using the plus (+) sign. The process, however, is one of joining, not of arithmetic addition. For example, the strings assigned to F$ and L$ can be concatenated and the new, longer string assigned to another variable N$ in an assignment statement like this:

```
110   LET N$ = F$ + L$
```

Strings assigned to variables can be concatenated with string constants, like this:

```
120   LET G$ = N$ + "CUSTOMER"
```

or

```
150   LET N$ = F$ + " " + L$
```

The statement above concatenates the strings associated with F$ and L$ and assigns them to N$, but it also places a space in the new N$ string between the parts of N$ that were assigned to F$ and L$. Look at the following program and show what will be printed when it is RUN.

(a)
```
10   LET F$ = "JANET"
20   LET L$ = "BARRINGTON"
30   LET N$ = F$ + " " + L$
40   PRINT N$
```

RUN

_____

– – – – – – – – – – – – – – – –

(a)   JANET BARRINGTON

IF. . .THEN STATEMENTS

The IF. . .THEN statement in BASIC gives the language real power. Its syntax varies from one BASIC system to another. Some BASICs permit only a GOTO statement to follow an IF. . .THEN expression.

```
140   IF X < Y THEN   GOTO 800
```

However, the GOTO can be, and usually is, omitted. The simplest form of IF. . .THEN is a COMPARISON between two numeric values or expressions. IF the comparison is true, THEN (GOTO) a given line number and continue executing the program with the statement at that line number. Since GOTO is usually omitted, just the line number follows THEN. The possible comparisons are:

```
=    equals
<    less than
>    greater than
< =  less than or equal to
> =  greater than or equal to
< >  not equal to
```

APPLESOFT BASIC also includes in the IF. . .THEN family of statements:

IF. . .THEN LET. . .	(Follow rules for regular LET statements. LET can be omitted.)
IF. . .THEN GOSUB. . .	(Line number follows GOSUB.)
IF. . .THEN RETURN. . .	(Unusual, but possible.)
IF. . .THEN PRINT. . .	(Follow all the rules for regular PRINT statements.)
IF. . .THEN INPUT. . .	
IF. . .THEN READ. . .	(These two are possible, but are not recommended because of confusion and debugging complications.)
IF. . .THEN STOP. . .	
IF. . .THEN END. . .	
IF. . .THEN IF...THEN...	(Possible, but confusing and unnecessary.)

(a) What statement is implied after the THEN in the simplest form of the IF. . .THEN statement? _____

(b) List at least five BASIC statements that can be part of an IF. . .THEN statement and that will be executed if the condition (comparison) is true.

_____

_____

_____

_____

_____

_____

- - - - - - - - - - - - - - - - -

(a) GOTO

(b) PRINT, GOTO (assuming a line number appears after THEN),
LET (direct assignment statement, with the option of omitting the word LET),
READ, INPUT, another IF. . .THEN statement (not recommended),
GOSUB, RETURN (any 5 answers)

IF. . .AND. . .THEN. . . and IF. . .OR. . .THEN. . . are called the logical AND and logical OR. They allow you to put more than one comparison in a single IF. . .THEN statement. The comparisons on both sides of an AND must be true for the entire IF. . .THEN comparison to be true. Only one comparison on either side of an OR must be true for the comparison to be true. You can use more than one AND and more than one OR between IF and THEN, and you may use both AND and OR in the same IF. . .THEN statement, which allows three or more comparisons in one IF. . .THEN statement! Be certain you understand how to use the logical AND and OR to produce the results you want. We find they are useful for certain checks on user INPUT entries. If an INPUT value should be between five and twenty, then the following statement would check that the value was within these parameters.

```
150  IF F < 5 OR F > 20 THEN  PRINT "ENTRY IS INCORRECT"
```

Alternately, the following line would check for "within bounds" parameters for the value assigned to F, instead of "out of bounds" values.

```
150  IF F > = 5 AND F < = 20 THEN  PRINT "ENTRY IS WITHIN BOUNDS"
```

Note: Be very careful to have your logic straight or such comparison statements will not do what you want. For some, flow charts help visualize the alternatives so you can properly construct your comparison statements. Thoroughly testing programs and program segments for every conceivable mistake that you could enter is a must.

(a) Write two IF. . .THEN statements, one using a logical AND and another using a logical OR. The statement should test to see if the value assigned to variable Y is greater than, but not equal to, zero, and less than, but not equal to, one. When the comparison is true, one statement should print the message BETWEEN ZERO AND ONE, and the other should print NOT BETWEEN ZERO AND ONE.

_____

_____

_____

– – – – – – – – – – – – – – – –

(a) ```
60 IF Y > 0 AND Y < 1 THEN PRINT "BETWEEN ZERO AND 1"
70 IF Y < = 0 OR Y > = 1 THEN PRINT "NOT BETWEEN ZERO AND 1"
```

Having seen how more than one comparison can be made within a single IF. . .THEN statement, now consider the other end of the comparison statement and how to have more than one instruction executed in the case of a true IF. . .THEN comparison.

APPLESOFT BASIC permits you to do nearly anything after an IF. . .THEN expression, frequently encouraging you to place multiple statements on one line.
```

```
150   IF X < Y THEN   PRINT "TOO LOW": LET C = C + 1: GOTO 10
160   IF X > Y THEN   LET C = C + 1: LET G = 0: GOTO 10
```

When you use this APPLESOFT BASIC feature, keep in mind that you may be hindering the portability of your program. If this doesn't concern you, forget it! We do urge you to complete your entire "activity" on one line after an IF. . .THEN statement, otherwise the program is extremely awkward to follow. If you cannot complete your activity on one line, then GOTO a section where all of the activity can be done together. Follow the acceptable example:

BAD

```
150   IF X < Y THEN   LET X = X + D: LET Y = Y / N: GOTO 200
160   IF X > Y THEN   LET X = X - D:Y = Y / N: GOTO 10
  .
  .
  .
200   LET C = C + 1: PRINT "TOO LOW": GOTO 10
```

ACCEPTABLE

```
150   IF X < Y THEN 200
160   IF X > Y THEN 250
  .
  .
  .
200   LET X = X + D
210   LET Y = Y / N
220   LET C = C + 1
230   PRINT "TOO LOW"
240   GOTO 10
```
. . . or all on one line

Most of us who program for fun ignore what is going on inside the computer because we don't have to pay attention. However, on occasion, little "bugs," inconsistencies, and our own ignorance can cause some interesting (and frustrating) problems. BASIC software sometimes does funny things, barely detectable because the problem exists at the seventh or eighth decimal location, which may be invisible to the BASIC user. We once spent hours trying to fix a "money changing" program that kept giving us 4.9999 pennies change instead of a nickel. (This points out a very important lesson: Your BASIC language interpreter does not always do things with the accuracy and consistency you might expect. Therefore, when you are comparing numeric values, especially numbers that have been computed by your computer, try to compare using less than (<), greater than (>), or not equal (< >).

GOOD

```
IF X<1125.75 THEN...
IF X>1125.75 THEN...
IF X <> 1125.75 THEN.....
```

NOT WISE

```
IF X = 1125.75 THEN....
```

(a)   Why should you avoid IF. . .THEN comparisons for equality?

_____

_____

_____

_ _ _ _ _ _ _ _ _ _ _ _ _ _ _

(a)   Internal round-off errors may produce very slightly inaccurate values in calculations. Therefore, a comparison for equality might fail (be false) where you would
expect the comparison to be true.

IF. . .THEN String Comparisons and the ASCII Code

So far the only comparisons used in IF. . .THEN examples have been between two
numeric expressions or values. Comparing *strings* in IF. . .THEN statements begins to get a
little tricky. However, comparisons for equality or inequality are fairly straightforward.
Examine these statements:

```
220   INPUT "ENTER YOUR LEGAL NAME:";N$
230   IF N$ = "STOP" THEN 999
```

Notice that in line 230 a string variable (N$) is compared with a string constant
("STOP"). A string constant in a comparison must be enclosed in quotation marks.
In order for a comparison for equality between two strings to be true, each and every
character in the two strings must be identical (upper and lower case are different), and
the length of the strings and any leading or trailing spaces must be the same. Any
difference *whatsoever* will make the equality comparison false.

In line 230 above, the string assigned to a string variable was compared to a
string constant. Likewise, the contents of two string variables can be compared.

```
310   INPUT "ENTER OLD TITLE:";T$
320   IF T$ < > D$ THEN  PRINT "WRONG TITLE. TRY ANOTHER."
```

The difficulty in string comparisons comes with the "less than" or "greater
than" comparisons. These have application in sorting strings, alphabetizing data, or
inserting new information into an alphabetically organized data file. In IF. . .THEN
comparisons, BASIC compares the two strings one character at a time, from left to
right.

Rather than comparing within the construct of a twenty-six-character alphabet,
*BASIC uses a standard code that represents every possible signal a terminal keyboard
can send to the computer (and vice versa).* Each key and each permitted combination
of keys, such as the shift or CONTROL key along with another key, sends a
unique electronic *code* pattern to the computer. *These patterns are represented by*

the decimal numbers 0 through 127 in the ASCII Code chart. Mercifully, here is one instance of standardization throughout the computer industry. ASCII stands for American Standard Code for Information Interchange. The ASCII code's 128-character set includes the upper and lower case letters of the alphabet, numbers, punctuation, and other special characters and special function keys. The ASCII code also includes 128 other special codes that are numbered 129 through 255, that do not concern us. Refer to the ASCII chart in the Appendix for your understanding of the following.

Notice that the numbers 0 through 9 have ASCII codes of 48 to 57. The alphabet has ASCII codes of 65 to 90 for upper case letters; lower case starts at 96. Therefore, the lower case equivalent of an upper case letter is the upper case letter's ASCII code number plus 31.

$$A = 65, \text{ so } a = 65 + 31 = 96$$

This fact will be of use later.

What actually happens in an IF. . .THEN string comparison? BASIC compares the ASCII code number for each character in the two strings, comparing just *one* character at a time. As soon as an inequality exists between characters, the string with the character that has the lower ASCII code number will be considered "less than" the other string. BASIC *does not* add up the ASCII code values for the two strings being compared to determine "less than" or "greater than." The following chart shows the results of comparing a series of strings assigned to A$ and B$.

```
A$        B$

ABC       ABD       A$ IS LESS THAN B$
MN!       MNO       A$ IS LESS THAN B$
STOP      STO       B$ IS LESS THAN A$   (A$ is greater than B$)
123A      123a      A$ IS LESS THAN B$
```

In the comparison process, if one string ends before the other and no other difference has been found, then the shorter string is said to be "less than" the longer one. One result is that a null string is always "less than" a non-null string, since the ASCII code for null is zero. Here are some more examples of string comparisons:

```
A$            B$

SMITH         SMITHE      A$ IS LESS THAN B$
ALCOTJONES    ALCOT       A$ IS GREATER THAN B$   (B$ is less than A$)
JOHNSEN       JOHNSON     A$ IS LESS THAN B$
KELLOG        KELLOGG     A$ IS LESS THAN B$
EQ-8          EQ 8        B$ IS LESS THAN A$
```

Now it's your turn to familiarize yourself with ASCII code comparisons. Fill in the blanks with the appropriate string variable. Of course you can refer to the Appendix!

	C$	D$		
(a)	JACOB	JACOBS	_____ is greater than	_____
(b)	LOREN	LORAN	_____ is less than	_____
(c)	SMITH—HILL	SMITH HILL	_____ is less than	_____
(d)	ABLE12	ABLE—12	_____ is less than	_____
(e)	Theater	THEATER	_____ is less than	_____
(f)	95.2	95—2	_____ is less than	_____

- - - - - - - - - - - - - - -

(a)	D$,C$	D$ has more characters, others being equal
(b)	D$.C$	Letter A is less than letter E
(c)	D$,C$	A space is less than a hyphen
(d)	D$,C$	A hyphen is less than the number 1
(e)	D$,C$	Uppercase letters are less than lower case letters
(f)	D$, C$	A hyphen is less than a decimal point

Two string functions are used in conjunction with the ASCII code. The ASC ( ) function gives the ASCII code number for the first character of the string contained in the parentheses or for the first character of the string assigned to the string variable contained in the parentheses. The ASCII number produced by ASC ( ) may be assigned to a variable, displayed by a PRINT statement, used in arithmetic expressions, and used as a value in an IF...THEN comparison. The following examples illustrate these points.

```
LET X = ASC(A$)
LET X = ASC("ANTWERP")
PRINT ASC(A$)
IF ASC(N$) = 0 THEN...
```

Give the ASCII number or value that will be printed for each of these program segments. Refer to the ASCII chart in the appendix.

(a)
```
LET D$ = "DOLLAR"
PRINT ASC (D$)
RUN
```
_____

(b)
```
PRINT  ASC ("YES")
RUN
```
_____

(c)
```
10   LET F$ = "FRANK"
20   LET L$ = "JONES"
30   LET N$ = L$ + ",  " + F$
40   PRINT   ASC (F$)
50   PRINT   ASC (L$)
60   PRINT   ASC (N$)
```

RUN

_____

_____

_____

- - - - - - - - - - - - - - - -

(d)
```
10   PRINT   ASC (" ")
```
RUN

_____

(a)   68
(b)   89
(c)   70
      74
      74
(d)   32

Describe the string that must be assigned to A$ in order for the following IF. . .THEN comparisons to be true.

(a)   IF ASC(A$) = 53 THEN 510   _____

(b)   IF ASC(A$) < > 48 THEN 810   _____

(c)   IF ASC(A$) = $\emptyset$ THEN 950 _____

- - - - - - - - - - - - - - - -

(a)   First character in A$ is 5
(b)   First character in A$ is not zero
(c)   A$ must be a null string

The opposite of the ASC( ) function is the CHR$( ) function. An ASCII number is placed in the parentheses: It causes the computer to send that ASCII code signal to the terminal, which can cause the printing of an alphanumeric character. CHR$( ) is also used to send special control signals to the CRT screen or printer (ASCII numbers 0 through 31) or in a PRINT statement to print characters corresponding to the ASCII number in the CHR$( ) parentheses.

```
840   PRINT   CHR$ (69); CHR$ (78); CHR$ (68)
```

(a)   By running this program or by reference to the ASCII chart, what will this
      program line print? _____

— — — — — — — — — — — — — — — —

(a)   END

    CHR$(7) sounds the beeper on the APPLE keyboard. CHR$(34) produces
quotation marks in situations where they would not otherwise be printed around a
string. Remember these possibilities. Check the ASCII codes, especially 0 through
31, in your APPLESOFT reference manual. There may be some interesting capabilities to explore.
    When a program user has limited options for a response to input statements, it
is necessary to check the input for the options available. For example, it is often
useful to have the computer user answer yes or no, or to select from a specific list
of options for the response to an input statement. Examine the following program
segment:

```
330   INPUT "DO YOU WISH TO CONTINUE DATA ENTRY (Y OR N)?";R$
340   IF R$ <  > "Y" AND R$ <  > "N" THEN  PRINT  CHR$ (7);"PLEASE TYPE 'Y'
      FOR YES OR 'N' FOR NO.": GOTO 330
350   IF R$ = "Y" THEN 450
```

    If line 340 were omitted and the user typed YES instead of Y, the program
would not operate as the programmer intended. Suppose a program displays the
following "menu" or list of possible responses!

ENTER 'I' TO INSERT DATA
ENTER 'C' TO CHANGE DATA
ENTER 'D' TO DELETE DATA
ENTER 'N' FOR NO CHANGE OF DATA
YOUR CHOICE:

The selection of each option directs the computer to branch to a different section of
the remaining program to accomplish this activity.

```
210   INPUT "YOUR CHOICE:";R$
220   IF R$ = "I" THEN 510
230   IF R$ = "C" THEN 610
240   IF R$ = "D" THEN 710
250   IF R$ = "N" THEN 150
```

    If the user entered a response other than I, C, D, or N, this program would not
detect the error. If the user pressed RETURN with no response, the computer would
not catch the error either.

(a) Now write a statement for line 215 that ensures that the response entered was among the list of options on the menu, and, if not, informs the user of the options available and branches back to the INPUT statement.

215

_____

_____

_____

– – – – – – – – – – – – – – – –

(a) 215 IF R$ ⟨ ⟩ "I" AND R$ ⟨ ⟩ "C" AND R$ ⟨ ⟩ "D" AND R$ ⟨ ⟩ "N" THEN PRINT "PLEASE TYPE ONLY THE LETTER I, C, D, OR N.": GOTO 210

THE LEN FUNCTION

Recall that while the maximum length of a string that can be assigned to a string variable is 255 characters, the *actual* length of the string is the number of characters *currently* assigned to a string variable. BASIC provides a function to "count" and report the actual length of a string, or of a string assigned to a particular variable; a function appropriately called the LEN (for LENgth) function. LEN can be used in a print statement to print the number of characters in the string in question. Since the execution of LEN results in a numeric value, it can be assigned as a value to a numeric variable, used as a value in an IF. . .THEN comparison, or used in calculations.

For example:

```
10   LET G$ = "WHAT A GAS"
20   PRINT  LEN (G$)

]RUN
10


100  PRINT  LEN ("NORTHERN MUSIC")

]RUN
14


10   LET H$ = "1582 ANCHORAGE DRIVE"
20   LET A =  LEN (H$)
30   PRINT A

]RUN
20


150  LET R$ = "YES"
160  IF  LEN (R$) = 3 THEN  PRINT "GO ON TO THE NEXT QUESTION."

]RUN
GO ON TO THE NEXT QUESTION
```

```
10   LET M$ = "AMERICAN"
20   LET N$ = "FOREIGN"
30   PRINT  LEN (M$) +  LEN (N$)
RUN

15
```

Show the results of executing each of the following program segments:

(a)
```
10   LET C$ = " "
20   PRINT  LEN (C$)
```

RUN

_____

(b)
```
10   LET F$ = "FRANK"
20   LET L$ = "JONES"
30   LET N$ = L$ + ", " + F$
40   PRINT N$
50   PRINT  LEN (N$)
```

RUN

_____

_____

– – – – – – – – – – – – – – – – –

(a)   1
(b)   JONES, FRANK
      12

SUBSTRING FUNCTIONS:
VERSATILE TOOLS TO MANIPULATE STRING DATA

Three APPLESOFT BASIC string functions (MID$, RIGHT$, LEFT$) allow you to manipulate the parts of a string called substrings. The MID$ function is by far the most useful substring manipulating function. It allows you to *select* substrings from within a larger string. The MID$ selection function has the following forms:

(1)   MID$("CHARGE IT", 1,6)

(2)   MID$(T$, 3, 15)

(3)   MID$(D$, 10)

(4)   MID$(W$, A, C*D)

In example (1), the MID$ function selects characters 1 through 6 inclusive as the substring within the string constant CHARGE IT, with the substring starting at character position 1 (the C) and including six characters total, making the substring

CHARGE. Example (2) assumes that a string has been assigned to T$, and the sub-string comprises fifteen characters of the T$ string, starting with the third character in the string and continuing on to the 15th character after the third one. In example (3), the "last character position" notation (the last value inside the MID$ parentheses) has been omitted, which tells the computer that the substring will start at character position 10, and will include all the rest of the string to the right of the character at position 10. Example (4) shows that the starting position for the substring, as well as the number of characters to be included in the substring, can be represented by variables or expressions that evaluate to a numeric value. Of course, these variables must have been previously assigned values, just as the string variable must have pre-viously been assigned a string. So in general, the MID$ function has the form

> MID$ (string variable or constant, substring starting position, how many characters in the substring from the start position)

Note that the three parameters in the MID$ function are separated by commas. The first is usually a string variable to which a string has previously been assigned. The second parameter is the starting position for the substring. The third parameter *does not* tell the last character position number in the substring, but rather tells how many characters to include in the substring — a point that sometimes confuses people.

Notice the use of the MID$ selection function in PRINT statements in the program below. Remember, it allows you to select and print any part or substring of the string assigned to the string variable in the MID$ parentheses. The other two values or parameters inside the parentheses still indicate where the substring to be printed starts and how many characters it includes.

```
150   LET N$ = "FOGHORNE WHILDEFLOWER"
160   PRINT  MID$ (N$,1,8)
170   PRINT  MID$ (N$,10,12)
180   PRINT N$

]RUN
FOGHORNE
WHILDEFLOWER
FOGHORNE WHILDEFLOWER
```

Notice the use of MID$ as a *selection* function in lines 160 and 170 above. This same selection function can be used to assign a substring from a string assigned to a string variable, without changing the original string from which the substring was selected. Notice in the program segment below that a substring from an existing string can be assigned to a new variable without changing the string from which it was selected. F$ (for first name) and L$ (for last name) are selected from the entire name (N$) without changing N$.

```
150   LET N$ = "FOGHORNE WHILDEFLOWER"
160   LET F$ =  MID$ (N$,1,8)
170   LET L$ =  MID$ (N$,10,12)
180   PRINT N$
190   PRINT "FIRST NAME IS ";F$
200   PRINT "LAST NAME IS ";L$
```

(a)   Show the RUN for the program segment above.

_____

_____

_____

_____

(b)   Which character in N$ is not selected for inclusion in either F$ or L$?

_____

— — — — — — — — — — — — — —

(a)   RUN
       FOGHORNE WHILDFLOWER
       FIRST NAME IS FOGHORNE
       LAST NAME IS WHILDEFLOWER

(b)   The space at character position 9 of N$

The LEFT$ and RIGHT$ string functions are not as versatile as MID$ and are not used as much in our programming. They both work the same way, however, as shown in these program segments:

```
160  PRINT  LEFT$ (A$,8)
```
means print the left-most eight characters of A$ (the first eight characters in the string assigned to A$)

```
170  LET R = 12
180  LET B$ =  RIGHT$ (A$,R)
```
means assign to B$ the twelve right-most characters of A$ (the last twelve characters in the string assigned to A$)

These examples demonstrate the substring selection capabilities of LEFT$ and RIGHT$. They are strictly *selection* functions, selecting one or more characters from one end or the other of an existing string to treat as a substring.
We often use LEFT$ for convenience to check for a user's YES or NO response to an INPUT prompting question. Using an IF. . .THEN statement, we have the computer look at the first character of the response string to determine whether or not the answer was YES, as shown in the following program segment:

```
240  INPUT "DO YOU NEED INSTRUCTIONS (YES OR NO)?",R$
250  IF  LEFT$ (R$,1) = "Y" THEN 600
```

(a)   What responses could a user make to the INPUT prompt above in order for the
IF. . .THEN comparison to be true?

_____

_ _ _ _ _ _ _ _ _ _ _ _ _ _ _ _

(a)   Could type YES or Y or any string that started with the letter Y

We have found less use for the RIGHT$ function than for MID$ or for LEFT$,
but here is an example. Remember, the numeric value inside the RIGHT$ function's
parentheses means to start counting the characters for the substring at the right-most
end of the string from which the substring is being selected, counting toward the
beginning of the string.

```
240   INPUT "WHICH HIGH SCHOOL CLASS DID YOU GRADUATE FROM?";Y$
250   PRINT "YOU GRADUATED IN 19"; RIGHT$ (Y$,2)
```

Assume that several people responded to the INPUT prompting question when the
above program segment was RUN. Show what the computer will print for each user's
response.

(a)   User responds: CLASS OF 1938

Line 250 prints: _____

(b)   User responds: CLASS OF '64

Line 250 prints: _____

(c)   User responds: 1958

Line 250 prints: _____

(d)   User responds: FORTY EIGHT

Line 250 prints: _____

_ _ _ _ _ _ _ _ _ _ _ _ _ _ _ _

(a)   YOU GRADUATED IN 1938   (c)   YOU GRADUATED IN 1958
(b)   YOU GRADUATED IN 1964   (d)   YOU GRADUATED IN 19HT

MULTI-BRANCHING WITH ON. . .GOTO

The ON. . .GOTO statement allows the computer to branch to a number of different
statements throughout a program. The format for the statement is a list of line numbers:

```
10   ON X GOTO 310,450,660,660,660,720,830,910
```

Note: X = any variable or expression from which a value will result.

If the value of X is 1 when the ON. . .GOTO statement is encountered and executed, the computer branches (goes to) the first line number in the list of line numbers (in our example, line 310). If the value of X is 2, the second line number in the list is branched to. As many line numbers can follow GOTO as will fit in a statement line. Notice also in our example that if X = 3, 4, or 5, the same line number (660) will be branched to.

If the value of X is a zero, a negative number, or larger than the number of line numbers in the list, then the ON. . .GOTO statement will be skipped without execution and the next statement executed.

Here is a method to arrive at an ON. . .GOTO value in a menu-section situation. In the following program segment, the ASC( ) function is used to convert a letter entered by the user to an ASCII value that is used to determine the value for an ON. . .GOTO statement. The ON. . .GOTO is a multi-branching instruction. In line 260, if the value of R is 1, then the program goes to the first line number given after GOTO. If R = 2, then the program branches to the second line number given, and so on. The value of R must be greater than 1 and no higher than the number of line numbers that follow GOTO.

```
200 :
210 :
220 :
230  INPUT "ENTER YOUR CHOICE, A-E:";R$
240  LET R =  ASC (R$)  - 64
250  IF R ( 1 OR R ) 5 THEN 270
260  ON R GOTO 300,400,500,600,700
270  PRINT "ENTRY ERROR. PLEASE REENTER AS REQUESTED": GOTO 230
280 :
290 :
```

(a)   In the program above, why is line 250 included?

_____

_____

— — — — — — — — — — — — — — —

(a)   If R evaluates to less than 1 due to a data entry error or larger than 5, an error would occur; so the checking is done by line 250.

FOR NEXT STATEMENTS

It is preferable to use a FOR NEXT loop when you have a controlled, repeating sequence of instructions.

PREFERRED   UNDESIRABLE

```
100   FOR X = 1 TO N         100   LET K = 1
110   PRINT X,X ^ 2          110   PRINT X,X ^ 2
120   NEXT X                 120   LET X = X + 1
                             130   IF X > N THEN 200
                             140   GOTO 110
```

As you can see, the FOR NEXT loop is more space-efficient (it could even have been done in one line), looks better, and is easier to read.

A general rule when using FOR NEXT loops is: DO NOT EXIT from the middle of a FOR NEXT loop, except to GOSUB to a subroutine. Leaving the controlled loop makes the program difficult to read and hard to understand. Further, internally your computer wants to complete the entire FOR NEXT sequence. If you exit prematurely, there is no certainty that your computer will behave "normally" the next time it encounters the loop variable (X in the example above). This uncertainty can cause some very serious program errors that are extremely hard to detect. An exit to a subroutine is acceptable because a subroutine will RETURN the program to the *inside* of the FOR NEXT loop to continue in sequence, as if there was no exit at all.

NEVER

```
100   FOR X = 1 TO N
110   IF A(X) = B(X) THEN 200
120   NEXT X
```

NOT DESIREABLE

```
100   FOR X = 1 TO N
110   IF A(X) = B(X) THEN 130
120   NEXT X
130   LET S = S + 1
140   GOTO 120
```

PREFERRED

```
100   FOR X = 1 TO N
110   IF A(X) ( ) B(X) THEN 130
120   LET S = S + 1
130   NEXT X
```

You can usually write your program to include everything you need to do *inside* the loop, rather than leaving the loop. (There will be exceptions.)

(a)   Write a program segment using nested FOR NEXT loops that will print the word HELLO three times, but will print the word GOODBY four times after each appearance of the word HELLO.

_____

_____

_____

_____

_____

```
(a)    10    FOR X = 1 TO 3
       20    PRINT "HELLO"
       30    FOR Y = 1 TO 4
       40    PRINT "GOODBY"
       50    NEXT Y
       60    NEXT X
```

MULTIPLE-STATEMENT LINES

Many language features in APPLESOFT BASIC are *not* available on other computer systems. Some of these features speed up the program's run time, others save memory space, and some do both. Some features enhance program readability while others confuse the reader. A popular feature is the ability to place multiple BASIC statements on one line separated by a colon, as we showed earlier in discussing IF. . .THEN.

```
140   FOR X = 1 TO 10: PRINT X,X ^ 2: NEXT X
```

or

```
200   IF X = Y THEN  PRINT "YOU WON!": GOTO 10
210   PRINT "SORRY, WRONG NUMBER": GOTO 60
```

A few cautions and suggestions are applicable as you use multiple-statement lines:

1. Multiple-statement lines are often hard to read and sometimes hard to understand. If you later change a program, readability may be a problem. It is more clear to use one statement to a line.
2. If you must use multiple-statement lines, carry out a complete procedure or action on *one* line, whenever possible. Carryover to other lines makes reading more difficult and less clear.
3. Finding program errors buried in multiple-statement lines is difficult.
4. Understand completely how IF. . .THEN statements work in a multiple-statement line. In line 200 above, if X *does* equal Y, then "You won" will be printed and the program will branch to line 10. If the X=Y condition is false, line 210 will be executed next. Some people incorrectly presume that GOTO 10 will be executed whether the condition is true or false.
5. REM statements must be the *last* statement on a multiple-statement line. Any executable statement after a remark will *not* be executed.

Special consideration of the GOSUB statement in multiple-statement lines is warranted. Remember that each GOSUB statement must have a corresponding RETURN statement that appears as the last statement in the subroutine which the GOSUB branches to.

Say, a GOSUB is executed when an IF. . .THEN condition is true. After completing the subroutine, the computer must always be instructed to RETURN. The statement it returns to will be:

(1) the next statement after GOSUB if it is a multiple-statement line, or

(2) the next lined numbered statement in normal line number order.

(a)   Assume that the comparison in line 120 below is true and the GOSUB statement is executed. Which statement will be executed next after the RETURN from subroutine execution?

```
120   IF X = 2 THEN  GOSUB 510: GOTO 360
130   PRINT "X IS LESS THAN TWO."
```

_ _ _ _ _ _ _ _ _ _ _ _ _ _ _ _

(a)   GOTO 360

TRAPPING ERRORS WITH ONERR GOTO

APPLESOFT BASIC has the ability to detect errors while your program is executing. If you wish, you can have the program stop execution altogether and print an error message. Or you can "trap" the error using the ONERR GOTO statement and then determine if you want the program to continue, terminate, or print a message to the program user.

The main reason for using the ONERR trap procedure is to avoid having your program terminate unexpectedly in the middle of execution. This is especially important when using data files in your programs. If you do not use the error trapping procedure, any programming or data entry errors will cause your program to terminate with an error message. And most error messages do not do an adequate job of explaining what is wrong to a naive computer user.

ONERR GOTO works much like an IF. . .THEN statement; if there is an error, THEN GOTO the statement number indicated.

```
10   ONERR  GOTO 300
```

If there is no error, then continue program operation.

The ONERR statement sets what we call a "flag." ANY error that occurs after the ONERR statement has been executed will cause the statement to execute. In that regard it is unlike an IF. . .THEN statement. You need execute the ONERR statement only once and the flag is "set" for the rest of the program or until the flag is "unset," or reset with another ONERR statement that may direct the computer to a different line number than the first ONERR.

To "unset" the ONERR flag, use the statement POKE 216, 0. Alternatively, a second ONERR statement executed after the first one in a program will cancel the first one.

Here is an example of the use of ONERR. The program reads information from DATA statements into an array. We do not know exactly how much data is contained in the DATA statements; less than fifty items is assumed. When we run "out of data" (an error condition), we wish to continue operation of the program at line 200, where the array information will then be used in some way.

```
100  REM     ONERR DEMO PROGRAM
110  :
120  DIM A(50)
130  LET K = 1
140  :
150  ONERR  GOTO 200
160  READ A(K)
170  LET K = K + 1
180  GOTO 160
190  :
200  POKE 216,0: REM    RESET ERROR TRAP
210  REM    PROGRAM CONTINUES
```

Notice that the ONERR statement is only executed once (line 150). That sets the flag until the flag is "unset" or reset at line 200. As the program continues at line 200, you may have wanted to set another error trap to send the program to line 300 if an error occurs.

(a)   Write the statement that will set another error trap in line 200 to send the program to line 300.

200

_ _ _ _ _ _ _ _ _ _ _ _ _ _ _

(a)   200 ONERR GOTO 300

A NOTE ON POKE AND PEEK

The BASIC statements PEEK and POKE provide the BASIC user with a way to get "inside" of the computer and observe or change the machine language codes.

You are aware that all data, even BASIC programs, are translated in the computer into a binary code. This code is called "machine langauge." The PEEK statement will show you the numeric machine language code-value at a particular memory location. These locations are numbered. For example, the following program segment "looks at" the numeric code found at memory location 222, assigns it to the variable A, and then displays it on the screen.

```
10  LET A =  PEEK (222)
20  PRINT A
```

The POKE statement, on the other hand, allows you to change the numeric machine langauge code found at a particular memory location. You need not learn machine language to use PEEK and POKE to accomplish specific jobs when you are provided with the necessary machine language code and/or memory location. Here is an example of a POKE statement.

```
50  POKE 216,0
```

This statement tells the computer to place a zero value at memory location 216. A zero at this memory location turns off, or cancels, a previous ONERR instruction. This is discussed further in the next section.

USING ONERR

You can use ONERR to trap bad data in data entry routines (discussed in more detail in Chapter 3). If a user responds with alphabetic information when numeric data is requested, that is a trapable error. Look these program segments over carefully.

```
100   REM      DATA ENTRY ERROR TRAP
110 :
120   ONERR  GOTO 200
130   INPUT "ENTER YOUR COMPLETE NAME:";N$
140   INPUT "ENTER YOUR AGE IN YEARS:";A
150 :
160   REM      PROGRAM CONTINUES
        :
        :
        :
200   PRINT "YOU HAVE MADE A DATA ENTRY ERROR. PLEASE TRY AGAIN."
210   RESUME
220 :
```

If the user makes a trapable error, the message at line 200 is printed. The RESUME statement in line 210 sends the computer back to the line in which the error was originally made (where the error was trapped). We do not normally encourage the use of the RESUME statement, however, as you will see in Chapter 3.

Each normal error message has a numeric error code. The code for "out of data" is 42. For "bad response to INPUT statement," the code is 254. Other error codes are in your reference manual and DOS manual. We will point out particular error codes as we use them. The numeric code for a particular error encountered by the ONERR error trap is saved in the computer memory in location 222. To see the error code, or to check to see if it is the one you expected, use PEEK(222) in a BASIC statement. For instance, in line 200 we might have said:

```
200   IF  PEEK (222) = 254 THEN  PRINT "YOU HAVE MADE A DATA ENTRY ERROR.
      PLEASE TRY AGAIN.": RESUME
205   PRINT "UNUSUAL ERROR CONDITION. PLEASE REENTER."
```

Now line 200 checks to be sure that it is a data entry error before the message is printed. If it is not a data entry error, the message in line 205 is displayed to caution the operator of an unusual error.

(a) Rewrite the error trapping routine for the first example to trap for bad data (alphabetic information) and for out of data. Print an appropriate message if the data are bad, then continue to the next data item.

_____

_____

_____

_____

_____

_____

_____

_____

_____

_____

_____

_____

_____

_____

_____

- - - - - - - - - - - - - - -

(a)
```
100  REM     SECOND ONERR DEMO PROGRAM
110  :
120  DIM A(50)
130  LET K = 1
140  :
150  ONERR  GOTO 200
160  READ A(K)
170  LET K = K + 1
180  GOTO 160
190  :
200  IF  PEEK (222) = 254 THEN  PRINT "BAD DATA ITEM REJECTED.": GOTO 160
205  IF  PEEK (222) = 42 THEN 220
210  PRINT "UNUSUAL ERROR CONDITION": STOP
220  REM     PROGRAM CONTINUES
```

CHAPTER 2 SELF-TEST

1. Why do the authors recommend using "greater than" and "less than" comparisons in IF. . .THEN numeric comparisons, rather than comparisons for equality?

    _____

    _____

    _____

    _____

2. When must quotation marks be placed around string data items in a DATA statement?

    _____

    _____

    _____

3. How can a null string be assigned to an INPUT string variable?

    _____

    _____

4. Show the results of a RUN of the following program:

```
10   LET A$ = "ALFRED"
20   LET B$ = "CONTRACT"
30   LET C$ = "32C"
40   PRINT  ASC (A$),  ASC (B$),  ASC (C$)
RUN
```

    _____

5. Describe the string that must have been assigned to D$ for each of these comparisons to be true:

    (a) `10  IF  ASC (D$) < 48 OR  ASC (D$) > 57 THEN 660`

    (b) `30  IF  ASC (D$) > 64 AND  ASC (D$) < 91 THEN  GOSUB 1520`

    (a) _____

    (b) _____

6. What value will the LEN function show for a string to which fifteen spaces have been assigned?

    _____

7. Write a statement to check that the user response to an INPUT is among the options requested. The INPUT prompt asks: DO YOU WANT INSTRUCTIONS (YES OR NO):

   _____

   _____

8. Give an example of a simple numeric variable and a simple string variable.

   _____

   _____

   _____

9. Give a reason for avoiding multiple-statements in one program line.

   _____

   _____

   _____

10. Examine the following statement:

    ```
    120 IF X > 10 THEN GOSUB 810 : GOTO 110
    ```

    After executing the subroutine starting at like 810, to which statement will the computer return?

    _____

11. If a variable name has more than two alphanumeric characters, how many of those characters does the computer use to identify the value assigned to that variable?

    _____

Answer Key

1. Round-off error in the computer's computational process may introduce tiny errors that make expected values slightly more or less. Therefore, an equality comparison may fail where you would expect it to succeed.

2. When the string data item includes a comma as part of the string or leading spaces are to be included as part of the string.

3. By pressing the ENTER key without entering anything else from the keyboard.

4.   65   67   57

5. (a)   First character of D$ must *not* be a number (∅ to 9).
   (b)   First character of D$ must be a capital letter (A to Z).

6. 15 (Spaces count as characters in a string.)

7.
```
220   IF R$ <  > "YES" AND R$ <  > "NO" THEN  PRINT "PLEASE TYPE 'YES' OR
      'NO'":  GOTO 310
```

8. Numeric variable: A (or any letter of the alphabet); string variable: A$ or any letter of the alphabet followed by a dollar sign.

9. May make it harder to read the program; may make errors in programming harder to detect. (either answer)

10. GOTO 110

11. Only the first two characters.

CHAPTER THREE

Building Data Entry and Error Checking Routines

Objectives: When you finish this chapter, you will be able to write statements in a data entry program module to check the following aspects of data items:

Proper length
Non-response (null strings)
Type of data (numeric or alphanumeric)
Inadvertant inclusion of wrong characters
Parameters for numeric data

In addition, you will be able to write data entry modules that:

Have clearly stated prompts
Use reasonable data fields
Concatenate data items into a single field
Check and "pad" entries, as necessary, for proper field length
Remove excess spaces from data taken from data fields
Replace data items contained in a data field
Provide complete explanations of a data entry error to the user

INTRODUCTION

If you are wondering when you are going to get into data files themselves, be patient. Experience has shown that you need a good background in some special techniques associated with data file programming which use BASIC statements you already know. This will make it much easier and faster to learn the new BASIC statements and functions specifically applied to data file handling. You shouldn't have to struggle to understand a new use for a familiar BASIC statement while trying to absorb the data file statements and techniques, so please don't gloss over this material.

Concern for data entry procedures was introduced in the section on INPUT in the previous chapter. For our purposes *data* are defined as any information that is or will be stored in a data file on disk. Common examples of data include mailing, subscription, or billing lists; inventories of retail merchandise; accounting information; files of books, recordings, journal articles, or notes for a book; statistical information. *Data entry* includes the process of getting such information into the computer so that it can be stored in a data file. *Data files* usually contain large amounts of data, which, to be useful, must be accurate, valid, and error-free in content and format. The accuracy and usefulness of your program output depends entirely on the accuracy of the data in these files. Furthermore, inaccurate or invalid data in a data file (or any place in a program) can cause your program to interrupt, halt, or abort in an error condition in the middle of its run. If your program terminates unexpectedly, there may be no telling what is happening inside the computer. Printed reports can be only partially completed, entered data can be lost or destroyed, data in the files can be half processed; the list goes on.

The result of an unexpected program interruption can be catastrophic, though it may not always be so. It is almost impossible to predict exactly what will happen. Therefore, always do everything you can in your programming to avoid errors that can precipitate program interruptions.

Unfortunately most errors occur at data entry time. That is why we emphasize the use of data entry checking procedures in this chapter — procedures to guarantee that data are entered as clean, valid, and accurate in content and format as your ingenuity and knowledge of programming techniques can make it. Throughout the remainder of this book "error-traps" and places where programming errors are likely to occur are illustrated.

This chapter focuses on constructing the data entry module of a program. This is where, usually with INPUT statements, the computer user is instructed to type in information that is going to be placed in a new data file, or to tell the computer to locate information in an already existing data file. After each response to an INPUT statement we will use one or more statements to check the response for possible errors. These error-checking statements comprise the largest part of a data entry program module.

DATA FIELD LENGTH

Many data entry problems are avoided by establishing a certain amount of space; a certain number of character positions into which a given element of data or data item is placed. Establish strings, or defined substring positions within one string, where data must be located (data fields). *A data field can be thought of as a string that contains more than one data item. These data items always fit between two defined character positions within the string.* A simple example would be one string variable to which both a customer's first and last names are assigned like this:

```
N$ = "VIVIAN VANCE"
```

The first name field is a six-character field in N$, occupying the first six character positions of that string (1 through 6). The separator field is a one-character field, located at character position 7.

The last name field has (a) _____ characters and occupies character positions

(b) _____ in the string assigned to (c) _____ .

_ _ _ _ _ _ _ _ _ _ _ _ _ _ _ _ _

(a)   five
(b)   8 to 12
(c)   N$

Below is a graphic look at the fields in N$ with a slash (/) marking the field designation:

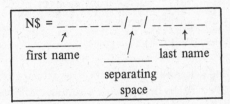

This particular data field works for the name in the example. However, the goal is to establish *reasonable* data fields. In this case, a reasonable data field should hold ANY first or last name that might be assigned to N$. Certainly, many names contain more than six letters for the first name and five letters for the last. On one hand, you want to provide reasonably sized fields for the data. On the other hand, much storage space will be wasted if you try to cover all possibilities. There really may be someone named *John Jacobjingleheimerschmidt*, but reserving twenty-four character positions for a last name data field would waste storage space; if 95 percent of the last names in a data file has twelve letters or less, then half or more of the last name data field goes unused 95 percent of the time. In a file of 1,000, 10,000, or 100,000 names, such as a mailing list, this can amount to a vast amount of unused string and disk storage space.

Data field lengths must be adequate and reasonable. If all the catalog numbers in an inventory data file are five characters, then obviously a five-character data field is sufficient.

To review, use a slash(/) to mark off the fields in a twenty-six character string assigned to A$, where the data fields hold the city, state, and zip code (the last line in a mailing address). Place a number in each field indicating which of the following data items are to occupy that field.

1.   City name (fifteen characters maximum)
2.   Two separator spaces
3.   State code (standard two-letter postal abbreviation)
4.   Two separator spaces
5.   Zip code (five characters)

(a)   A$ = _

— — — — — — — — — — — — — — —

(a)   A$ = _ _ _ _ _ _ _ _ _ _ ①_ _ _ _ _ / ②_ _ / ③_ _ / ④_ _ / ⑤_ _ _ _ _

Next, consider the following data entry module to enter the city, state, and zip code. These data are to be placed into the data fields you just defined above.

```
100   INPUT "ENTER NAME OF CITY:";C$
110   INPUT "ENTER STATE CODE:";S$
120   INPUT "ENTER ZIP CODE:";Z$
130   LET A$ = C$ + " " + S$ + "   " + Z$
140   PRINT A$
```

Notice the concatenating statement in line 130 — an attempt to get the data items into data fields. But these two RUNs demonstrate a serious problem that relates to the length of the city name.

(a)   ]RUN
```
ENTER NAME OF CITY:IOWA CITY
ENTER STATE CODE:IA
ENTER ZIP CODE:52240
IOWA CITY IA   52240
```

(b)   ]RUN
```
ENTER NAME OF CITY:SOUTH SAN FRANCISCO
ENTER STATE CODE:CA
ENTER ZIP CODE:94080
SOUTH SAN FRANCISCO CA   94080
```

Fill in the spaces to show the results of line 130 in the program for each of the sample RUNs:

(a)   A$ = _ _ _ _ _ _ _ _ _ _ _ _ _ _ _ / _ _ / _ _ / _ _ / _ _ _ _ _

(b)   A$ = _ _ _ _ _ _ _ _ _ _ _ _ _ _ _ / _ _ / _ _ / _ _ / _ _ _ _ _

— — — — — — — — — — — — — —

(a)   A$ = <u>I O W A   C I T Y _ _ I A _ _</u> / <u>5 2</u> / <u>2 4</u> / <u>0 _</u> / _ _ _ _ _

(b)   A$ = <u>S O U T H _ S A N _ F R A N C</u> / <u>I S</u> / <u>C O</u> / _ _ / <u>C A _ _ 9 4 0 8 0</u>

The fact that all cities don't have fifteen letters means that simple concatenation of this data does not place it into the defined character positions for the data fields.

Checking Data Entries for Acceptable Length

One programming technique to check data entries for acceptable length uses the LEN function in an IF . . . THEN comparison. If the data requested always have a defined number of characters, then an important check for mistakes in data entry would be to see whether the entry has the exact length it should. A U.S. zip code always has five characters, so a check for that data item would look like line 170:

```
160   INPUT "ENTER ZIP CODE:";Z$
170   IF  LEN (Z$) <  > 5 THEN  PRINT "REENTER AS 5 DIGIT CODE": PRINT :
      GOTO 160

]RUN
ENTER ZIP CODE:9543
REENTER AS 5 DIGIT CODE

ENTER ZIP CODE:954316
REENTER AS 5 DIGIT CODE

ENTER ZIP CODE:
REENTER AS 5 DIGIT CODE
```

If the entry for the zip code does not have exactly five characters, then a mistake has been made, the user is so advised, and the computer repeats the prompting message and waits for another entry. With new zip code formats, a bit of reprogramming will be necessary.

Now you write a statement to check for proper length of the entry for the INPUT statement below:

(a)   `140   INPUT "ENTER STATE CODE:";S$`

150 _____

— — — — — — — — — — — — — —

(a)   `150   IF  LEN (S$) <  > 2 THEN  PRINT "REENTER AS STANDARD 2-LETTER CODE.":`
      `PRINT : GOTO 140`

How can you check something like a city name, which is allowed fifteen characters or less? The city name could have less than fifteen characters, exactly fifteen, or more than fifteen. If it has more, you must advise the user that a shorter entry is needed and allow the user to reenter the data item with an intelligent abbreviation.

```
120   INPUT "ENTER CITY NAME:";C$
130   IF  LEN (C$) > 15 THEN  PRINT "REENTER USING 15 CHARACTERS OR LESS.":
      PRINT : GOTO 120

]RUN
ENTER CITY NAME:SOUTH SAN FRANCISCO
REENTER USING 15 CHARACTERS OR LESS.

ENTER CITY NAME:
```

Write a statement (similar to line 130 above) to check the entry for the INPUT statement below, where the data field for the entry is twenty characters maximum;

(a)   `310   INPUT "ENTER STREET ADDRESS:";S$`

320 _____

– – – – – – – – – – – – – – – –

```
(a)   320   IF  LEN (S$) > 20 THEN  PRINT "REENTER USING 20 CHARACTERS OR LESS.":
            PRINT : GOTO 310
```

"Padding" Entries With Spaces to Correct Field Lengths

You are probably wondering how to *increase* the length of an entry that has fewer characters than its data field. The solution involves automating the addition of spaces to "pad" the short entry (say, a short city name) with trailing spaces, so that the resulting city name *string,* which includes the padding spaces, exactly fits the data field. Remember, spaces occupy character positions and count as characters in the length of the string. Line 140 shows how to pad with spaces:

```
120   INPUT "ENTER CITY NAME:";C$
130   IF LEN (C$) > 15 THEN  PRINT "REENTER USING 15 CHARACTERS OR LESS.":
      PRINT : GOTO 120
140   IF  LEN (C$) < 15 THEN  LET C$ = C$ + " ": GOTO 140
```

In line 140, if the city name entered and assigned to C$ has less than fifteen characters, then a space is concatenated on to the end of the string. The new string assigned to C$ is the old string plus a space. The statement "goes back to itself" (GOTO 140) and keeps adding another space to the end of the C$ string until the string contains exactly fifteen characters, including the spaces. Clever?

Now you write a statement to pad an entry with spaces if it has less than the eight characters required to fit in its data field.

```
(a)   120   INPUT "ENTER YOUR FIRST NAME:";F$
            130   IF  LEN (F$) > 8 THEN  PRINT "SHORTEN ENTRY TO 8 CHARACTERS OR LESS.":
            PRINT : GOTO 120

      140 _____
```

– – – – – – – – – – – – – – – –

```
(a)   140   IF  LEN (F$) < 8 THEN  LET F$ = F$ + " ": GOTO 140
```

Now apply the techniques you have been using in a data entry module.

(a)   Write a program routine to request that a user enter an alphanumeric product identification code with three characters, plus a product description with up to twenty characters maximum, followed by a two-character code identifying the person making the entries, using their first and last name initials. Once these three data items have been entered and tested, combine the data into one string of twenty-five characters assigned to a single string variable.

```
(a) 100   REM      DATA ENTRY MODULE
    110   :
    120   INPUT "ENTER A THREE CHARACTER CODE:";C$
    130   IF  LEN (C$) <  > 3 THEN  PRINT "ENTRY MUST BE 3 CHARACTERS. PLEASE
          REENTER.": PRINT : GOTO 120
    140   INPUT "ENTER DESCRIPTION:";D$
    150   IF  LEN (D$) > 20 THEN  PRINT "ENTRY TOO LONG. PLEASE REENTER USING
          20 CHARACTERS OR LESS.": PRINT : GOTO 140
    160   IF  LEN (D$) < 20 THEN  LET D$ = D$ + " ": GOTO 160
    170   INPUT "ENTER YOUR TWO INITIALS:";N$
    180   IF  LEN (N$) <  > 2 THEN  PRINT "PLEASE USE THE FIRST LETTERS OF YOUR
          FIRST AND LAST NAME ONLY.": PRINT : GOTO 170
    190   LET R$ = C$ + D$ + N$
    200   REM  FOR DEMONSTRATION PURPOSES ONLY WE DISPLAY R$
    210   PRINT : PRINT R$
```

What's the advantage in setting up data fields in a single string and putting more than one data item into it? The reasons will become clear in later chapters. For now, the answer has to do with how data files can store information using some automated data entry procedures and equipment and with the ease with which BASIC allows the manipulation of substrings using MID$ for particular applications.

Examine the program below and answer the questions that follow it.

```
100   REM      EXAMPLE DATA ENTRY MODULE
110 :
120   INPUT "ENTER CITY NAME:";T$
130   IF   LEN (T$) > 15 THEN   PRINT "REENTER USING 15 CHARACTERS OR LESS.":
      PRINT : GOTO 120
140   IF   LEN (T$) < 15 THEN   LET T$ = T$ + " ": GOTO 140
150   INPUT "ENTER STATE CODE:";S$
160   IF   LEN (S$) < > 2 THEN   PRINT "PLEASE REENTER AS 2 CHARACTERS.":
      PRINT : GOTO 150
170   INPUT "ENTER ZIP CODE:";Z$
180   IF   LEN (Z$) < > 5 THEN   PRINT "REENTER AS A 5 DIGIT CODE": PRINT :
      GOTO 170
190   LET C$ = T$ + " " + S$ + "  " + Z$
200 :
210   REM     FOR DEMONSTRATION PURPOSES ETC.
220   PRINT : PRINT C$
```

(a)   What is the purpose of line 130?

_____

_____

_____

_____

(b)   What does T$ = T$ + "   " in line 140 do?

_____

_____

_____

_____

(c)   In line 190, what is the purpose of "   " in the concatenation?

_____

_____

_____

- - - - - - - - - - - - - - - -

(a)   Tests to be sure user has not entered more than the acceptable number of characters (fifteen) for the city name field

(b)   Fills in, adds on, or concatenates spaces from the last character of the T$ string up to and including character field position 15. Changes T$ to a fifteen-character string if there were fewer than fifteen characters in the string entered for T$.

(c)   Places spaces in the C$ string, one between the fields for city and state and two between state code and zip code.

Stripping the Padding Spaces From Substrings in Fields

You know how to pad a string with extra spaces to arrive at the proper field length for that data item. Now let's explore a way to eliminate the extra blank spaces when you extract data packed into a string. In the example where we wanted to change a person's last name, it was necessary to pad names with spaces to the proper field length so that corrections could be made, if necessary, and so the first and last names could be found separately. But for name printing purposes, you want to eliminate all the extra blank spaces. The method shown below uses the MID$ function. In our example, N$ really consists of eight characters, one space separating the two fields, twelve characters for L$, and one final space. If the name concatenated into N$ is Jenny Smiles, then:

$$N\$ = \text{“JENNY SMILES ”}$$

This includes the field-separating space at character position 9. The string N$ has this format:

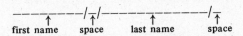

first name   space   last name   space

The procedure used in the following example is called "parsing." It means searching through the string variable, one character at a time, until you find the character(s) you are seeking. We use a FOR NEXT loop to help us "parse" the string variable N$ to find the first space in the first name field and first space in the last name field. If no padding spaces were used, the spaces at the end of each field are found. The example program below shows how to use first and last names separately, without extra spaces, in a computer-printed "thank you" letter.

```
100   REM      PARSING DEMO PROGRAM
110 :
120   REM      VARIABLES USED
130   REM        F$=FIRST NAME
140   REM        L$=LAST NAME
150   REM        N$=CONCATENATED NAMES
160   REM         S AND S1=CHARACTER POSITION OF SPACE
170   REM        X=FOR-NEXT LOOP CONTROL VARIABLE
180 :
190   REM      DATA ENTRY MODULE
200 :
210   INPUT "ENTER FIRST NAME:";F$
220   IF  LEN (F$) ) 8 THEN  PRINT "NAME TOO LONG. REENTER USING 8
      CHARACTERS OR LESS.": PRINT : GOTO 210
230   IF  LEN (F$) ( 8 THEN  LET F$ = F$ + " ": GOTO 230
240   INPUT "ENTER LAST NAME:";L$
250   IF  LEN (L$) ) 12 THEN  PRINT "NAME TOO LONG. REENTER USING 12
      CHARACTERS OR LESS.": PRINT : GOTO 240
260   IF  LEN (L$) ( 12 THEN  LET L$ = L$ + " ": GOTO 260
270 :
280   REM     CONCATENATES ENTIRE NAME INTO N$
290 :
300   LET N$ = F$ + " " + L$ + " "
310 :
320   REM    PARSING ROUTINE TO DETECT FIRST SPACE IN FIELD
330 :
340   FOR X = 1 TO 9
350   IF  MID$ (N$,X,1) = " " THEN  LET S = X: GOTO 380: REM
      S=CHAR.POSITION OF FIRST SPACE FOUND IN FIRST NAME FIELD
360   NEXT X
370 :
380   FOR X = 10 TO 23
390   IF  MID$ (N$,X,1) = " " THEN  LET S1 = X: GOTO 440: REM   S1 IS FIRST
      SPACE FOUND IN LAST NAME FIELD
400   NEXT X
410 :
420   REM      LETTER PRINT ROUTINE
430 :
440   PRINT : PRINT : PRINT
450   PRINT "DEAR "; MID$ (N$,1,S - 1);",": REM   PRINTS FIRST NAME IN SALUTATION
460   PRINT "IT SURE WAS GOOD TO SEE YOU AND MRS. "; MID$ (N$,10,S1 - 10);"
      AT THE GET TOGETHER THE OTHER EVENING."
```

```
]RUN
ENTER FIRST NAME:DANIEL
ENTER LAST NAME:ROBERTS


DEAR DANIEL,
IT SURE WAS GOOD TO SEE YOU AND MRS. ROBERTS AT THE GET TOGETHER THE OTHER
    EVENING.
```

NOTE: Lines 350 and 390 are one of those exceptions when the program leaves or
exits a FOR NEXT loop without necessarily completing all of the loops.

(a)   In lines 350 and 390, what does the MID$ function search for?

_____

(b)   What value is assigned to S and S1 in the same lines?

_____

(c)   In line 450, why does S appear in the MID$ function?

_____

(d)   In line 460, why is 10 subtracted from S1 in the MID$ function?

_____

_____

— — — — — — — — — — — — — — — —

(a)   Looks for the first space in each name field
(b)   Character position number of first space in each field
(c)   Counts the number of characters in the first name field, with the space at the end subtracted from the character count
(d)   Subtracts the characters in the first name field (B), the space at character position nine (1), and the first space in the last name field (1) from the MID$ character count.

CHECKING ENTRIES FOR NULL STRINGS

One idiosyncracy of the INPUT statement already pointed out is that if the user merely presses the RETURN key when the computer is waiting for a response to an INPUT statement, a null string is assigned to the string variable. If the computer then encounters a checking statement that pads the entry with spaces to the proper field length, the entire entry would end up as a string of spaces and be duly included in the data field for that entry. So checking data entries for null string assignments is a must and should be part of your data entry program modules.

You can use two different techniques to test whether a string variable has been assigned a null value. They work equally well.

```
IF A$ = "" THEN...
```

or

```
IF LEN(A$) = 0 THEN...
```

The decision the programmer must make (and it will vary with each situation) is what to do after the THEN when the IF. . .THEN condition is true and a null assignment has been mistakenly made. Whatever you do, do *not* have the computer merely repeat the INPUT prompt, as in the "what-not-to-do" example below.

```
170  INPUT "ENTER CUSTOMER NUMBER:";C$
180  IF  LEN (C$) = 0 THEN 170
]RUN
ENTER CUSTOMER NUMBER:
ENTER CUSTOMER NUMBER:
ENTER CUSTOMER NUMBER:
ENTER CUSTOMER NUMBER:
```

A user who persists in not entering the customer number gets no information as to what is wrong. Always provide a helpful error message, perhaps even a beep, bell, or other sound if available on the terminal, so the user knows something is amiss with the present response or entry.

```
170   INPUT "ENTER CUSTOMER NUMBER:";C$
180   IF  LEN (C$) = 0 THEN   GOSUB 1010
      :
      :
1010  PRINT "PLEASE, WE MUST HAVE THE CUSTOMER NUMBER TO CONTINUE."
1020  :

]RUN
ENTER CUSTOMER NUMBER:
PLEASE, WE MUST HAVE THE CUSTOMER NUMBER TO CONTINUE.
```

With this information in mind, write the data entry routine that will produce the prompts shown below. Test each data item for null response immediately after it is entered with a message to the user that if reentry is made then all data entered are assigned to string variables.

(a)   ENTER CUSTOMER NUMBER:
       ENTER CUSTOMER NAME:
       ENTER PRODUCT NUMBER:
       ENTER QUANTITY ORDERED:

```
(a)  210 :
     220  INPUT "ENTER CUSTOMER NUMBER:";C$
     230  IF  LEN (C$) = 0 THEN  PRINT "ENTRY ERROR. PLEASE REENTER.": PRINT :
          GOTO 220
     240  INPUT "ENTER CUSTOMER NAME:";N$
     250  IF  LEN (N$) = 0 THEN  PRINT "PLEASE RESPOND AS REQUESTED.": PRINT :
          GOTO 240
     260  INPUT "ENTER PRODUCT NUMBER:";P$
     270  IF  LEN (P$) = 0 THEN  PRINT "WE CANNOT CONTIUE WITHOUT THIS DATA.":
          PRINT : GOTO 260
     280  INPUT "ENTER QUANTITY:";Q$
     290  IF  LEN (Q$) = 0 THEN  PRINT "PLEASE ENTER THE CORRECT VALUE.": PRINT :
          GOTO 280
```

(or some similar messages)

Depending upon the program user's sophistication, even more detailed error messages for problems like the null string entry and others may be necessary. Our examples have given minimum messages to keep the examples short, uncluttered, and easy to understand, but they may not be adequate to ensure a proper response. Return to this example.

```
170  INPUT "ENTER CUSTOMER NUMBER:";C$
180  IF  LEN (C$) = 0 THEN  GOSUB 1010: PRINT : GOTO 170
        :
        :
1010  PRINT "YOU APPARENTLY PRESSED THE 'RETURN' KEY WITHOUT MAKING AN
      ENTRY."
1020  PRINT "WE NEED A CUSTOMER NUMBER WITH THIS FORMAT: A-121."
1030  RETURN
```

Another example:

```
230  INPUT "ENTER COMPANY NAME:";C$
240  IF  LEN (C$) > 12 THEN  GOSUB 1010: PRINT : GOTO 230
        :
        :
1010  PRINT : PRINT : PRINT "YOU ENTERED: ";C$
1020  PRINT "PLEASE ABBREVIATE THE COMPANY NAME TO 12 CHARACTERS OR LESS."
1030  PRINT "EXAMPLE: ALPHA PRODUCTS COMPANY COULD BE SHORTENED TO 'ALPHA
      PRO CO'"
1040  RETURN
```

Subroutines need to be protected from the main program that calls or branches to them. Depending on how a program is constructed, a subroutine could be encountered and executed as if it were part of the main program, especially if the subroutine section is one of the program's last modules. *Use a STOP or END statement between the main program and the module(s) containing the subroutines.* This protects the first subroutine in the subroutine module from being executed in normal line number order. If the first subroutine is executed, the computer will stop executing the program and give an error message when it encounters a RETURN statement for which the program has no matching GOSUB statement that sent it to the subroutine.

(a)   Write an error message subroutine accessed by a GOSUB statement executed after a true IF. . .THEN comparison; one that displays an INPUT entry and describes how to comply with the limit of twenty characters (because of data field length) for entries to the following statement:

```
320  INPUT "ENTER PRODUCT DESCRIPTION:";P$
```

Sample entry to above statement:

```
RUN
ENTER PRODUCT DESCRIPTION:LEFT HANDED MONKEY WRENCH
```

_____

_____

_____

_____

_____

– – – – – – – – – – – – – – – –

(a)   Your solution should be similar to this:

```
330  IF  LEN (P$) > 20 THEN  GOSUB 1120: PRINT : GOTO 320
     :
     :
     :
1110 STOP
1120 PRINT : PRINT : PRINT "YOU ENTERED >> ";P$;" << FOR PRODUCT
     DESCRIPTION."
1130 PRINT "PLEASE REENTER, BUT SHORTEN YOUR ENTRY BY USING ABBREVIATIONS"
1140 PRINT "SO THAT THE PRODUCT DESCRIPTION IS 20 CHARACTERS OR LESS IN
     LENGTH,"
1150 PRINT "INCLUDING THE SPACES AND PUNCTUATION."
1160 RETURN
```

REPLACEMENT OF DATA ITEMS CONTAINED IN A DATA FIELD

You may encounter problems when you attempt to change a data item in a data field. The most practical solution is *always use data fields of predefined lengths for each data item in a string.* That way any changes or replacements with MID$ will be complete, rather than partial, as happened above.

Now design program modules to accomplish assignment and extraction of data in fields within strings, using first and last names as examples.

Step 1. Define the field for the first name to have eight characters and that for the last name, twelve characters, with a space after each name field.

Step 2. Create the data entry routine.

```
100   INPUT "ENTER FIRST NAME:";F$
110   IF  LEN (F$) = 0 THEN  PRINT : PRINT "PLEASE, WE MUST HAVE THE NAME.":
      PRINT : GOTO 100
120   IF  LEN (F$) > 8 THEN  PRINT : PRINT "FIRST NAME TOO LARGE. 8 CHAR.
      MAX.": PRINT : GOTO 100
130   IF  LEN (F$) < 8 THEN  LET F$ = F$ + " ": GOTO 130
140   INPUT "ENTER LAST NAME:";L$
150   IF  LEN (L$) = 0 THEN  PRINT : PRINT "PLEASE, WE MUST HAVE THE LAST
      NAME.": PRINT : GOTO 140
160   IF  LEN (L$) > 12 THEN  PRINT : PRINT "LAST NAME TOO LONG. 12
      CHAR.MAX.": PRINT : GOTO 140
170   IF  LEN (L$) < 12 THEN  LET L$ = L$ + " ": GOTO 170
180   :
190   REM     CONCATENATED NAMES
200   :
210   LET N$ = F$ + " " + L$ + " "
220   PRINT : PRINT N$: PRINT
230   :
```

Step 3. Replacement routine for last name field.

```
240   REM  NEW LAST NAME TO REPLACE OLD LAST NAME
250   :
260   INPUT "ENTER NEW LAST NAME:";L1$
270   IF  LEN (L1$) = 0 THEN  PRINT : PRINT "PLEASE, WE MUST HAVE A LAST
      NAME.": PRINT : GOTO 260
280   IF  LEN (L1$) > 12 THEN  PRINT : PRINT "LAST NAME TOO LONG. 12
      CHAR.MAX.": PRINT : GOTO 260
290   IF  LEN (L1$) < 12 THEN  LET L1$ = L1$ + " ": GOTO 290
300   LET N$ = MID$ (N$,1,9) + L1$ + " "
310   :
```

Step 4. Name printing routines.

```
320   REM     NAME PRINTING ROUTINE
330   :
340   REM     TO PRINT FIRST NAME ONLY
350   :
360   PRINT : PRINT  MID$ (N$,1,8)
370   :
380   REM     TO PRINT LAST NAME ONLY
390   :
400   PRINT : PRINT  MID$ (N$,10,12)
410   :
420   REM     TO PRINT COMPLETE NAME
430   :
440   PRINT : PRINT N$
```

Check your understanding of the routines above by answering the following questions.

(a)   In line 170, what is the purpose of L$ = L$ + " "?

_____

_____

(b)   What does line 210 do? _____

_____

_____

(c)   In line 300, what does the MID$ function do? _____

_____

_____

_____

_____

_____

(d)   If F$ = "VAL" and L$ = "JEANS", how will N$ appear when printed or dis-
played by line 220? _____

(a)   Fills in unused character positions with blanks to the correct field length (same
technique used in lines 160 and 420)
(b)   Packs first and last names into N$
(c)   Concatenates the first nine characters of original N$ with the new last name
(F1$), creating a new N$ assignment
(d)   VAL   JEANS
(All "padding" spaces are included when N$ is printed.)

THE VAL FUNCTION IN DATA ENTRY CHECKS

If the product number and quantity ordered in a program must be numeric quantities,
VAL( ) can easily convert these numbers stored as strings to numeric values.

```
330    LET A$ = "128.95"
340    PRINT  VAL (A$)
350    LET A =   VAL (A$)
360    PRINT A

]RUN
128.95
128.95
```

In the conversion, either a leading space is added for the implied plus sign, or a minus
sign is provided if the quantities were negative.
But the VAL( ) function does not completely solve the problem of converting
string numbers to numeric values. For example, alphabetic information included in a
string you wish to convert to a numeric value presents a very real problem that can
range from accidentally using the letter O (oh) for a zero, to a quantity that includes
the units that measure that quantity (12 quarts). Therefore, always test to be sure
that if numeric values are needed, that is what was entered.

Following are some sample values run on our APPLE II.

```
100  REM      VAL FUNCTION TEST#1
110  :
120  LET A$ = "ABC"
130  PRINT A$, VAL (A$)
140  :
150  REM      TEST#2-NULL STRING
160  :
170  LET A$ = ""
180  PRINT A$, VAL (A$)
190  :
200  REM      TEST#3
210  :
220  LET A$ = "123ABC"
230  PRINT A$, VAL (A$)
240  :
250  REM      TEST#4
260  LET A$ = "ABC123"
270  PRINT A$, VAL (A$)
```

The RUN:

```
]RUN
ABC              0
                 0
123ABC           123
ABC123           0
```

Notice in the RUN above that alphabetic characters result in a value of $\emptyset$, as do a null string and the mixed alphanumeric data where the alpha information *precedes* the numeric (ABC123). Notice also that the mixed data 123ABC results in a value of 123. The APPLESOFT BASIC's VAL function disregards the alphabet information that *follows* numeric information in the same string. This is convenient if you wish to enter the quantity and the units, such as 14 gallons, but inconvenient if you wish to check for the validity of the data entered. Here, you want to ascertain that the data entered are numeric, so when the VAL function entry test is used you get valid numeric values. At this point, for mixed numbers and letters, assume that the user did enter the correct value.

The test to validate numeric information would be:

```
100  IF  VAL (A$) = 0 THEN  PRINT "ENTER NUMERIC VALUES ONLY."
```

Note that the entry passes the test if only the first character entered is numeric.

(a) Now do some programming. For the data entry problem on page 60, you wrote a program to produce a data entry sequence with null string checks added. Now add data checks that ensure that the product number and quantity ordered are numeric values. Also include a data check to be certain that the product number is a four-digit number.

_____

_____

_____

_____
_____
_____
_____
_____
_____
_____
_____
_____
_____
_____
_____
_____
_____
_____
_____
_____
_____
_____
_____
_____
_____
_____
_____
_____

– – – – – – – – – – – – – – – – –

(a)
```
210 :
220   INPUT "ENTER CUSTOMER NUMBER:";C$
230   IF  LEN (C$) = 0 THEN  PRINT "ENTRY ERROR. PLEASE REENTER.": PRINT :
      GOTO 220
240   INPUT "ENTER CUSTOMER NAME:";N$
250   IF  LEN (N$) = 0 THEN  PRINT "PLEASE RESPOND AS REQUESTED.": PRINT :
      GOTO 240
260   INPUT "ENTER PRODUCT NUMBER:";P$
270   IF  LEN (P$) = 0 THEN  PRINT "WE CANNOT CONTINUE WITHOUT THIS DATA.":
      PRINT : GOTO 260
272   IF  VAL (P$) = 0 THEN  PRINT : PRINT "PLEASE ENTER NUMBERS ONLY.":
      PRINT : GOTO 260
274   IF  LEN (P$) <  > 4 THEN  PRINT : PRINT "THIS ENTRY MUST BE A 4-DIGIT
      NUMBER, SO REENTER.": PRINT : GOTO 260
280   INPUT "ENTER QUANTITY:";Q$
290   IF  LEN (Q$) = 0 THEN  PRINT "PLEASE ENTER THE CORRECT VALUE.":
      PRINT : GOTO 280
295   IF  VAL (Q$) = 0 THEN  PRINT : PRINT "ENTER NUMBERS ONLY, PLEASE.":
      PRINT : GOTO 280
```

USING STR$ TO CONVERT VALUES TO STRINGS

The STR$( ) function serves the opposite purpose of the VAL( ) function. It converts numeric values into strings. This allows you to manipulate numbers with string functions. You can use it to convert numeric values to strings assigned to variables, in concatenating several small strings into a string variable, as done earlier in this chapter. For example, you may have combined product number, product description, and quantity in inventory into one long string. You may then need the quantity in inventory for an accounting procedure or another calculation. Such operations require a *numeric* value. You would convert the string to a numeric value by using the VAL( ) of the entry string. When the quantity is stored, you can convert back to a string by taking the STR$( ) of the numeric value to place it into the P$ string.

P$	17633	BOOK TITLE	144

```
P$ = P$ + STR$(Q)
```

or

```
Q$ = STR$(Q)
P$ = P$ + Q$
```

When the computer converts a numeric value to a string with STR$( ), a minus sign is included in the string if the value is negative.

Try this demonstration program:

```
140   LET X = 847.25
150   LET X$ =    STR$ (X)
160   PRINT "X =";X
170   PRINT "X$ =";X$


]RUN
X =847.25
X$ =847.25
```

In the example above, the LEN(X$) is six — five numeric characters and the decimal point. (Remember, blank spaces, decimal points, and other punctuation marks are characters.) If you fail to provide enough string length or field space, you will inadvertently lose significant digits or characters due to computer truncation. A six-digit number with a decimal point does *not* fir in a six-character field.

How many characters will the following data items have if they are converted from values to strings with the STR$ function?

(a)   171.83 _____

(b)   2001 _____

(c)   −999 _____

— — — — — — — — — — — — — —

(a)   6
(b)   4
(c)   4

CHECKING FOR ILLEGAL CHARACTERS

Using the ASC function in a data entry checking statement is a powerful tool to determine whether illegal or unlikely characters have been included in an INPUT string. Checking is done by a combination of the ASC function, the MID$ function, an IF. . .THEN statement, and a FOR NEXT loop. First the length of the entry is determined by the LEN function, which is used as the upper limit of the FOR control variable, like this:

```
350  INPUT "ENTER 6 CHARACTER CATALOG CODE:";C$
360  FOR X = 1 TO  LEN (C$)
```

Then the MID$ function, using the FOR control variable (value of X for any iteration) to determine which character to examine, selects each character in the string for comparison to an ASCII number, like this:

```
370  IF  ASC ( MID$ (C$,X,1)) = 32 THEN  PRINT "REENTER BUT DO NOT INCLUDE
     SPACES.": PRINT : GOTO 350
380  NEXT X
```

(Note: Here is one of those exceptions when the computer leaves or exits a FOR NEXT loop before completing all iterations of the loop.)

Notice that any character that can be entered as part of a string can be checked to see that legal characters that should be there are included, or that illegal characters are not included. Notice, too, that the error message could be located in a subroutine outside of the FOR NEXT loop. In addition, you can use the logical AND and OR to check for more than one character or group of characters in the same IF. . .THEN statement.

What if a user made the following response to line 350 in the example above? Answer the questions based on this response and this program segment:

```
]RUN
ENTER 6 CHARACTER CATALOG CODE:A - 1341
REENTER BUT DO NOT INCLUDE SPACES.

ENTER 6 CHARACTER CATALOG CODE:A-1341
```

(a)   What is the length of the substring selected by the MID$ function in line 370?

_____

(b)   What ASCII value is compared to 32 the first time through the FOR NEXT

loop? _____

(c)   The second time through? ————————————

(d)   On which iteration of (time through) the FOR NEXT loop is the comparison in

line 370 true? ————————————

(e)   What value does the FOR statement control variable have as an upper limit for

this user's response? ————————————————————

— — — — — — — — — — — — — — — —

(a)   1
(b)   64 (for A)
(c)   32 (for a space)
(d)   second iteration
(e)   LEN(C$) = 8

(a)   Write a data entry checking routine similar to the one before that prints an
error message if an illegal character is encountered. Use more than one IF. . .
THEN statement with the ASC function in the comparison, or a single IF. . .
THEN statement that uses the logical AND and OR. The only *legal* characters
for the entry are the digits Ø (zero) through 9 inclusive and the decimal point,
such as would be entered for a dollar and cents entry without a dollar sign.
Include a null entry test.

————————————————————————————————

————————————————————————————————

————————————————————————————————

————————————————————————————————

————————————————————————————————

————————————————————————————————

————————————————————————————————

————————————————————————————————

————————————————————————————————

————————————————————————————————

————————————————————————————————

– – – – – – – – – – – – – – – –

```
(a) 100    INPUT "ENTER A VALUE:";V$
    110    IF  LEN (V$) = 0 THEN  PRINT : PRINT "PLEASE ENTER AS REQUESTED.":
           PRINT : GOTO 100
    120    FOR X = 1 TO  LEN (V$)
    130    IF  ASC ( MID$ (V$,X,1)) >  = 49 AND  ASC ( MID$ (V$,X,1)) <  = 57 OR
           ASC ( MID$(V$,X,1)) = 46 THEN 150
    140    PRINT "INVALID ENTRY. ENTER NUMBERS AND DECIMAL PT. ONLY.": PRINT :
           GOTO 100
    150    NEXT X
    160    REM    PROGRAM CONTINUES
```

THE HOME INSTRUCTION

It is sometimes desireable to remove "clutter" from the screen, especially when asking the computer user for specific input, or after a data entry or data display operation is completed. Use APPLESOFT HOME instruction to accomplish this. HOME should generally be used just before a new display operation. (If HOME is placed in the program after a display or entry instruction, the screen may be cleared before the user has a chance to absorb the information). HOME may also be used in direct mode to clear a screen.

```
100    HOME
110    INPUT "ENTER A VALUE:";V$
120    HOME
130    IF LEN (V$) = 0 THEN  PRINT : PRINT "PLEASE ENTER AS REQUESTED.":
       HOME : PRINT : GOTO 110
140    HOME
150    FOR X = 1 TO  LEN (V$)
160    IF  ASC ( MID$ (V$,X,1)) >  = 49 AND  ASC ( MID$ (V$,X,1)) <  = 57 OR
       ASC ( MID$(V$,X,1)) = 46 THEN 190
170    HOME : PRINT "INVALID ENTRY. ENTER NUMBERS AND DECIMAL PT. ONLY.":
       PRINT : HOME : GOTO 110
180    HOME
190    NEXT X
200    REM    PROGRAM CONTINUES
```

(a)   The HOME instruction appears five times in this segment. Which ones should be

removed so that adequate information is displayed for the user.? _____

– – – – – – – – – – – – – – – –

(a)   All except line 100.

A DISCUSSION OF DATA ENTRY AND CHECKING PROCEDURES

This chapter has included recommendations, hints, and techniques for dealing with and checking data. This section describes and summarizes procedures used to check and validate all data entries.

There are two schools of thought regarding at what point incoming data should be checked for errors. One states that since the data entry operator's time is costly, the operator should merely enter data using the fastest possible procedures, with no checks for accuracy at the time data are entered. This position requires that more time be spent training the data-entry operator in fast, accurate computer entry techniques. Then, later, another program does the error checking on the data at fast computer speeds. Whenever a data error is encountered, the computer "kicks out" or rejects the entire data entry transaction for that set of data and prints the rejected information in a special report. The rejected data set is then reprocessed or reentered by the data-entry staff. This procedure works well if the number of rejects is low.

In contrast, we prefer the second approach — checking data on the way in. As each item is entered, it is error-checked immediately. If an error is detected, the computer operator is advised to reenter the data. One advantage is that the person making the entry error is responsible for correcting it. This method also gives management a better measure of an operator's work flow since only accurate, accepted information is completed during a work day. In the alternate method, data entry rates may seem high, but so may be the reject rate, and special procedures are need to verify who is making the entry errors. A less subtle technique is to signal an entry error with a terminal beeper or bell. Each time faulty data are detected, the sound signals the operator (and the manager, if present) that an error was made and draws attention to the "culprit." But these are concerns in a business environment. The immediate error check is more in keeping with the small business or personal nature of most programming applications presented here. And since all the error checking routines follow the data entry immediately, you can easily read the program to see what kinds of error checks are being made.

Two general data entry techniques are universally accepted. One uses a graphic reproduction on the video screen of the paper form from which data are entered. It makes sense to reproduce that form on the screen and have the computer prompt the operator to "fill in the blanks" just as they appear on the paper form or data source sheet.

A second generally accepted technique is one that repeats back to the operator one or more sets of data entered. The operator is then given the chance to reenter any incorrect items, even after the entry checking has been performed by the computer. This is the "last chance" to pick up spelling errors, number transpositions, typographical errors, and anything else for which entry error checks cannot be designed into the program itself. An example of such a post-data entry display appears below:

```
THANK YOU. HERE IS THE DATA YOU ENTERED.

     CUST. #        PROD. #         QUANTITY

 1 - 98213          17892           18
 2 - 98213          24618           12
 3 - 98213          81811           144

ARE THERE ANY CHANGES (YES OR NO)? YES
ENTER THE NUMBER OF THE LINE IN WHICH A CHANGE IS NECESSARY:
```

Before a summary report such as the one above is displayed, clear the screen of previously displayed information. If fact, clearing the screen before each new entry or after the entry of a data set is important in the entire concept of avoiding errors. If the graphic display of a data source form is used, then the screen should be cleared and the form redisplayed with the just-entered data. The operator can then double check with the option to make any corrections directly on the new form.

Many error-checking procedures depend on personal preference or company policy. Either way, plan ahead. Look carefully at the complete problem or job for which you are using your computer. In what form and format should the data be entered? Are there subtle limits or tests that you can apply to data to detect operator errors? For instance, if you are entering addresses with zip codes and a large percentage of your business is in California, then you know that most zip codes should start with the number 9. It would be appropriate to test whether the entered zip code value begins with a 9, and if not, to inform the operator of a *possible* error.

```
140   INPUT "ENTER ZIP CODE:";Z$
150   IF  LEN (Z$) ( ) 5 THEN  PRINT : PRINT "ZIP CODE MUST BE EXACTLY 5
      DIGITS. PLEASE REENTER.": PRINT : GOTO 140
160   IF  LEFT$ (Z$,1) = "9" THEN 210
170   PRINT : PRINT "THE ZIP CODE YOU ENTERED, ";Z$;" IS NOT FOR CALIFORNIA."
180   INPUT "IS IT CORRECT ANYWAY?";R$
190   IF  LEFT$ (R$,1) ( ) "Y" AND  LEFT$ (R$,1) ( ) "N" THEN  PRINT :
      PRINT "ENTER 'Y' FOR YES OR 'N' FOR NO.": PRINT : GOTO 170
200   IF  LEFT$ (R$,1) ( ) "Y" THEN  PRINT "PLEASE REENTER.": PRINT :
      GOTO 140
210   REM     PROGRAM CONTINUES
```

We also strongly recommend consistency in your data entry formats, especially for such things as data field lengths. Don't confuse yourself or others who use your programs. If you write several programs that use personal names, use the same size delimiters or data fields. This also allows you to have compatible data files for various uses. The same goes for address sizes and formats, product descriptions, and other alphanumeric data. Remember, your company may have already made the decision for you, so be sure you know the policies!

For numeric values, quantities, and entries involving monetary values, you may have to dig a little to discover the limits for which the data should be tested. Company policy, common sense, and actual experience may give you the logical limits for a "not less than" or "not to exceed" data entry check. And you can always use the operator override procedure for possibly erroneous data, as shown below:

```
330  INPUT "ENTER QUANTITY ORDERED:";Q$
340  IF  VAL (Q$) <  = 96 THEN 400
350  PRINT : PRINT "THE QUANTITY ENTERED EXCEEDS ORDER LIMIT OF 96 UNITS.
     PLEASE REENTER.": PRINT : GOTO 330
360  :
370  :
380  REM    ANOTHER PROCEDURE
390  :
400  INPUT "ENTER PRICE QUOTED:";P$
410  IF  VAL (P$) <  = 75.00 THEN 460
420  PRINT : PRINT "THE PRICE QUOTED EXCEEDS NORMAL LIMITS OF $75.00."
430  INPUT "IS IT CORRECT ANYWAY?";R$
440  IF  LEFT$ (R$,1) <  > "Y" AND  LEFT$ (R$,1) <  > "N" THEN  PRINT :
     PRINT "PLEASE ENTER 'Y' OR 'N'.": PRINT : GOTO 420
450  IF  LEFT$ (R$,1) <  > "Y" THEN  PRINT : PRINT "PLEASE REENTER.":
     PRINT : GOTO 400
460  REM    PROGRAM CONTINUES
```

Let's review the general data entry error-checking procedures for alphabetic and numeric information.

1. Enter all data into string variables after a clearly stated prompt request from the computer.
2. Enter only one data item per prompt.
3. If you are going to pack a number of data items (a data set) into one string, enter the data into separate string variables and then concatenate after all checking has been accomplished. Do *not* enter data directly into a substring position.
4. Checking should include a test for non response (a null string) of the type IF LEN(R$) = ∅. . .
5. When an error is discovered, include a message not only to tell the operator that an error was made, but also to describe as completely as possible what the error was. Do not merely request a reentry.
6. Check alphabetic data for field length using the LEN function.
7. It may be necessary to pad the entry with spaces to the proper field length, especially for alphabetic data.
8. Thoroughly test numeric data (which we recommend be entered into a string variable) in this order:
    (a) for non-response (a null string)
    (b) for excess string length, if applicable
    (c) for the inadvertent inclusion of alphabetic characters in numeric values, using VAL or ASC
    (d) for any company policy tests or size limit
    (e) if the datum is an integer value, test the value to see if it is an integer with a statement like IF $X <> INT(X)$. . . .
    (f) for negative values if they are not acceptable.

If this sounds like a lot of work, remember that your otherwise excellent program must have valid and accurate data to do its job. Don't skimp. Be complete. For example, the capability of the IF. . .THEN statement to PRINT a message may lull you into trying to oversimplify an error message in order to fit it into the same programming line as the IF. . .THEN statement. Don't fall into this trap. Use GOSUBs and provide complete, clear messages to the operator.

You may want to place all error tests and messages into subroutines. This gives your program neatness and clarity. Various entries may be put to the same tests, allowing the check statements to work for various entries if variables and other factors are compatable.

Be alert to other occasions throughout your programs where data errors may occur. While we encourage sensitivity to errors at data entry time, always check for data errors later in your program, especially if the data are subject to various manipulations after the entry routines. Watch for strange results from functions such as VAL. Get to know the version of BASIC you are using inside and out by thoroughly exploring the reactions of statements and functions in various circumstances. The error conditions you encounter will depend largely on your programming skills and the kinds of applications you program. Be alert to the errors that occur and include tests for them. Don't get psychologically locked in to your first, second, or third version of a program or programming technique.

Finally, be aware that many programmers test their programs with only sensible data, neglecting the ridiculous mistakes that can, and without a doubt will, be made. When you think you have covered every possibility, let a child with no computer experience try it out. If the program survives, you've checked it all out!

CHAPTER 3 SELF–TEST

1. Write an IF. . .THEN comparison that will be true if:
   (a) the entry has exactly seven characters.
   (b) the entry does not have exactly seven characters.
   (c) the first character in any entry is not a number.
   (d) the first character in an entry is a number other than zero.
   (e) the entry is not a null string.

   (a) _____

   (b) _____

   (c) _____

   (d) _____

   (e) _____

2. Write a statement line that checks to see if an entry has less than twelve characters, and if so, pads the entry with spaces so that the resulting string has exactly twelve characters.

   _____

   _____

3. Write a data entry checking routine that checks to see that no numbers have been included in a string entry. Write an accompanying subroutine, to be called when a number is found, that tells the user what was entered, and to reenter without including numbers in the entry.

_____

_____

_____

_____

_____

_____

_____

_____

_____

_____

4.   You now have the background to write a data entry module for most kinds of data to be later placed into a data file (covered in the next chapter). Write the data entry module and complete it with data entry error checks, as described below:

(a)   Write a data entry routine that prompts the use to enter:
     (1)   a five-character alphanumeric product code (must always have five characters)
     (2)   a product name with a twelve-character maximum length
     (3)   the quantity ordered into a three-digit field with a limit of 288 per order
     (4)   the price, into a five-digit field, with no price exceeding $99.99

(b)   Pack the information entered into one long string (M$) with the following fields:

M$ = _ _ _ _ _ / _ _ _ _ _ _ _ _ _ _ _ _ / _ _ _ / _ _ _ _ _
         C$ N$ Q$ P$

Note: Do not include slashes in the data field string.

(c)   Print parts of M$ in a "report" with the format shown below:

```
]PRICE: 1.25
QUANTITY: 24
PROD. CODE: 11234
```

Refer back through this chapter for ideas, and try debugging your solution program before looking at our way of doing it. Our solutions are not the only ones possible. The real test is whether the program works, and how foolproof it is.

Answer Key

1. (a) IF LEN (A$) = 7 THEN . . . . .

   (b) IF LEN (A$) < > 7 THEN . . . . .

   (c) IF ASC (A$) < 48 AND ASC (A$) > 57 THEN . . . . .

   (d) IF VAL (A$) < > 0 THEN . . . . .

   (e) IF LEN (A$) < > 0 THEN . . . . .

2. 120 IF LEN (A$) < 12 THEN LET A$ = A$ + " ": GOTO 120

(Your string variable and line number may be different, of course.)

3.
```
100   REM     SOLUTION, CH3, PROB3, SELF-TEST
110 :
300   INPUT "ENTER YOUR NAME:";A$
310   IF LEN (A$) = 0 THEN  PRINT : PRINT "NO ENTRY MADE. PLEASE TRY
      AGAIN.": PRINT : GOTO 300
320   FOR X = 1 TO  LEN (A$)
330   IF  ASC ( MID$ (A$,X,1)) > 47 AND  ASC ( MID$ (A$,X,1)) < 58 THEN
      GOSUB 1100: PRINT : GOTO 300
340   NEXT X
      :
      :
1090  STOP
1100  PRINT : PRINT "YOU ENTERED: ";A$
1110  PRINT "PLEASE REENTER, BUT DO NOT INCLUDE ANY NUMBERS.": PRINT
1120  RETURN
```

```
4.   100   REM     SOLUTION, CH3, PROB4 SELF-TEST
     110   :
     120   REM     VARIABLE LIST
     130   REM        C$=PRODUCT CODE(5 CHAR.)
     140   REM        N$=PRODUCT NAME(12 CHAR.MAX.)
     150   REM        Q$=QUANTITY ORDERED(3 CHAR.MAX.)
     160   REM        P$=PRICE(5 CHAR.MAX.)
     170   REM        M$=CONCATENATED DATASET(25 CHAR.)
     180   :
     190   REM     DATA ENTRY MODULE
     200   :
     210   INPUT "ENTER PRODUCT CODE:";C$
     220   IF  LEN (C$) <  > 5 THEN  PRINT : PRINT "CODE MUST BE 5 CHARACTERS
           EXACTLY. PLEASE REENTER.": PRINT : GOTO 210
     230   INPUT "ENTER PRODUCT NAME:";N$
     235   IF  LEN (N$) = 0 THEN  PRINT : PRINT "NO ENTRY MADE. PLEASE ENTER AS
           REQUESTED.": PRINT : GOTO 230
     240   IF  LEN (N$) > 12 THEN  PRINT : PRINT "ENTRY TOO LONG. PLEASE REDUCE
           TO 12 CHARACTERS MAX.": PRINT : GOTO 230
     250   IF  LEN (N$) < 12 THEN  LET N$ = N$ + " ": GOTO 250
     260   INPUT "ENTER QUANTITY ORDERED:";Q$
     263   IF  LEN (Q$) = 0 THEN  PRINT : PRINT "PLEASE ENTER AS REQUESTED.":
           PRINT : GOTO 260
     265   IF  VAL (Q$) = 0 THEN  PRINT : PRINT "ENTRY ERROR. NUMBERS ONLY,
           PLEASE.": PRINT : GOTO 260
     270   IF  LEN (Q$) > 3 THEN  PRINT : PRINT "TOO MANY DIGITS.  3 MAX.":
           PRINT : GOTO 260
     280   IF  LEN (Q$) < 3 THEN  LET Q$ = Q$ + " \": GOTO 280
     290   IF  VAL (Q$) > 288 THEN  PRINT : PRINT "ORDER EXCEEDS LIMIT OF 288
           UNITS. PLEASE REENTER.": PRINT : GOTO 260
     300   INPUT "ENTER UNIT PRICE:";P$
     305   IF  LEN (P$) = 0 THEN  PRINT : PRINT "NO ENTRY MADE. PLEASE ENTER AS
           REQUESTED.": PRINT : GOTO 300
     310   IF  VAL (P$) > 99.99 THEN  PRINT : PRINT "PRICE ERROR. MAXIMUM PRICE
           MUST BE LESS THAN 100.": PRINT : GOTO 300
     320   IF  LEN (P$) < 5 THEN  LET P$ = P$ + " ": GOTO 320
     330   :
     340   REM     CONCATENATE DATA
     350   :
     360   LET M$ = C$ + N$ + Q$ + P$
     370   :
     380   REM     DISPLAY DATA
     390   :
     400   HOME
     460   PRINT "PRICE: "; RIGHT$ (M$,5)
     470   PRINT "QUANTITY: "; MID$ (M$,18,3)
     480   PRINT "PROD. CODE: "; LEFT$ (M$,5)
     490   :
```

CHAPTER FOUR

Creating and Reading Back Sequential Data Files

Objectives: When you complete this chapter, you will be able to store and retrieve numeric and/or alphanumeric data in sequential disk data files, using the following BASIC data file statements in their special formats: OPEN, CLOSE, DELETE, READ and INPUT, and WRITE and PRINT.

INTRODUCTION

A data file is stored alphanumeric information that is separate and distinct from any particular BASIC program. It is located (recorded) on either a magnetic disk, diskette, or cassette tape. This chapter discusses using sequential (also called serial) data files on disks and diskettes.

In your previous BASIC programming experiences you probably hand-entered all data needed by your programs using INPUT statements. You did this each time you ran your programs. Or, if you had larger amounts of data, you might have entered the data with DATA statements and used the READ statement to access and manipulate the data. In either case, the data were program-dependent; that is, they were part of that one program and not usable by other programs.

A data file is *program-independent*. It is *separate* from any one program and can be accessed and used by many different programs. In most cases, you will use only one program to load a data file with information. But once your data file is loaded (entered and recorded) on a disk, you can read the information from that file using many different programs, each performing a different activity with that file's data.

For example, perhaps you have computerized your personal telephone and address directory using data files stored on a disk. You may need just one program to originally load information into that file and add names to it. (This chapter will show you how.) Another program allows you to select phone numbers from the file using NAME as the selection criterion. You can use still another program to change addresses or phone numbers for entries previously made in the file. Another program could print gummed mailing labels in zip code order using the same data file. You could design yet another program to print names and phone numbers by phone number area code. The possibilities go on and on. Notice that one data file can be accessed by many different computer programs. The data file is located separately on the disk in a defined place. Each program mentioned above copies the information from the disk into the electronic memory of the computer as it is needed by that particular program. Alternatively, the program could transfer information from the computer's memory to be recorded onto the disk.

If you already use your disk to SAVE and/or LOAD BASIC programs, then you have some experience with disk files. When you SAVE a BASIC program, it is recorded on this disk in a file. Such files containing BASIC programs are called *program files*. In contrast, the files discussed in this chapter contain data and are therefore called *data files* or text files. *Program files and data files* are different and are used differently. A BASIC program file contains a copy of a BASIC program that you can LOAD, RUN, LIST, and SAVE. A data file contains information only. You access this information using a BASIC program that includes special BASIC statements that access data files; that is, transfer all or part of the data from the magnetic recording on the disk into the computer's electronic memory so the program can use it. You *cannot* LOAD, RUN, LIST, or SAVE a data file. You can access the information only by using a BASIC program.

You can tell what type of files is contained on your diskette by listing a CATALOG on your screen or printer. Type the word CATALOG and press RETURN. Here is a CATALOG of one of our diskette contents:

```
*A 002 HELLO
*I  002 APPLESOFT
*B 027 MUFFIN
 A 013 RENUMBER
*T 023 QUIZ
 T 015 APPLE CHAPTERS
```

The column to the far left with the letter A, I, B, or T indicates whether the file is an Applesoft BASIC program file, Integer BASIC program file, Binary program file, or Text (or data) file. The asterisk (*) indicates whether or not the file is "locked," If it is, you cannot accidentally erase that file. See the APPLE II DOS Manual for the locking procedures.

The numeric entry in the second column indicates how many "sectors" of disk space are taken by the file, and, of course, the file name. A file name can be from one to thirty characters in length. The only "rule" is that the file name must begin with a letter. "Sectors" are explained in next section.

(a)   Describe in general-terms how you can access data in a data file.

_____

_____

- - - - - - - - - - - - - - - - -

(a)   Using a BASIC program that includes special file accessing BASIC statements.

DATA STORAGE ON DISKS

A magnetic disk (or diskette) has limited data storage capacity that varies from one computer to another, from one size disk to another, and from one recording system to another. For our APPLE II computer using version 3.3 DOS with sixteen-sector diskettes, the user storage capacity of the diskette is nearly 127,000 bytes of information. (The term "byte" will be explained shortly.) Using the 3.2 DOS, with diskettes of only thirteen sectors, the storage capacity is slightly over 103,000 bytes of information.

A disk refers to several styles of magnetic storage. Floppy disks are made of a flexible, magnetic-coated plastic, and come in two sizes − 8-inch and 5¼-inch. The smaller is often called a diskette. Hard disks are also available for microcomputers. Although more expensive, they have larger data storage capacities. Fortunately, these physical variations do not affect the BASIC statements used to store and access data files.

Other variations occur in the way data are recorded on disks. A disk can be recorded on one or both sides and in more or less space, depending on the disk drive system. A double-density system records twice as much data in the same space as a single-density system. A quad-density system is double-density recording on a system that can record both sides of a disk without "turning it over." Again, such variations do not affect the BASIC statements used to store and access data files.

Let's take a closer look at the single-density, 5-¼ inch diskette that is used by the standard disk drive available with your APPLE computer. The disk is divided into thirty-five concentric circles called tracks. Each track, in turn, is divided into thirteen or sixteen sectors, depending on whether you use DOS 3.2 or 3.3   Each sector has the capacity to store 256 bytes of information. The DOS uses three complete tracks. Therefore, the DOS 3.3 diskette has a user capacity of 496 sectors, while the DOS 3.2 user has only 403 sectors of storage capacity.

What is this thing called a byte? A *byte* is computer jargon for both a unit of computer memory and a unit of disk storage. Each byte has an electronic pattern that corresponds to one alphanumeric character of information. One letter of the alphabet, one special character, or one numeric character entered as a string (such as LET B$ = "3") takes up one byte of storage space. A twenty-character name takes twenty bytes of disk storage space. The general rule for storing strings in data files is that the amount of storage needed for each string is equal to the actual length of the string plus one byte for "overhead."

(a)   How many bytes of disk storage are required by the string assigned to N$?

```
N$ = "BASIC DATA FILES ARE FUN"
```

– – – – – – – – – – – – – – – –

(a)   Twenty-four, plus one for "overhead" (Spaces also take one byte.)

Keeping track of disk storage requirements for alphanumeric data in strings is easy, since one character equals one byte. Numeric values not entered as strings work in much the same way. Each character in the number, the sign (if negative), and the decimal point all take one byte, plus one byte for "overhead." The trick is knowing in advance about how large each number will be so that you can approximate how much storage space will be needed for numeric entries. With string entries you can limit the size of the data field, as we showed you in Chapter 3. You cannot, however, limit the size of a numeric entry. Therefore, you must plan ahead and estimate the space requirements for your numeric file entries. The examples below give the space requirements for each entry.

$$234 \quad = 3 \text{ characters} +1 = 4 \text{ bytes}$$
$$-127.5 = 6 \text{ characters} +1 = 7 \text{ bytes}$$
$$12.509 = 6 \text{ characters} +1 = 7 \text{ bytes}$$
$$.0002 \quad = 5 \text{ characters} +1 = 6 \text{ bytes}$$

For a personal telephone and address directory application, let's see how much disk storage space is required for each person on file. Each data item has a defined field length.

Name	20 characters	
Address (street)	25	
City	10	
State	2	
Zip code	5	
Phone (xxx-xxx-xxxx)	12	
Age	2	(Entered as an integer number)
Birthdate (xx/xx/xx)	8	
Subtotal	84	
Overhead	7	
Total	91	

(a)   How many bytes would be required to store the zip code as numeric value instead of a string? _____

(b)   Why was a twelve-character string rather than a numeric value used for the phone number? _____

_____

(c)   How many sectors would 150 entries in the address and phone directory take up in storage? _____

_____

(d)   What is the maximum number of people you could file in your directory on one disk with a capacity of 103,000 bytes? _____

_____

– – – – – – – – – – – – – – – – –

(a)   5, plus 1 "overhead"
(b)   Could not have included hyphens, which make number easier to read
(c)   92 times 150 = 13,800 bytes. 13,800 divided by 256 = 53.9, or 54 sectors
       (Note that if you placed all eight data items into one long string, you could
       save seven bytes of overhead, leaving eighty-five bytes per entry for a total of
       fifty sectors. This technique can save bytes per entry and, therefore, valuable
       storage space.)
(d)   103,000 divided by 92 = 1119

The eight items in each entry in the personal directory are called a *dataset*. A dataset consists of all data that are included in one complete transaction or entry into a data file. Grouping information by dataset and then accessing or otherwise manipulating the dataset as a group of data items makes programming and reading programs much easier.

Sequential data files can be visualized as one long, continuous stream of information, with datasets recorded one after the other. Imagine datasets recorded continuously on a magnetic tape cassette (a single, long ribbon of tape) and you have a fairly accurate image of how a sequential file looks in theory. That is how you as a file user should think of it. The truth is, a file can be partially located on one track or one sector, and partially on another, depending on the computer system and how the file was filled. Fortunately, the physical location of the file on a disk is "invisible" to the user. All you need remember is the long, continuous stream of information.

SEQUENTIAL VS RANDOM ACCESS DATA FILES

Data filing systems can use sequential data files or random access data files. The latter are explained fully in Chapters 6 and 7. Sequential data files use disk storage space more efficiently than random access data files. It will quickly become clear to you that a disk is easy to fill to capacity, despite the seemingly large number of bytes that can be stored on it. Thus, sequential files are *space-efficient*. However, it is somewhat difficult to change data stored in a sequential file. *Sequential files are designed for "permanent" information* that changes infrequently. You can change data in sequential files, but it is not as easy or efficient as in random access files, Thus, another criterion for choosing between sequential and random access data files is how often changes in data can be expected.

A third consideration is the time it takes to access information stored on a disk. When you have a large data file with loads of information, it takes more computer time to find or access a particular dataset at the end of a sequential file than it would in a random access file. To access the 450th data set in a sequential file of 475 data sets, the computer must sequentially search through 449 datasets before coming upon the 450th dataset. Using random access files, the computer can immediately access the 450th dataset without having to search through the other 449 datasets. Therefore access time is another factor in selection of sequential or random access data files.

(a)   What are three factors to consider when choosing between sequential and random access data files? _____

_____

_ _ _ _ _ _ _ _ _ _ _ _ _ _ _ _

(a)   Storage space efficiency, changing data, and time for accessing data

INITIALIZING SEQUENTIAL DATA FILES

To prepare to use data files, you must first tell your APPLE how many different data files you plan to use at one time in your programs. When you first load the DOS, your APPLE assumes that you will use no more than three separate data files at one time and reserves enough buffer memory space for those three files. If you know that you will use more than three files at the same time in one BASIC program, then you must execute a MAXFILES command.

APPLE will allow up to sixteen files to be used at one time. The MAXFILES command tells the computer how many files you plan to use. To allocate space for eight files, use this format:

MAXFILES8

You should execute the MAXFILES command before you even load your BASIC program, since its execution will sometimes interfere with the internal pointers (explained later) set by your program. If you must execute a MAXFILES command as part of a program, make the MAXFILES command the first executable statement in your program.

The MAXFILES command actually sets aside 595 bytes of memory for each file that will be used. This space is called a buffer; it acts as a go-between for the computer and the disk data file (see Figure 1). Input information accessed from a disk file is first copied into the buffer, 256 bytes at a time. It is then available for manipulation by the program. Likewise, data to be output from the computer for recording onto the disk are first accumulated in the buffer. When the buffer is full, the information is copied from the buffer to the disk file. The buffer is a holding area for all data coming to or from a data file.

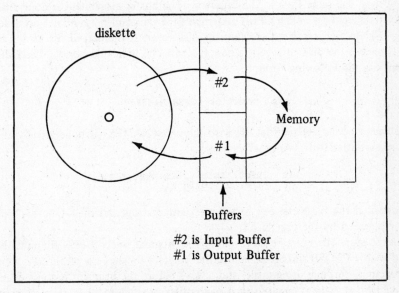

Figure 1: Data flow through buffers.

APPLESOFT BASIC statements that deal with data files fall into a special category of BASIC statements that require an unusual format to execute. These statements look like PRINT statements but are not really the same. The special format requires a PRINT followed by a CONTROL D character, followed by the executable statement:

```
100  PRINT "CONTROL D";MAXFILES5
```

While this looks easy, when you see a line such as 100 in a program listing, you will not see the CONTROL D. Control characters do not print in a program listing, so at some later time you may forget what you were trying to do. To establish a clean, readable procedure, we do the following in our programs:

1.   Define the string variable D$ with the Control D character in the initialization routine at the beginning of each program, as shown below.

```
150  LET D$ = CHR$ (4): REM    SET CONTROL D
```

2.   Use D$ in all special file statements.

```
200  PRINT D$;"MAXFILES 5"
```

Notice the punctuation in line 200. A semicolon (;) follows the PRINT statement and the BASIC file statement is inside quotations marks.

Normally, the first statement in your program that relates directly to data files is the OPEN statement(s) that identify to the computer the names of the files that will be used in the program. The OPEN statement causes the computer to assign one of the buffers to the file named in the OPEN statement. A buffer is needed for each file that is open at the same time in the program. The buffer assignment is done automatically on execution of the OPEN statement; the user and programmer need do nothing. The OPEN statement searches the disk to see if the named file aready exists. If not, it readies the disk to accept a new file with the indicated home. The OPEN statement has the following form:

```
140   PRINT D$;"OPEN NAMES1"
```

This statement opens a sequential file with the name NAMES1 if none already exists, and assigns a buffer to it. Another example:

```
140   INPUT "ENTER FILE NAME:";F$
150   PRINT D$;"OPEN"F$
```

This shows that the file name can be assigned with a string variable. Line 150 opens the file designated by the user in F$.

Just as every file must be OPENed by the program, every OPEN file must be CLOSEd with a CLOSE statement before the program finishes execution. As soon as your program is through using a file, and always before the program terminates, include a CLOSE statement to close each of the files or to close all of them at once. This also completes any transaction inside the computer system that the buffer was involved in, as explained in more detail in the next section. Once a file has been closed and the buffer unassigned, the same buffer may be used again by the program if you open new files. Here are some examples of CLOSE statements:

```
800   PRINT D$;"CLOSE NAMES1"

810   PRINT D$;"CLOSE"F$

820   PRINT D$;"CLOSE"
```

The Buffer Problem

CLOSE is a vitally important statement and, in most cases, is used to maintain the integrity and accuracy of your data files. Recall that the buffer acts as a go-between for the computer and the disk system. When you *output* data from the computer to the disk file, the data go first to the buffer. Then, when the buffer is full (256 bytes), the data are output and recorded onto the disk. This is often referred to as *updating the disk file.*

What happens if the buffer is only partly full of data and there are no more data to finish filling it? You might expect the half-full buffer to simply transfer its contents to the disk for recording when the program finishes execution. But it won't do that. The data in the half-filled buffer will not necessarily be recorded into the file; your file, therefore, may not contain all the information you expected. One important purpose of the CLOSE statement is to force the buffer to transfer its contents to the data file even though the buffer is not full. As a rule of thumb, any program with an

OPEN statement should have a CLOSE statement that is always executed before the program terminates. If you get trapped with a program that aborts or terminates and the buffer still contains data, CLOSE can be executed in direct mode, forcing the buffer to transfer its contents to the disk file. However, to have to do so indicates poor programming technique and would be completely unacceptable in a work environment. Further instructions on writing your programs to always execute a CLOSE statement are given later in the chapter.

(a)   What are two purposes of the CLOSE statement?

_____

_____

- - - - - - - - - - - - - - - -

(a)   To unassign the buffer and to force the buffer to transfer its contents to the disk data file.

Our APPLE reference material states that the buffer will automatically "flush" (transfer its contents to the disk data file) under normal conditions if the program executes an OPEN to the same file, CLOSE or MAXIFILES, or if the user switches languages by typing INT or FP (for Integer Basic or Floating-Point Basic). Don't count on anything else to flush the buffer! To repeat: Always include a CLOSE statement that is executed before the program terminates, so that buffer-flushing is automatic. You should only force buffer-flushing under emergency conditions, and then you should use the CLOSE statement in direct mode.

The buffer-flushing problem — and it is a real problem — makes it imperative that you *never* remove a disk from the disk drive if the disk contains an open file. Be certain all files are closed before you remove the disk from the drive, or you may find yourself with data from a half-filled buffer placed in the wrong file on the wrong disk, which can create some nasty errors. Be cautious, and remember that data go first to the buffer. They then transfer to the disk file once the buffer is full. If the buffer is not full, force it to transfer the data to the disk file with the CLOSE statement.

(a)   If you are outputting data in a program to a data file and the program accidentally terminates without executing a CLOSE statement, what should you do?

_____

_____

- - - - - - - - - - - - - - -

(a)   Close the file with a CLOSE statement in direct mode.

WRITING DATA TO A SEQUENTIAL DATA FILE

You have learned to set up communication between your APPLE and the disk system with the OPEN and CLOSE statement. Now you will learn how to place data into a file; that is, actually record data onto the disk. APPLESOFT BASIC does this using a special WRITE statement followed by a PRINT statement. The procedure is a little tricky, mainly because you have to plan the sequence of operation in your program.

To write to a file, you must use a PRINT D$ statement with a WRITE statement to begin the WRITE operation.

360 PRINT D$; "WRITE DEMO1"

Once you start the WRITE operation, any normal PRINT statement that follows will cause data to be printed to the file, rather than printed to the screen or printer. You can see how this is done in the next program segment in lines 360 and 370. The PRINT statement, then, actually causes the data to be printed to the file (after going first to the buffer). The WRITE operation is terminated by a blank PRINT D$ statement, like this:

410 PRINT D$

An INPUT statement INPUT N$ by itself will also terminate the file WRITE operation. However, an INPUT with a prompt string (INPUT "ENTER NAME:"; N$) will place unwanted data in your file by printing the prompt string message (ENTER NAME:) to your file before terminating the write-to-file operation.

In our example, we want to enter data from the keyboard, and then write the data to the disk file. We then enter more data and write it to the file. We will continue this procedure until we "signal" the computer that no more data are forthcoming, then close the file. The program creates a data file containing the information found in a school transcript showing classes taken, grades received, and units of college credit for the course. The general programming steps are shown below.

1. OPEN the file.
2. Enter the data.
3. Tell the computer to start the WRITE procedure.
4. PRINT to the file.
5. Terminate the WRITE operation.
6. Return to step 2 above.
7. CLOSE the file.

Here is our program. Read it over carefully.

```
100  REM       FILE PRINT DEMO #1
110  :
120  REM       VARIABLES USED
130  REM        N$=COURSE NAME
140  REM        G$=COURSE GRADE
150  REM        N=NUMBER OF ACADEMIC UNITS
160  :
170  REM       FILES USED
180  REM        SEQUENTIAL FILE NAME: DEMO1
190  REM        DATASET FORMAT:N$,G$,N
200  :
210  REM       INITIALIZE
220  :
230  LET D$ =  CHR$ (4)
240  PRINT D$;"OPEN DEMO1"
250  :
260  REM       'BARE BONES' DATA ENTRY MODULE
270  :
280  PRINT "TYPE 'STOP' INSTEAD OF COURSE NAME TO END DATA ENTRY."
290  INPUT "ENTER COURSE NAME:";N$
300  IF N$ = "STOP" THEN 460
310  INPUT "ENTER COURSE GRADE:";G$
320  INPUT "ENTER NUMBER OF UNITS:";N
330  :
340  REM       START FILE WRITE OPERATION
350  :
360  PRINT D$;"WRITE DEMO1"
370  PRINT N$: PRINT G$: PRINT N
380  :
390  REM       TERMINATE WRITE OPERATION
400  :
410  PRINT D$
420  PRINT : GOTO 280
430  :
440  REM       CLOSE FILE
450  :
460  PRINT D$;"CLOSE DEMO1"
470  END
```

(a) What is the name of the file used in this program? _____

(b) Data entry takes place in what statements? _____

(c) What signal is used to tell the computer there are no more data forthcoming?

_____

(d) What is the purpose of line 410?

_____

_____

(a) DEMO1
(b) 290, 310, 320
(c) STOP
(d) It turns OFF the file write operation before you return for more data entry.

Line 360 tells the computer to begin the write-to-file operation, also referred to as print-to-file, copy-to-file, or record-to-file operations. The PRINT statements in line

370 actually cause the data to be printed to the file (buffer). You can only PRINT one data item to the file with each PRINT statement. You cannot easily use one statement to print all three items as you would likely do if you were using a PRINT statement to display data on the screen or printer. Rather than use three separate PRINT statements on three different lines, we have chosen to complete the file PRINTing on one multiple-statement line (see line 370). The three data items are called a dataset, PRINTed to the file by us on one line. This method creates one file PRINT statement in the program, making it easier to check the program for errors.

Before the program returns for more data entry, the WRITE operation must be terminated. The blank or empty PRINT D$ statement at line 410 terminates the WRITE. Notice that there is no punctuation following the D$. Strange happenings can occur in programs when you accidentally place a semicolon after the D$.

The final operation is the CLOSE routine at line 460.

(a)   What causes the program to execute line 460?

_____

_____

- - - - - - - ┬ - - - - - - - -

(a)   The operator enters "STOP" as the course name: line 300 tests for "STOP" and branches to 460 to CLOSE the file.

There are other ways to use PRINT statements to print to a file. We mention them here in case you encounter them in programs written by other people. We do NOT recommend these procedures, primarily because it is too easy to make errors as you type the statements.

For *numeric data only,* you can use either of the PRINT statements shown below to print to a file. Notice that this procedure requires only one PRINT statement to print three data items.

```
100   PRINT A;",";B;",";C
110   PRINT A;";";B;";";C
```

(a)   What is the difference between the two statements?

_____

_____

- - - - - - - - - - - - - - - - -

(a)   Line 100 uses commas (",") to separate the variables; line 110 uses semicolons (";").

Notice the use of semicolons and quotations. With all that typing, you are bound to make errors. We think the procedure described earlier is easier and clearer: use one PRINT statement for each numeric variable holding data for the file.

For *alphanumeric data*, you *must* use separate PRINT statements for each string variable, as described before:

```
130  PRINT A$: PRINT B$: PRINT C$
```

A possible problem arises when you want to write information that includes commas to your file.

```
210  LET B$ = "PUBLIC, JOHN Q."
```

You would expect that the file print sequence below would cause the complete name to be printed to the file:

```
220  PRINT D$;"WRITE FILENAME"
230  PRINT B$
```

But it doesn't: The quotation marks are essentially ignored. The computer accepts the word "Public" and rejects the words ""John Q.." The only item placed on your file is the word "Public." Replacing line 210 with this statement compounds the problem even more:

```
210  INPUT "ENTER NAME:";N$
```

When RUN, the operator responds with:

```
]RUN
ENTER NAME:"PUBLIC,JOHN Q."
```

Enclosing the name in quotes, you would expect the complete name to be written to the file. Again, the computer confounds us by accepting the word "PUBLIC," rejecting "JOHN Q.," printing the error message "EXTRA INPUT IGNORED," and placing both the word PUBLIC *and* the error message on your file! And you thought this was going to be easy!

As you might expect, there is a way to program the APPLE to accept alphabetic data that includes embedded commas. The solution is to "force" quotation marks on either side of the name string variable by using the CHR$() function. CHR$(34) is the ASCII code for the quote (") symbol. Here is a PRINT statement that will accept and print to the file any alphabetic information that includes commas:

```
230  PRINT  CHR$ (34);: PRINT N$;: PRINT  CHR$ (34)
```

Note carefully the format and the use of semicolons and colons. The typing alone in the statement above may cause you anxiety. However, you need to worry about forcing quotation marks only when your string includes commas. This should not happen often and with careful planning it may never be necessary.

As noted earlier, using files requires planning. Your plan should consider:
1. What to include in each dataset.
2. How large each data item or dataset will be.
3. Whether technical points, such as imbedded commas in strings, must be handled with special techniques.
4. How to test each data item in the dataset as completely as possible for accuracy and validity.

With these considerations in mind, here is a program to help you place a simple inventory from your home or business into a disk file. The introductory module and possible checks for data validity are included.

```
100   REM        INVENTORY FILE LOAD PROGRAM
110   :
120   REM        VARIABLES USED
130   REM          T$=DESCRIPTION(20 CHAR.MAX.)
140   REM          N = NUMBER OF ITEMS
150   REM          V = DOLLAR VALUE
160   REM          D$ = CONTROL D
170   REM          R$=USER RESPONSE
180   :
190   REM        FILES USED
200   REM          SEQUENTIAL FILE NAME: PROPERTY
210   REM          DATASET FORMAT: T$,N,V
220   :
230   REM        INITIALIZE
240   :
250   LET D$ = CHR$ (4)
260   PRINT D$;"OPEN PROPERTY"
270   :
280   REM        DATA ENTRY ROUTINES
290   :
300   INPUT "ENTER ITEM DESCRIPTION:";T$
310   IF  LEN (T$) = 0 THEN  PRINT : PRINT "PLEASE ENTER AS REQUESTED.":
      PRINT : GOTO 300
320   IF  LEN (T$) > 20 THEN  PRINT : PRINT "PLEASE ABBREVIATE TO 20
      CHARACTERS OR LESS.": PRINT : GOTO 300
330   INPUT "HOW MANY ITEMS:";N
340   IF N <  > INT (N) THEN  PRINT : PRINT "ENTER INTEGERS ONLY, PLEASE.":
      PRINT : GOTO 330
350   IF N <  = 0 THEN  PRINT : PRINT "THERE MUST BE SOME UNITS! PLEASE
      ENTER A QUANTITY." : PRINT : GOTO 330
360   INPUT "WHAT IS THE DOLLAR VALUE OF EACH:";V
370   IF V <  = 0 THEN  PRINT : GOTO 460
380   PRINT D$;"WRITE PROPERTY"
390   PRINT T$: PRINT N: PRINT V
400   PRINT D$
410   :
420   PRINT : GOTO 300
430   :
440   REM        ERROR MESSAGE MODULE
450   :
460   INPUT "DID YOU REALLY MEAN ZERO VALUE, YES OR NO:";R$
470   IF  LEFT$ (R$,1) <  > "Y" AND  LEFT$ (R$,1) <  > "N" THEN  PRINT :
      PRINT "PLEASE,TYPE 'Y' FOR YES OR 'N' FOR NO.": PRINT : GOTO 460
480   IF  LEFT$ (R$,1) = "N" THEN  PRINT : PRINT "REENTER THE CORRECT
      VALUE.": PRINT : GOTO 360
490   GOTO 380
500   :
510   REM        FILE CLOSE ROUTINE
520   :
530   PRINT D$;"CLOSE PROPERTY"
540   :
550   END
```

(a)   What is the purpose of the blank PRINT D$ statement in line 400?

_____

_____

_____

_____

(b)   The above program has one small but important "bug." Find and describe the error.

_____

_____

_____

_____

— — — — — — — — — — — — — — —

(a)   To turn OFF the WRITE operation so you can resume data entry
(b)   The program never executes the file closing routine at line 530; the CLOSE statement is needed to assure flushing the last data items from the buffer to the file.

The problem of how to indicate to the program when to close the file is part of replanning. The program should include a way for the user to indicate to the computer that the user is done with the program for now, or that all data have been entered. Either of the two procedures shown below could be included in the previous program for this purpose. The choice is yours.

```
295  PRINT "TYPE 'STOP' IF NO MORE DATA. OTHERWISE,"
315  IF T$ = "STOP" THEN 530
```

or

```
405  INPUT "IS THERE MORE DATA TO ENTER (Y OR N)?";R$
406  IF  LEFT$ (R$,1) (  ) "Y" AND  LEFT$ (R$,1) (  ) "N" THEN  PRINT :
     PRINT "PLEASE TYPE 'Y' FOR YES OR 'N' FOR NO": PRINT : GOTO 405
407  IF  LEFT$ (R$,1) = "N" THEN 530
```

Now enter and RUN the program, creating a sequential data file named PROPERTY, which you will use later. This procedure works for terminating a program and closing files which contain discrete datasets, as have been described in the inventory program. But what about a variable length dataset — one with no predefined field lengths, such as a data file of recipes or a file of letters? How do you indicate to the program when one recipe or letter ends and another begins? And then, how can the computer "sense" the end of such data when inputting or reading back from the recorded data file?

One popular procedure is to place a flag or "dummy" character at the end of each dataset as a separator. The dummy character could be any character that would never be part of or found in the data. An asterisk (*) is often used as a dummy separator. Here is one way to insert such markers into the data file.

```
322   INPUT "IS THIS THE END OF ONE DATASET?";R$
323   REM    Y OR N DATA TEST GOES HERE
324   IF  LEFT$ (R$,1) = "Y" THEN  PRINT D$;"WRITE FILENAME": PRINT "*":
      PRINT D$: GOTO 410
```

A word of advice! When you write file programs (or any program for that matter) prepare some written documentation for yourself and other users. At least some description of the file layout is needed. Without written documentation, even you may have trouble seeing how the program works six months from now. A good procedure is to include such information in REM statements in the program itself as part of the introductory module.

(a)   Why is it important to inform the computer that all data to be included in the data file have been entered?

_____

- - - - - - - - - - - - - - -

(a)   so that a CLOSE statement can be executed to flush an unfilled buffer

And a word of extreme caution: When you WRITE to a file after an OPEN statement, you destroy any previous data that may be in that file! If you reuse a file, and place data into it from the beginning, you destroy the previous information that was placed in the file — but not completely. What happens is that some of the new data overwrite the old data (old data are erased and new data are recorded on the same disk space), but some of the old data may still be in the file! That means that when you use the file, you may have some of the new data you want and some old data you thought were destroyed. There is a way out of this mess. Follow these steps when you first initialize your file and you can be sure you have completely destroyed all previous data. Remember though, reuse only data files in which the old data are no longer of use.

```
140   PRINT D$;"OPEN FILENAME"
150   PRINT D$;"DELETE FILENAME"
160   PRINT D$;"OPEN FILENAME"
```

You must first OPEN the file before you DELETE it. This is done because the DELETE instruction first looks for a data file with the specified file name. If there is no file by that name, the DELETE statement will cause an error message and your program will stop altogether. You can see that using the first OPEN statement prevents the potential error condition. The moral of this lesson is think twice before you begin to WRITE to a file. Make sure the file is either new or deleted before you start to write new data into it; otherwise, you may end up with a file that contains a lot of "garbage."

Now you create a data file using the inventory program shown above. The data file should include several datasets and a procedure to inform the computer that all data have been entered, so that the file can be properly closed. Do NOT include a routine that places a dummy separator between datasets. The file you create will be used in another program later in this chapter.

READING DATA FROM A FILE

Now that you can output data from the computer to the data file, let's examine how to input or read data back into the computer's memory from an existing disk file. To do this, the most important thing to know is how the data were placed in the file in the first place; that is, what order and format a dataset has in the file. After that, reading from a file is simple and straightforward, with none of the complications that can accompany writing to a file.

To read from a file, first OPEN the file as you did for the PRINT to file operation. You then use a PRINT D$ statement to begin the READ operation. Any INPUT statements that follow the READ statement will input data to the computer from the file. The READ operation is terminated by a blank PRINT D$ statement, as before.

```
120    PRINT D$;"OPEN FILENAME"
130    PRINT D$;"READ FILENAME"
140    INPUT A$,B,C$
150    PRINT D$
```

Notice the use of commas to separate the variables in line 140 above.

It is important that the variables in the INPUT statements be the correct variable type (string or numeric) to match the data that appear next in the file. If the INPUT statement "looks" for numeric data in the file to assign to a numeric variable (B), and the next file data item is alphanumeric, then your program may terminate in an error condition or, perhaps worse, it will continue with bad data. If the INPUT statement looks for string data and the next file item is numeric, the number will be accepted and assigned to the string variable.

Is that good or bad? While the problem of having an open file and the program stopping in an error condition is avoided and the new problem of having invalid data takes its place — and after all that error checking at data entry time to place accurate data into the file in the first place! To avoid such hassels, be sure you know how the data were initially placed into the file, whether numeric or string data; and if strings, how long. Your documentation should show the format of your dataset, at least in the section of the program showing the variables used.

Returning to the simple inventory file named PROPERTY described earlier in the chapter, recall that the alphanumeric description (T$), followed by number of units (N), followed by value (V) were placed in the file in that order. The variable names T$, N, and V were used in the program when the data were printed to the file. The variable names themselves are separate from the data items. Therefore, you can use any appropriate string or numeric variable name in the INPUT statement when data are read from the file, as long as they match the variable type in the file, numeric or string.

(a)   Which of the following statements is appropriate to input data from the inventory data file named PROPERTY?

1)   270 INPUT A,B,C
2)   270 INPUT A$,B,C
3)   270 INPUT D1$,Q,D

_ _ _ _ _ _ _ _ _ _ _ _ _ _ _

(a)   Statements 2 and 3 are both acceptable.

Below is the companion program to the property inventory file program, to read the PROPERTY file and print a simple screen report with the data. Enter and RUN the program. Make sure the disk containing the datafile called PROPERTY is in the disk drive.

```
100  REM      READ DATA FROM PROPERTY FILE
110  :
120  REM      VARIABLES USED
130  REM        T$=DESCRIPTION
140  REM        N=NUMBER OF ITEMS
150  REM        V=DOLLAR VALUE
160  REM        D$ = CONTROL D
170  :
180  REM      FILES USED
190  REM        SEQUENTIAL FILE NAME: PROPERTY
200  REM        DATASET FORMAT:T$,N,V
210  :
220  REM      INITIALIZE
230  :
240  LET D$ =  CHR$ (4)
250  PRINT D$;"OPEN PROPERTY"
260  :
270  REM      PRINT HEADINGS
280  :
290  PRINT : PRINT "DESCRIPTION"; TAB( 22);"QUANTITY"; TAB( 33);"VALUE":
     PRINT
300  :
310  REM      FILE READ ROUTINE/PRINT REPORT
320  :
330  PRINT D$;"READ PROPERTY"
340  INPUT T$,N,V
350  PRINT D$
360  PRINT T$, TAB( 22);N; TAB( 33);V
370  GOTO 330
380  :
390  REM      CLOSE FILE ROUTINE
400  :
410  PRINT D$;"CLOSE PROPERTY"
420  END
```

```
RUN
DESCRIPTION          QUANTITY    VALUE

FILES                   2          49
COMPUTERS               1          4500
GLASSES                 24         5
DISKS                   15         4.25
```

(a)   What is the line number of the statement that begins the READ operation?

_____

(b)   What is the line number of the statement that terminates the READ operation?

_____

(c)   What is the purpose of line 360?

_____

— — — — — — — — — — — — — — — —

(a)   line 330
(b)   line 350
(c)   Displays the report on the screen

   This RUN terminated in an error condition with the message END OF DATA. This was an aborted end to the program execution. What if you wanted to do more with the data and did not want the program to terminate when the end of the data file was reached? A technique exists that allows the program to read to the end of the file without the program stopping at that point. To understand the technique, you must know how the data file "pointer" works. What follows is not an exact explanation of how the APPLE works, but it serves to explain how to detect the end of the file. The procedures used do, indeed, work on the APPLE.

   Just as with regular READ and DATA statements in BASIC, the data file uses a pointer to point "to" the next data item available in the buffer holding data from the disk file. When a file is opened, the pointer is positioned automatically at the beginning of the file and points to the first data item. Each execution of a file INPUT statement or a file PRINT statement pushes that pointer forward as many places as there are variables in the statement-variable list.

10   PRINT A$ moves the pointer one position, to the place where the second data item may be recorded.

20   INPUT N,N$ moves the pointer past data items 1 and 2 to item 3. The pointer is always looking at the position of the next available data ietm.

30   INPUT W,X,Y,Z moves the pointer four places, so the next data item read by an INPUT statement will be the fifth data item

When your program uses a PRINT statement to add data to a file, each PRINT statement moves the pointer and an end-of-file marker ahead one position. When all data have been entered, the end-of-file marker is located just past the last data item. The end-of-file marker is automatically put in place by the computer.

When you INPUT data from the file, the file pointer is always looking at the next data item available in the file (or in the buffer, to be more exact). An attempt to INPUT the end-of-file marker or anything beyond the last item of data results in an error condition that can be detected using the ONERR statement. The end-of-file error number is number five (5). Here are the statements needed to detect the end-of-file condition.

```
220   ONERR   GOTO 300
230   PRINT D$;"READ FILENAME"
240   INPUT A$,B
      :
      :
300   IF  PEEK (222) = 5 THEN   PRINT D$;"CLOSE": GOTO 800
```

Line 220 sets the error condition test. Notice that we placed it before the READ operation, since it does not have to be set more than once. One execution of line 220 sets the error condition trap, which continues in effect until the program stops execution or until another ONERR statement is executed during the program RUN. Line 300 tests to be sure that the error detected is the end-of-file condition. If it is, the file is closed.

You can modify the previous program so that it does not terminate with an END-OF-DATA error condition. Make these changes to your program.

```
325   ONERR   GOTO 410
      :
410   IF  PEEK (222) = 5 THEN 430
420   PRINT "UNUSUAL FILE ERROR. PROGRAM TERMINATED."
430   PRINT D$;"CLOSE PROPERTY"
440   END
```

An alternative modification would be as follows:

```
410  IF  PEEK (222) = 5 THEN   PRINT D$;"CLOSE PROPERTY": GOTO 440
```

With either "fix," the file will be properly closed.

A reminder: This is NOT a precise description of how the end-of-file mark works on the APPLE. However, while the explanation has been simplified, the procedures described to detect the end of a file do work correctly on your APPLE.

(a)   In the program to read and display PROPERTY, with the end-of-data error trap included, under what conditions is line 420 executed?

_____

– – – – – – – – – – – – – – – –

(a)   If the error detected by ONERR is not the out-of-data error

PERMANENTLY REMOVING FILES FROM DISKS

Situations will arise when you want to erase a data file from a disk. It may be a temporary file such as those created for demonstration programs in this book or a file that is of no further use to you for other reasons. Use the DELETE command. Using this command deletes the file named after the command from the disk, destroying the file's contents and deleting all reference to the file from the disk file directory. DELETE is a system command that is entered and executed like RUN or LIST. DELETE can also be used in an executable statement in APPLESOFT BASIC, but we discourage this use except, perhaps, for very temporary files. Here is the form:

DELETE FILENAME

Use the file destroying command very carefully, as the action is irreversible. Once the file has been deleted, there is no going back. Accidentally destroying the wrong file, especially if you have not made a backup copy, can mean that you wasted hours or days entering data into a file. Think carefully before using DELETE.

Be sure you understand the difference between DELETE and CLOSE. CLOSE merely disassociates a buffer from the file it was assigned to and flushes the buffer contents onto the disk if you are outputting data. After a CLOSE statement, the data file is still recorded on the disk. DELETE eliminates the file entirely from the disk, as well as all reference to it in the file directory.

We have used the word "copy" to describe how the INPUT statement works when data are transferred from the disk data file into the computer's memory. Copy implies that the data in the file do not change when they are input into the part of the computer's electronic memory designated as the buffer. The data in the file are unaffected and unchanged and remain in the file for another use. The only way to change data in a data file is with a WRITE and PRINT statement.

You can fill a file with data and read from the same file in the same program. But you must always CLOSE a file after outputting or recording information into it *before* you can reopen the file for input or copying data back into the computer memory. You must OPEN to output, then CLOSE and OPEN to read back the data. This procedure resets the file pointer to the beginning of the file.

The following program illustrates the procedure to open and close the files at the appropriate times. Quality assurance data are entered from a manufacturing process into a file. The program will read the QA values from the file and accumulate the number of responses in each category (1 through 6) in an array, and then print the results. The program is self-documented by REM statements.

```
RUN
QUALITY CONTROL MEASUREMENTS:
ACCUMULATED RESULTS

QA NUMBER        QUANTITY
1                6
2                5
3                2
4                10
5                9
6                2
```

```
100   REM     FILE INPUT/OUTPUT DEMO
110  :
120   REM     PROGRAM TO ENTER QUALITY CONTROL RESULTS
130   REM     INTO FILE.  PREPARE SIMPLE REPORT
140   REM     FROM FILE
150  :
160   REM     VARIABLES USED
170   REM        F$ = FILE
180   REM        N = QUALITY ASSURANCE MEASURE
190   REM        V = QUALITY ASSURANCE MEASURE
200   REM        C() = COUNTING ARRAY
210   REM        D$ = CONTROL D
220  :
230   REM     FILES USED
240   REM        SEQUENTIAL FILE NAME (USER ENTERED): QUALITY CONTROL
250   REM        DATASET FORMAT:N (EACH DATASET IS ACTUALLY ONE NUMERIC VALUE)
260  :
270   REM     INITIALIZE
280  :
290   LET D$ =  CHR$ (4)
300  :
310   INPUT "ENTER FILE NAME:";F$
320   PRINT D$;"OPEN"F$
330  :
340   REM     DATA ENTRY ROUTINE
350  :
360   PRINT : PRINT "ENTER INTEGER NUMBERS 1-6 ONLY "
370   PRINT "ENTER '99' WHEN DONE ENTERING DATA.": PRINT
380   INPUT "QA NUMBER:";N
390   IF N = 99 THEN 510
400   IF N < 1 OR N > 6 THEN  PRINT "PLEASE ENTER 1-6 ONLY": GOTO 380
410  :
420   REM   WRITE-TO-FILE ROUTINE
430  :
440   PRINT D$;"WRITE"F$
450   PRINT N
460   PRINT D$
470   GOTO 380
480  :
490   REM     CLOSE FILE
500  :
510   PRINT D$;"CLOSE"F$
520  :
530   REM     OPEN FILE TO READ
540  :
550   PRINT D$;"OPEN"F$
560  :
570   REM     READ FILE AND ACCUMULATE IN ARRAY
580  :
590   ONERR  GOTO 670
600   PRINT D$;"READ"F$
610   INPUT V
620   LET C(V) = C(V) + 1
630   GOTO 610
640  :
650   REM     ERROR TEST
660  :
670   IF  PEEK (222) = 5 THEN 730
680   PRINT "UNUSUAL ERROR. STOP PROGRAM"
690   STOP
700  :
710   REM     PRINT REPORT FROM ARRAY
720  :
730   POKE 216,0
740   HOME
750   PRINT : PRINT "QUALITY CONTROL MEASUREMENTS:"
760   PRINT "ACCUMULATED RESULTS": PRINT
770   PRINT "QA NUMBER","QUANTITY": PRINT
780   FOR V = 1 TO 6
790   PRINT V,C(V)
800   NEXT V
810  :
820   REM     CLOSE FILE
830  :
840   PRINT D$;"CLOSE"F$
850   END
```

Refer to the program on p. 101 to answer the following questions:

(a)   Through which statement does the computer obtain the name of the data file?

_____

(b)   Which statement checks the parameters for the quality control numbers?

_____

(c)   How does the computer know that all data have been entered? _____

_____

(d)   Why are two CLOSE statements used in the same program? _____

_____

(e)   What does line 590 do? _____

_____

(f)   In line 620, how many different values can V have? _____

– – – – – – – – – – – – – – – –

(a)   line 310
(b)   line 400
(c)   user enters 99 as input value
(d)   the data file must be closed after output and after input
(e)   sets trap for end-of-data error
(f)   six (1 to 6)

Help us write another program that first creates a data file called TEST, and then displays the contents of that data file. Complete lines 280, 320, 410, 470, 550, 590, 630, 670, 710, and 750. (Read the REMs and comments.)

```
100   REM      DATAFILE DEMONSTRATION
110 :
120   REM      VARIABLES USED
130   REM         A$ = OUTPUT VARIABLE
140   REM         B$ = INPUT VARIABLE
150   REM         D$ = CONTROL D
160   REM         X = FOR NEXT LOOP CONTROL VARIABLE
170 :
180   REM      FILE USED
190   REM         SEQUENTIAL FILE NAME: TEST
200   REM         DATASET FORMAT: A$ (DATASET IS ONE STRING DATA ITEM)
210 :
220   REM      INITIALIZE
230 :
240   LET D$ =  CHR$ (4)
250 :
260   REM      OPEN THE FILE
270 :
280   _____
290 :
300   REM      START WRITE OPERATION
310 :
320   _____
330 :
340   REM      USING A FOR-NEXT LOOP, PLACE 8 STRINGS INTO A DATA FILE
350 :
360   FOR X = 1 TO 8
370   LET A$ = "TEST" +  STR$ (X)
380 :
390   REM      PRINT TO THE FILE
400 :
410   _____
420 :
430   NEXT X
440 :
450   REM   CLOSE THE FILE
460 :
470   _____
480 :
490   REM      A PRINT STATEMENT TO TELL US ALL IS WELL, SO FAR
500 :
510   PRINT "FILE WRITTEN AND CLOSED"
520 :
530   REM      REOPEN THE FILE
540 :
550   _____
560 :
570   REM      SET END-OF-DATA ERROR TRAP
580 :
590   _____
600 :
610   REM      START THE READ OPERATION
620 :
630   _____
640 :
650   REM      INPUT DATA ITEM
660 :
670   _____
680 :
690   REM      TERMINATE READ OPERATION
700 :
710   _____
720 :
730   REM      PRINT TO THE SCREEN
740 :
750   _____
760   GOTO 630
770 :
780   REM      CLOSE FILE
790 :
800   IF  PEEK (222) = 5 THEN 820
810   PRINT : PRINT "UNUSUAL ERROR. PROGRAM TERMINATED.": PRINT
820   PRINT D$;"CLOSE TEST"
830   PRINT "FILE CLOSED."
840   END
```

— — — — — — — — — — — — — —

```
(a)   280   PRINT D$;"OPEN TEST"
(b)   320   PRINT D$;"WRITE TEST"
(c)   410   PRINT A$
(d)   470   PRINT D$;"CLOSE TEST"
(e)   550   PRINT D$;"OPEN TEST"
(f)   590   ONERR  GOTO 800
(g)   630   PRINT D$;"READ TEST"
(h)   670   INPUT B$
(i)   710   PRINT D$
(j)   750   PRINT B$
```

(a)   Now show everything that will be printed or displayed when this program is RUN.

_____

_____

_____

_____

_____

_____

_____

_____

_____

_____

_____

— — — — — — — — — — — — — —

```
(a)   ]RUN
      FILE WRITTEN AND CLOSED
      TEST1
      TEST2
      TEST3
      TEST4
      TEST5
      TEST6
      TEST7
      TEST8
      FILE CLOSED
```

One unique feature of file programs is that sometimes nothing appears to be happening when the program is RUN. There may be no printed report or any CRT display other than RUN and READY. To the novice, this seeming lack of activity may be alarming. Be forewarned.

(a)   Which statements in the previous program help assure the user that "invisible"

data file activity has taken place? _____

– – – – – – – – – – – – – – – –

(a)   lines 290 and 450

A final word about the blank PRINT D$ statement that we have used to terminate the READ or WRITE operation: If you follow our examples and procedures in your own programming, everything should work in your file-related programming. However, when you start to deviate from our procedures, you can run into some real problems.

We have been repeatedly warned by other people that there are times when the blank PRINT D$ statement will not work. On investigation (it never happened to us), we discovered that file PRINT statements must always end with a carriage return. If your most recent PRINT to file statement ends with a comma or semicolon, then a blank PRINT D$ statement will not terminate the WRITE operation. As a matter of fact, it will place the code for a Control D in your file and your file will end up filled with garbage.

```
250   PRINT D$;"WRITE FILENAME"
260   PRINT A$,
270   PRINT D$
```

Line 270 does NOT turn off the WRITE operation because of the comma at the end of line 260.

If you ignore our file programming procedures, which never use a PRINT to file statement that ends with a comma or semicolon, you must use the ASCII code signal for a carriage return, which is CHR$(13), before a READ or WRITE operation can be terminated. The procedure is to first PRINT CHR$(13), to force a carriage return, and then to PRINT D$. This forces a carriage return into your file. Some programmers do the following:

```
340   PRINT  CHR$ (13) +  CHR$ (4)
```

CHR$(13) puts in the carriage return. CHR$(4) turns off the READ or WRITE condition.

Now you are probably saying, "I'll just always use the CHR$(13) + CHR$(4) technique. That will solve the problem forever." Not so! If you always print a carriage return before the blank PRINT D$, you will be placing an "extra" carriage return in your file. This could ruin your future file reading because of the dataset format problem (the extra carriage return here and there looks like a distinct data item to the computer) and would certainly foul the operation of the end-of-file check that you use. The easiest way to resolve this problem is to make sure your program is nice and "clean."

CHAPTER 4 SELF-TEST

The problems in this self-test require you to write programs to store data in data files and then to write companion programs to display the data in those data files. All data files that you create in this self-test will be used in Chapter 5, *so don't skip this section.* The introductory module is given so your solutions will look something like the solution provided. Save the programs and files for later use, modification, and reference. Try your solutions (and debugging the programs) before looking at the solutions provided. Believe me, our "first draft" programs had to be debugged, too! Good luck and keep on hackin'.

1 a.   Write a program to fill a data file with the information and format specified below:

Four data items per dataset.
First two data items are strings.
Second two data items are numeric values entered as strings.
Include data entry checks for null strings.
For the numeric values assigned to strings, include data entry tests to see
    that only numeric values were entered. Then convert these strings to
    numeric values assigned to numeric variables before storing them in the
    data file.
Place at least three datasets in the data file. Name this file CUST.

```
100   REM     SOLUTION TO CH4 SELFTEST PROB 1A
110   :
120   REM     VARIABLE LIST
130   REM        A$, B$ = ALPHA DATA
140   REM        M$,M, N$,N =NUMERIC DATA
150   REM        D$ = CONTROL D
160   REM        R$ = USER RESPONSE
170   :
180   REM     FILE USED
190   REM        SEQUENTIAL FILE NAME: CUST
200   REM        DATASET FORMAT: A$,B$,M,N
```

1 b. Write a companion program to display the contents of the data file named CUST that you created in 1 a.

_____

_____

_____

_____

_____

_____

_____

_____

_____

_____

_____

_____

_____

_____

_____

_____

_____

_____

_____

_____

2 a. Write a program to make a data file called GROCERY that stores your grocery shopping list. Include the description or name of each grocery item (maximum of twenty characters) and a numeric value telling the quantity of that item to buy. Store at least six datasets in the file.

```
100   REM     SOLUTION CH4 SELFTEST PROB 2A
110   :
120   REM     VARIABLES USED
130   REM       N$ = ITEM DESCRIPTION
140   REM       Q  = QUANTITY TO ORDER
150   REM       D$ = CONTROL D
160   REM       R$ = USER RESPONSE
170   REM       F$ = USER ENTERED FILE NAME
180   :
190   REM     FILES USED
200   REM       SEQUENTIAL FILE NAME: GROCERY (USER ENTERED)
210   REM       DATASET FORMAT: N$,Q
```

2 b. Write a companion program to display the contents of GROCERY.

```
]RUN
ENTER NAME OF FILE:GROCERY

ITEM            QUANTITY

BEANS           80
BREAD           3
MILK            5
BUTTER          3

FILE CLOSED
```

3 a.   Write a program to enter the following data in a data file for a customer credit
       file maintained by a small business. Each dataset consists of three items:
       1. five-digit customer number (must have exactly five digits)
       2. customer name (twenty characters maximum)
       3. customer credit rating (a single digit number 1, 2, 3, 4, or 5)
       Include data entry checks for null entries and for the parameters set forth in the
       list above. Enter at least three datasets in the data file. Remember, the customer
       numbers must be different for each customer and should be in *ascending* order,
       i.e., each larger than the previous one, such as 19652, 19653, 19654, etc. Name
       this file CREDIT.

```
100   REM       SOLUTION CH4 SELFTEST PROB 3A
110   REM       CREDIT FILE LOADER
120   :
130   REM       VARIABLES USED
140   REM        F$ = FILE NAME
150   REM        C$ = CUSTOMER # (5 CHAR.)
160   REM        N$ = CUST. NAME (20 CHAR.MAX.)
170   REM        R$ AND R = CREDIT RATING (1 CHAR)
180   REM        D$ = CONTROL D
190   REM        Q$ = USER RESPONSE
200   :
210   REM       FILES USED
220   REM        SEQUENTIAL  FILE NAME: CREDIT (USER ENTERED)
230   REM        DATASET FORMAT: C$,N$,R
240   :
```

3 b. Write a companion program to display the contents of the file named CREDIT.
Our RUN looks like this.

```
ENTER FILE NAME:TRANSACTION-1
10762
1
57

18102
2
6.12

43611
1
4.34

43611
2
58.95

43611
2
88.5

80223
1
450

98702
2
43.45

ALL DATA DISPLAYED AND FILE CLOSED
```

_____

_____

_____

_____

_____

_____

_____

_____

_____

_____

_____

_____

_____

_____

_____

4 a. Write a program to enter data into a transaction data file. A transaction file is the data on a business transaction, such as that of a bank, a retail store, or a mail-order business. For our example, each transaction produces a dataset with three items, as shown below:

Account number = five characters
Transaction code = two characters (for a bank, 1 = check, 2 = deposit, etc.)
Cash amount = seven characters (9999.99 maximum amount)

Include data entry checks for null entries and for the parameters set forth above. Check cash amount entries for non-numeric characters, except the decimal point. Your program should allow the user to select (input) a name for the data file.

Create two different data files with your program, with seven datasets (seven transactions) in each data file. Name file #1, TRANSACTION-1, and name file #2, TRANSACTION-2. Use the account numbers given below for the two files. For duplicate account numbers, make a complete dataset entry, so that each of the two files contain seven datasets.

file #1	file #2
10762	10761
18102	18203
43611	43611
43611	80111
43611	80772
80223	80772
98702	89012

Note: Only the account numbers are shown here; the complete datasets also include transaction codes and amounts.

```
110  :
120  REM      VARIABLES USED
130  REM        F$ = USER ENTERED FILE NAME
140  REM        D1$ = DATASETS FROM FILE 1,2
150  REM        A$ = ACC'T NUMBER (5 CHAR.)
160  REM        T$ = TRANSACTION CODE (1 CHAR.)
170  REM        C$ = CASH AM'T (9999.99 OR 7 CHAR.MAX.)
180  REM        I = FOR NEXT LOOP CONTROL VARIABLE
190  REM        D$ = CONTROL D
200  :
210  REM      FILES USED
220  REM        SEQUENTIAL FILE NAMES: TRANSACTION 1, TRANSACTION 2 (USER
       SELECTED AND ENTERED)
230  REM        DATASET FORMAT: A$,T$,C$
240  :
```

_____

_____

_____

_____

_____

4 b. Write a companion program to display the contents of a data file with the above dataset format. Again, the file name should be user entered so that it can be used to display the contents of TRANSACTION-1 or TRANSACTION-2.

Our sample RUN:

```
]RUN
FILE NAME:TRANSACTION-2

A/C#              T-CODE          AMOUNT
10761             1               33.33
18203             2               21
43611             2               500
80111             1               54.58
80772             1               54.68
80772             1               88.88
89012             2               485.77
FILE PRINTED AND CLOSED
```

5 a. Write a program to load a data file named ADDRESS with (surprise!) names and addresses. The data has the format shown below, with each dataset containing five items in fields with one string

			55		
/1	20/21	40/41	50/12/53	57/	
name	address	city	state	zip code	

Include appropriate data entry checks and field padding routines. Enter at least four addresses in the data file.

```
100   REM    SOLUTION CH4 SELFTEST PROB 5A
110   :
120   REM     VARIABLES USED
130   REM        N$ = NAME(20)
140   REM        A$ = STREET ADDRESS(20)
150   REM        C$ = CITY(10)
160   REM        S$ = STATE(2)
170   REM        Z$ = ZIP CODE(5)
180   REM        E$ = CONCATENATED DATASET(57)
190   REM        D$ = CONTROL D
200   REM        R$ = USER RESPONSE
210   :
220   REM     FILE USED
230   REM        SEQUENTIAL FILE NAME: ADDRESS
240   REM        DATASET FORMAT:C$ (ONE STRING)
```

5 b. Write a companion program to display the contents of ADDRESS. Here is our
sample RUN.

```
]RUN
JERALD R. BROWN
13140 FRATI LANE
SEBASTOPOL
CA
95472

REGGIE JACKSON
#1 BALLPARK RD
EVERYWHERE
US
00000

JACK SPRAT
1 LEAN DRIVE
SKINNYVILL
EA
00003

FILE CLOSED
```

6 a.   Write one program and use it to create three different data files called LETTER1, LETTER2, and LETTER3. Each file should contain the text of a form letter with at least three lines of text per letter. Each line of text in the letters is to be entered and stored as one dataset.

```
100   REM     SOLUTION CH4 SELFTEST PROB6A
110   :
120   REM     VARIABLES USED
130   REM       T$ = TEXT LINE
140   REM       F$ = FILE NAME
150   REM       D$ = CONTROL D
160   REM       R$ = USER RESPONSE
170   :
180   REM     FILES USED
190   REM       SEQ. FILE NAME: LETTER#
200   REM       (# IS USER SELECTED & ENTERED)
210   :
```

6 b. Write a companion program to display the data files above selected by the user. Our sample RUN:

```
]RUN
ENTER FORM LETTER NUMBER:1
YOU ARE HEREBY INFORMED THAT ALL ELECTRICAL SERVICE TO YOUR AREA WILL BE
DISCONTINUED AS OF JAN. 1. WE HOPE THIS WILL NOT INCONVENIENCE YOU.
FILE CLOSED
```

Answer Key

1 a.

```
100   REM     SOLUTION TO CH4 SELFTEST PROB 1A
110   :
120   REM      VARIABLE LIST
130   REM        A$, B$ = ALPHA DATA
140   REM        M$,M, N$,N =NUMERIC DATA
150   REM        D$ = CONTROL D
160   REM        R$ = USER RESPONSE
170   :
180   REM     FILE USED
190   REM        SEQUENTIAL FILE NAME: CUST
200   REM        DATASET FORMAT: A$,B$,M,N
210   :
220   REM     INITIALIZE
230   :
240   LET D$ =  CHR$ (4)
250   PRINT D$;"OPEN CUST"
260   :
270   REM        DATA ENTRY ROUTINE
280   :
290   INPUT "ENTER DATA ITEM:";A$
300   IF  LEN (A$) = 0 THEN  PRINT "PLEASE ENTER SOMETHING": GOTO 290
310   INPUT "ENTER DATA ITEM 2:";B$
320   IF  LEN (B$) = 0 THEN  PRINT "LEASE ENTER SOME DATA": GOTO 310
330   INPUT "ENTER NUMERIC DATA:";M$
340   IF  LEN (M$) = 0 THEN  PRINT : PRINT "PLEASE ENTER SOMETHING": PRINT :
      GOTO 330
350   IF  VAL (M$) = 0 THEN  PRINT : PRINT "PLEASE ENTER NUMBERS ONLY":
      PRINT : GOTO 330
360   LET M =  VAL (M$)
370   INPUT "ENTER NUMERIC ITEM 2:";N$
380   IF  LEN (N$) = 0 THEN  PRINT : PRINT "PLEASE ENTER SOMETHING": PRINT :
      GOTO 370
390   IF  VAL (N$) = 0 THEN  PRINT : PRINT "PLEASE ENTER NUMBERS ONLY":
      PRINT : GOTO 370
400   LET N =  VAL (N$)
410   :
420   REM     WRITE TO FILE
430   :
440   PRINT D$;"WRITE CUST"
450   PRINT A$: PRINT B$: PRINT M: PRINT N
460   PRINT D$
470   INPUT "MORE DATA?";R$
480   IF  LEFT$ (R$,1) <  > "Y" AND  LEFT$ (R$,1) <  > "N" THEN  PRINT :
      PRINT "TYPE 'Y' FOR YES OR 'N' FOR NO.": PRINT : GOTO 470
490   IF R$ = "Y" THEN 290
500   :
510   REM     CLOSE FILE
520   :
530   PRINT D$;"CLOSE CUST"
540   PRINT "FILE CLOSED"
550   END
```

1 b.

```
100   REM     SOLUTION TO CH4 SELFTEST PROB 1B
110   :
120   REM     VARIABLES USED
130   REM       A$,B$ = ALPHA DATA
140   REM       M,N = NUMERIC DATA
150   REM       D$ = CONTROL D
160   :
170   REM     FILE USED
180   REM       SEQUENTIAL FILE NAME: CUST
190   REM       DATASET FORMAT:A$,B$,M,N
200   :
210   REM     INITIALIZE
220   :
230   LET D$ =  CHR$ (4)
240   PRINT D$;"OPEN CUST"
250   :
260   REM     INPUT DATA FROM FILE & DISPLAY
270   :
280   ONERR  GOTO 370
290   PRINT D$;"READ CUST"
300   INPUT A$,B$,M,N
310   PRINT D$
320   PRINT A$: PRINT B$: PRINT M: PRINT N: PRINT
330   GOTO 290
340   :
350   REM     CLOSE FILE
360   :
370   IF  PEEK (222) = 5 THEN 390
380   PRINT : PRINT "UNUSUAL ERROR. PROGRAM TERMINATED.": PRINT
390   PRINT D$;"CLOSE CUST"
400   PRINT "ALL DATA DISPLAYED AND FILE CLOSED"
410   END
```

2 a.

```
100   REM     SOLUTION CH4 SELFTEST PROB 2A
110   :
120   REM      VARIABLES USED
130   REM       N$ = ITEM DESCRIPTION
140   REM       Q = QUANTITY TO ORDER
150   REM       D$ = CONTROL D
160   REM       R$ = USER RESPONSE
170   REM       F$ = USER ENTERED FILE NAME
180   :
190   REM      FILES USED
200   REM       SEQUENTIAL FILE NAME: GROCERY (USER ENTERED)
210   REM       DATASET FORMAT: N$,Q
220   :
230   REM      INITIALIZATION
240   :
250   LET D$ =  CHR$ (4)
260   INPUT "ENTER NAME OF FILE:";F$
270   PRINT D$;"OPEN"F$
280   PRINT D$;"DELETE"F$
290   PRINT D$;"OPEN"F$
300   :
310   REM      DATA ENTRY ROUTINE
320   :
330   HOME
340   PRINT "ENTER 'STOP' WHEN ALL DATA IS ENTERED.": PRINT
350   INPUT "ENTER ITEM DESCRIPTION:";N$
360   IF N$ = "STOP" THEN 550
370   IF  LEN (N$) = 0 THEN  PRINT : PRINT "PLEASE ENTER A DESCRIPTION OR
      'STOP'": PRINT :_ GOTO 350
380   IF  LEN (N$) > 20 THEN  PRINT : PRINT "SHORTEN DESCRIPTION TO 20
      CHARS. AND REENTER": PRINT : GOTO 350
390   INPUT "ENTER QUANTITY:";Q
400   IF Q >  = 1 AND Q < 10 THEN 480
410   PRINT "YOU ENTERED A QUANTITY OF ";Q
420   INPUT "IS THAT WHAT YOU WANTED?";R$
430   IF  LEFT$ (R$,1) <  > "Y" AND  LEFT$ (R$,1) <  > "N" THEN  PRINT :
      PRINT "TYPE 'Y' FOR YES OR 'N' FOR NO": PRINT : GOTO 410
440   IF  LEFT$ (R$,1) = "N" THEN 390
450   :
460   REM      WRITE TO FILE ROUTINE
470   :
480   PRINT D$;"WRITE"F$
490   PRINT N$: PRINT Q
500   PRINT D$
510   GOTO 330
520   :
530   REM      CLOSE FILE
540   :
550   PRINT D$;"CLOSE"F$
560   PRINT "FILE CLOSED"
570   END
```

2 b.

```
100   REM       SOLUTION CH4 SELFTEST PROB 2B
110   :
120   REM       VARIABLES USED
130   REM         N$ = ITEM DESCRIPTION
140   REM         Q = QUANTITY TO ORDER
150   REM         D$ = CONTROL D
160   REM         F$ = USER ENTERED FILE NAME
170   :
180   REM       FILES USED
190   REM         SEQUENTIAL FILE NAME: GROCERY (USER ENTERED)
200   REM         DATASET FORMAT: N$,Q
210   :
220   REM       INITIALIZATION
230   :
240   LET D$ =  CHR$ (4)
250   INPUT "ENTER NAME OF FILE:";F$
260   PRINT D$;"OPEN"F$
270   :
280   REM       READ AND PRINT FILE
290   :
300   PRINT : PRINT "ITEM","QUANTITY": PRINT
310   ONERR  GOTO 400
320   PRINT D$;"READ"F$
330   INPUT N$,Q
340   PRINT D$
350   PRINT N$,Q
360   GOTO 320
370   :
380   REM       CLOSE FILE
390   :
400   IF  PEEK (222) = 5 THEN 420
410   PRINT : PRINT "UNUSUAL ERROR. PROGRAM TERMINATED": PRINT : GOTO 420
420   PRINT D$;"CLOSE"F$
430   PRINT : PRINT "FILE CLOSED"
440   END
```

3 a.

```
100   REM       SOLUTION CH4 SELFTEST PROB 3A
110   REM       CREDIT FILE LOADER
120   :
130   REM       VARIABLES USED
140   REM       F$ = FILE NAME
150   REM       C$ = CUSTOMER # (5 CHAR.)
160   REM       N$ = CUST. NAME (20 CHAR.MAX.)
170   REM       R$ AND R = CREDIT RATING (1 CHAR)
180   REM       D$ = CONTROL D
190   REM       Q$ = USER RESPONSE
200   :
210   REM       FILES USED
220   REM         SEQUENTIAL  FILE NAME: CREDIT (USER ENTERED)
230   REM         DATASET FORMAT: C$,N$,R
240   :
250   REM       INITIALIZE
260   :
270   LET D$ =  CHR$ (4)
280   HOME
290   INPUT "ENTER FILE NAME:";F$
300   PRINT D$;"OPEN"F$
310   PRINT D$;"DELETE"F$
320   PRINT D$;"OPEN"F$
330   :
340   REM       DATA ENTRY ROUTINE
350   :
360   PRINT "ENTER 'STOP' WHEN FINISHED ENTERING DATA.": PRINT
370   INPUT "ENTER CUSTOMER NUMBER:";C$
380   IF C$ = "STOP" THEN 670
390   IF  LEN (C$) = 0 THEN  PRINT : PRINT "ENTER NUMBERS OR TYPE 'STOP'":
      PRINT : GOTO 370
400   IF  LEN (C$) ( ) 5 THEN  PRINT : PRINT "ENTRY ERROR. NUMBER HAS 5
      DIGITS.": PRINT : GOTO 370
410   IF  VAL (C$) = 0 THEN  PRINT : PRINT "ENTRY ERROR. NUMBERS ONLY,
      PLEASE.": PRINT : GOTO 290
420   :
430   PRINT : INPUT "ENTER CUSTOMER NAME:";N$
440   IF  LEN (N$) = 0 THEN  PRINT "PLEASE ENTER A NAME, NOW.": GOTO 430
450   IF  LEN (N$) ) 20 THEN  PRINT "PLEASE LIMIT NAME TO 20 CHARS AND
      REENTER.": GOTO 430

460   :
470   PRINT : INPUT "CREDIT RATING:";R$
480   IF  LEN (R$) ( ) 1 THEN  PRINT "ONLY A ONE DIGIT NUMBER IS
      ACCEPTABLE.": GOTO 470
490   IF  VAL (R$) ( 1 OR  VAL (R$) ) 5 THEN  PRINT "NUMBERS 1-5 ONLY,
      PLEASE.": GOTO 470
500   LET R =  VAL (R$)
510   :
520   REM       PRINT TO FILE
530   :
540   PRINT D$;"WRITE"F$
550   PRINT C$: PRINT N$: PRINT R
560   PRINT D$
570   :
580   REM       MORE DATA ROUTINE
590   :
600   HOME
610   INPUT "DO YOU HAVE MORE DATA TO ENTER?";Q$
620   IF  LEFT$ (Q$,1) ( ) "Y" AND  LEFT$ (Q$,1) ( ) "N" THEN  PRINT :
      PRINT "ENTER 'Y' FOR YES OR 'N' FOR NO": PRINT : GOTO 610
630   IF  LEFT$ (Q$,1) = "Y" THEN 360
640   :
650   REM       CLOSE FILE
660   :
670   PRINT D$;"CLOSE"F$
680   PRINT "JOB COMPLETED"
690   END
```

3 b.

```
100   REM        SOLUTION CH4 SELFTEST PROB 3B
110   REM        CREDIT FILE DISPLAY
120   :
130   REM        VARIABLES USED
140   REM         F$ = USER ENTERED FILE NAME
150   REM         C$ = CUST. #
160   REM         N$ = CUST. NAME
170   REM         R = CREDIT RATING
180   REM         D$ = CONTROL D
190   :
200   REM        FILES USED
210   REM         SEQUENTIAL FILE NAME: CREDIT (USER ENTERED)
220   REM         DATASET FORMAT: C$,N$,R
230   :
240   REM        INITIALIZE
250   :
260   LET D$ = CHR$ (4)
270   HOME
280   INPUT "ENTER FILE NAME:";F$
290   PRINT D$;"OPEN"F$
300   :
310   REM        READ/PRINT FILE
320   :
330   ONERR  GOTO 420
340   PRINT D$;"READ"F$
350   INPUT C$,N$,R
360   PRINT D$
370   PRINT C$: PRINT N$: PRINT R: PRINT
380   GOTO 340
390   :
400   REM        CLOSE FILE
410   :
420   IF  PEEK (222) = 5 THEN 440
430   PRINT : PRINT "UNUSUAL ERROR. PROGRAM TERMINATED": PRINT
440   PRINT D$;"CLOSE"F$
450   PRINT " ALL DATA DISPLAYED AND FILE CLOSED"
460   END
```

4 a.

```
100   REM     SOLUTION CH4 SELFTEST PROB 4A
110   :
120   REM       VARIABLES USED
130   REM       F$ = USER ENTERED FILE NAME
140   REM       D1$ = DATASETS FROM FILE 1,2
150   REM       A$ = ACC'T NUMBER (5 CHAR.)
160   REM       T$ = TRANSACTION CODE (1 CHAR.)
170   REM       C$ = CASH AM'T (9999.99 OR 7 CHAR.MAX.)
180   REM       X = FOR NEXT LOOP CONTROL VARIABLE
190   REM       D$ = CONTROL D
200   :
210   REM       FILES USED
220   REM       SEQUENTIAL FILE NAMES: TRANSACTION 1, TRANSACTION 2 (USER
      SELECTED AND ENTERED)
230   REM       DATASET FORMAT: A$,T$,C$
240   :
250   REM       INITIALIZATION
260   :
270   LET D$ =   CHR$ (4)
280   INPUT "ENTER FILE NAME:";F1$
290   PRINT D$;"OPEN"F1$
300   PRINT D$;"DELETE"F1$
310   PRINT D$;"OPEN"F1$
320   :
330   REM       DATA ENTRY/TESTS
340   :
350   HOME
360   PRINT "ENTER -1 TO END DATA ENTRY"
370   PRINT : INPUT " ENTER ACCOUNT NUMBER (5 DIGITS):";A$
380   IF A$ = "-1" THEN 620
390   IF  VAL (A$) = 0 THEN  PRINT "PLEASE MAKE AN ENTRY.": GOTO 370
400   IF  LEN (A$) <  > 5 THEN  PRINT "YOU ENTERED ";A$;" PLEASE REENTER.":
      GOTO 370
410   INPUT "ENTER TRANSACTION CODE(1 DIGIT):";T$
420   IF  VAL (T$) = 0 THEN  PRINT "PLEASE MAKE AN ENTRY.": GOTO 410
430   IF  LEN (T$) <  > 1 THEN  PRINT "YOU ENTERED ";T$;" PLEASE REENTER.":
      GOTO 410
440   INPUT "ENTER THE AMOUNT:";C$
450   IF  VAL (C$) = 0 THEN  PRINT "PLEASE MAKE AN ENTRY.": GOTO 440
460   IF  VAL (C$) > 9999.99 THEN  PRINT : PRINT "MAXIMUM AMOUNT IS 9999.99.
      PLEASE REENTER.": PRINT : GOTO 440
470   FOR X = 1 TO  LEN (C$)
480   IF  ASC ( MID$ (C$,X,1) )  = 48 AND  ASC ( MID$ (C$,X,1)) <  = 57 OR
      ASC ( MID$ (C$,X,1)) = 46 THEN 500
490   PRINT "INVALID ENTRY. ONLY NUMBERS AND DECIMAL POINTS ALLOWED.": GOTO
      440
500   NEXT X
510   :
520   REM       PRINT TO FILE
530   :
540   PRINT D$;"WRITE"F1$
550   PRINT A$: PRINT T$: PRINT C$
560   PRINT D$
570   HOME
580   GOTO 360
590   :
600   REM       CLOSE FILE
610   :
620   PRINT D$;"CLOSE"F1$
630   PRINT "FILE CLOSED"
640   END
```

4 b.

```
100   REM       SOLUTION CH4 SELFTEST PROB 4B
110   :
120   REM       VARIABLES USED
130   REM        F$ = USER ENTERED FILE NAME140
140   REM        A$ = ACCOUNT NUMBER
150   REM        T$ = TRANSACTION CODE
160   REM        C$ = CASH AMOUNT
170   REM        X = FOR NEXT LOOP CONTROL VARIABLE
180   REM        D$ = CONTROL D
190   :
200   REM       FILES USED
210   REM        SEQ.FILE NAMES: TRANSACTION-1, TRANSACTION-2 (USER SELECTED
      AND ENTERED)
220   REM        DATASET FORMAT:A$,T$,C$
230   :
240   REM       INITIALIZATION
250   :
260   LET D$ =  CHR$ (4)
270   INPUT "FILE NAME:";F$
280   PRINT D$;"OPEN"F$
290   HOME
300   :
310   REM       READ/DISPLAY
320   :
330   PRINT : PRINT "A/C#","T-CODE","AMOUNT": PRINT
340   ONERR  GOTO 430
350   PRINT D$;"READ"F$
360   INPUT A$,T$,C$
370   PRINT D$
380   PRINT A$,T$,C$
390   GOTO 350
400   :
410   REM       CLOSE FILE
420   :
430   IF  PEEK (222) = 5 THEN 450
440   PRINT : PRINT "UNUSUAL ERROR. PROGRAM TERMINATED.": PRINT
450   PRINT D$;"CLOSE"F$
460   PRINT "FILE PRINTED AND CLOSED"
470   END
```

5 a.

```
100   REM     SOLUTION CH4 SELFTEST PROB 5A
110   :
120   REM        VARIABLES USED
130   REM           N$ = NAME(20)
140   REM           A$ = STREET ADDRESS(20)
150   REM           C$ = CITY(10)
160   REM           S$ = STATE(2)
170   REM           Z$ = ZIP CODE(5)
180   REM           E$ = CONCATENATED DATASET(57)
190   REM           D$ = CONTROL D
200   REM           R$ = USER RESPONSE
210   :
220   REM        FILE USED
230   REM           SEQUENTIAL FILE NAME: ADDRESS
240   REM           DATASET FORMAT:C$ (ONE STRING)
250   :
260   REM        INITIALIZE
270   :
280   LET D$ =   CHR$ (4)
290   PRINT D$;"OPEN ADDRESS"
300   HOME
310   :
320   REM        DATA ENTRY
330   :
340   INPUT "ENTER NAME:";N$
350   IF  LEN (N$) < 20 THEN   LET N$ = N$ + " ": GOTO 350
360   :
370   INPUT "ENTER ADDRESS:";A$
380   IF  LEN (A$) < 20 THEN   LET A$ = A$ + " ": GOTO 380
390   :
400   INPUT "ENTER CITY NAME:";C$
410   IF  LEN (C$) < 10 THEN   LET C$ = C$ + " ": GOTO 410
420   :
430   INPUT "ENTER STATE CODE:";S$
440   IF  LEN (S$) <  > 2 THEN   PRINT "PLEASE ENTER A 2 CHAR CODE.": GOTO
      430
450   :
460   INPUT "ENTER ZIP CODE:";Z$
470   IF  LEN (Z$) <  > 5 THEN   PRINT "PLEASE ENTER 5-DIGIT CODE.": GOTO 460
480   :
490   LET E$ = N$ + A$ + C$ + S$ + Z$
500   :
510   PRINT D$;"WRITE ADDRESS"
520   PRINT E$
530   PRINT D$
540   :
550   INPUT "MORE ENTRIES?";R$
560   IF  LEFT$ (R$,1) <  > "Y" AND  LEFT$ (R$,1) <  > "N" THEN   PRINT :
      PRINT "ENTER 'Y' FOR YES OR 'N' FOR NO": PRINT : GOTO 550
570   IF  LEFT$ (R$,1) = "Y" THEN   HOME : GOTO 340
580   :
590   REM        CLOSE FILE
600   :
610   PRINT D$;"CLOSE ADDRESS"
620   PRINT "FILE CLOSED"
630   END
```

5 b.

```
100   REM       SOLUTION CH4 SELFTEST PROB 5B
110   :
120   REM       VARIABLES USED
130   REM         E$ = CONCATENATED DATASET
140   REM         D$ = CONTROL D
150   :
160   REM        FILE USED
170   REM          SEQ. FILE NAME: ADDRESS
180   REM          DATASET FORMAT: E$ (ONE STRING)
190   :
200   REM       INITIALIZE
210   :
220   LET D$ =  CHR$ (4)
230   PRINT D$;"OPEN ADDRESS"
240   HOME
250   :
260   REM       READ FILE/PRINT
270   :
280   ONERR  GOTO 420
290   PRINT D$;"READ ADDRESS"
300   INPUT E$
310   PRINT D$
320   PRINT  LEFT$ (E$,20)
330   PRINT  MID$ (E$,21,20)
340   PRINT  MID$ (E$,41,10)
350   PRINT  MID$ (E$,51,2)
360   PRINT  RIGHT$ (E$,5)
370   PRINT
380   GOTO 290
390   :
400   REM       CLOSE FILES
410   :
420   PRINT D$;"CLOSE ADDRESS"
430   PRINT "FILE CLOSED"
440   END
```

6 a.

```
100   REM       SOLUTION CH4 SELFTEST PROB6A
110   :
120   REM       VARIABLES USED
130   REM         T$ = TEXT LINE
140   REM         F$ = FILE NAME
150   REM         D$ = CONTROL D
160   REM         R$ = USER RESPONSE
170   :
180   REM       FILES USED
190   REM          SEQ. FILE NAME: LETTER#
200   REM          (# IS USER SELECTED & ENTERED)
210   :
220   REM       INITIALIZE
230   :
240   LET D$ =  CHR$ (4)
250   INPUT "ENTER LETTER FILE NUMBER:";F$
260   LET F$ = "LETTER" + F$
270   PRINT D$;"OPEN"F$
280   :
290   REM       DATA ENTRY
300   :
310   HOME
320   PRINT "ENTER TEXT LINE.  USE QUOTES AT BEGINNING AND END"
330   INPUT "TEXT LINE:";T$
340   :
350   PRINT D$;"WRITE"F$
360   PRINT  CHR$ (34);: PRINT T$;: PRINT  CHR$ (34)
370   PRINT D$
380   INPUT "MORE ENTRIES:";R$
390   IF  LEFT$ (R$,1) <  > "Y" AND  LEFT$ (R$,1) <  > "N" THEN  PRINT :
      PRINT "ENTER 'Y' FOR YES AND 'N' FOR NO": PRINT :310
400   IF  LEFT$ (R$,1) = "Y" THEN 310
410   :
420   REM       CLOSE FILE
430   :
440   PRINT D$;"CLOSE"F$
450   PRINT "FILE CLOSED"
460   END
```

6 b.

```
100    REM      SOLUTION CH4 SELFTEST PROB 6B
110    :
120    REM      VARIABLES USED
130    REM      T$ = TEXT LINE
140    REM      F$ = FILE NAME
150    REM      D$ = CONTROL D
160    REM      R$ = USER RESPONSE
170    :
180    REM      FILES USED
190    REM        SEQ. FILE NAME: LETTER#
200    REM        (WHERE # IS USER SELECTED & ENTERED)
210    REM        DATASET FORMAT:T$ (ONE STRING)
220    :
230    REM      INITIALIZE
240    :
250    LET D$ =  CHR$ (4)
260    INPUT "ENTER FORM LETTER NUMBER:";F$
270    LET F$ = "LETTER" + F$
280    PRINT D$;"OPEN"F$
290    :
300    REM    READ FILE
310    :
320    HOME
330    ONERR  GOTO 420
340    PRINT D$;"READ"F$
350    INPUT T$
360    PRINT D$
370    PRINT T$
380    GOTO 340
390    :
400    REM      CLOSE FILE
410    :
420    IF  PEEK (222) = 5 THEN 440
430    PRINT : PRINT "UNUSUAL ERROR. PROGRAM TERMINATED.": PRINT
440    PRINT D$;"CLOSE"F$
450    PRINT "FILE CLOSED"
460    END
```

CHAPTER FIVE

Sequential Data File Utility Programs

Objectives: When you finish this chapter you will be able to:

1. Write a program to add data to an existing sequential file.
2. Write a program to make a copy of a sequential data file.
3. Write a program to change the data in an existing sequential file.
4. Write a program to examine the contents in a sequential file and to change, add, or delete data.
5. Write a program to merge the contents of two sequential files into one file, maintaining the numeric or alphabetic order of the data.
6. Write a program that uses or combines selected data from more than one sequential file.

Now that you understand the BASIC statements to create and use sequential data files, let's build on this with more advanced techniques, including writing some file utility programs that help in your overall programming using data files. You will also develop embryonic file applications to practice what you have learned and provide a basis from which to develop personally useful programs. Most of the data files used in this chapter are created with programs you should have written for the Chapter 4 Self-Test, so if you skipped that, go back and write those programs before starting this chapter.

ADDING DATA TO THE END OF A SEQUENTIAL FILE

Unlike other versions of BASIC, it is quite easy to add data to the end of an existing APPLESOFT sequential file. To accomplish this you must APPEND your file rather than OPEN it. When you OPEN a file, the file pointer is moved to the first position in that file so that all subsequent file WRITE operations take place from the beginning of the file (recall the problem that arises when you attempt to overwrite an existing file). When you APPEND to an existing file, however, the file pointer is moved to the end of the file data, so that subsequent file WRITE operations take place starting after the last piece of existing data, and new data are added or appended beyond the previous end of the file. The file WRITE procedure is the same as the one used when the file was OPENed. The file APPEND statement looks like the other file operation statements:

```
100  PRINT D$;"APPEND FILENAME"
```

The only "hitch" we have found with the file APPEND operation is that you can only APPEND to an existing file. If you attempt an APPEND operation to a file not previously OPENed, the error condition – FILE NOT FOUND – will abort your program. To get around this problem (there's always a way), we will use this procedure:

```
200  PRINT D$;"OPEN FILENAME"
210  PRINT D$;"CLOSE FILENAME"
220  PRINT D$;"APPEND FILENAME"
```

Let's try an easy application. Assume you are using your personal computer to prepare a grocery list for your periodic trips to the grocery store (see problem 2 of the Chapter 4 Self-Test). Or better yet, in this modern electronic age, your list can be telecommunicated to the store of your choice and the goods will be ready for your pickup, with no shopping needed! In any event, every few days you think of new items to be added to the list to be entered into your APPLE and added to the file. Each dataset consists of one twenty-character string for the item description and one numeric value for the quantity of the item needed. With one program, you can enter the first items into the file and subsequent items as you think of them.

Here is the introductory module:

```
100  REM     APPEND DATA TO EXISTING FILE
110  :
120  REM     VARIABLES USED
130  REM      N$ = ITEM DESCRIPTION
140  REM      Q = QUANTITY TO ORDER
150  REM      D$ = CONTROL D
160  REM      R$ = USER RESPONSE
170  REM      F$ = USER ENTERED FILE NAME
180  :
190  REM     FILES USED
200  REM      SEQUENTIAL FILE NAME: GROCERY (USER ENTERED)
210  REM      DATASET FORMAT* N$,Q
220  :
```

(a)   To complete the next program segment, fill in 270, 280, and 290.

```
220  :
230  REM     INITIALIZE
240  :
250  LET D$ =  CHR$ (4)
260  INPUT "ENTER FILE NAME:";F$
270
280
290
300  :
```

– – – – – – – – – – – – – – – –

(a)
```
220 :
230 REM     INITIALIZE
240 :
250 LET D$ =  CHR$ (4)
260 INPUT "ENTER FILE NAME:";F$
270 PRINT D$;"OPEN"F$
280 PRINT D$;"CLOSE"F$
290 PRINT D$;"APPEND"F$
300 :
```

Here is the data entry routine with five blank lines for you to fill in. Use these clues:

Line 370 – test for stop entry.

Line 380 – test for null entry.

Line 390 – test for maximum entry length.

Line 420 – test for minimum entry of 1 and maximum entry of 10.

Line 460 – test for user response of N or NO and branch accordingly.

(a)
```
300 :
310 REM      DATA ENTRY ROUTINE
320 :
330 HOME
340 PRINT "TYPE 'STOP' WHEN ALL ITEMS ARE ENTERED."
350 PRINT
360 INPUT "ENTER ITEM DESCRIPTION:";N$
370
380
390
400 :
410 INPUT "ENTER QUANTITY:";Q
420
430 PRINT "YOU ENTERED A QUANTITY OF:";Q
440 INPUT "IS THAT WHAT YOU WANTED?";R$
450 IF  LEFT$ (R$,1) <  > "N" AND  LEFT$ (R$,1) <  > "Y" THEN  PRINT
    CHR$ (7);"PLEASE TYPE 'Y' FOR YES OR 'N' FOR NO.": PRINT : GOTO 430
460
470 :
```

- - - - - - - - - - - - - - -

(a)
```
300 :
310 REM      DATA ENTRY ROUTINE
320 :
330 HOME
340 PRINT "TYPE 'STOP' WHEN ALL ITEMS ARE ENTERED."
350 PRINT
360 INPUT "ENTER ITEM DESCRIPTION:";N$
370 IF N$ = "STOP" THEN 570
380 IF  LEN (N$) = 0 THEN  PRINT : PRINT "PLEASE ENTER A DESCRIPTION OR
    'STOP'": PRINT : GOTO 360
390 IF  LEN (N$) > 20 THEN  PRINT : PRINT "PLEASE LIMIT DESCRIPTION TO 20
    CHARS.MAX.": PRINT : GOTO 360
400 :
410 INPUT "ENTER QUANTITY:";Q
420 IF Q >  = 1 AND Q <  = 10 THEN 500
430 PRINT "YOU ENTERED A QUANTITY OF:";Q
440 INPUT "IS THAT WHAT YOU WANTED?";R$
450 IF  LEFT$ (R$,1) <  > "N" AND  LEFT$ (R$,1) <  > "Y" THEN  PRINT  CHR$
    (7);"PLEASE TYPE 'Y' FOR YES OR 'N' FOR NO.": PRINT : GOTO 430
460 IF  LEFT$ (R$,1) = "N" THEN 410
470 :
```

The file WRITE routine should be familiar since it is the same procedure you used in the last chapter. Fill in lines 500, 510, and 520.

(a)
```
470  :
480  REM      WRITE TO FILE ROUTINE
490  :
500
510
520
530  GOTO 330
540  :
550  REM      CLOSE FILE
560  :
570  PRINT D$;"CLOSE"F$
580  PRINT : PRINT "NEW DATA APPENDED AND FILE CLOSED."
590  END
```

-- -- -- -- -- -- -- -- -- -- -- -- --

(a)
```
470  :
480  REM      WRITE TO FILE ROUTINE
490  :
500  PRINT D$;"WRITE"F$
510  PRINT N$: PRINT Q
520  PRINT D$
530  GOTO 330
540  :
550  REM      CLOSE FILE
560  :
570  PRINT D$;"CLOSE"F$
580  PRINT : PRINT "NEW DATA APPENDED AND FILE CLOSED."
590  END
```

Following is a complete listing of the program you have developed:

```
100   REM      APPEND DATA TO EXISTING FILE
110   :
120   REM       VARIABLES USED
130   REM        N$ = ITEM DESCRIPTION
140   REM        Q = QUANTITY TO ORDER
150   REM        D$ = CONTROL D
160   REM        R$ = USER RESPONSE
170   REM        F$ = USER ENTERED FILE NAME
180   :
190   REM       FILES USED
200   REM         SEQUENTIAL FILE NAME: GROCERY (USER ENTERED)
210   REM         DATASET FORMAT* N$,Q
220   :
230   REM      INITIALIZE
240   :
250   LET D$ =  CHR$ (4)
260   INPUT "ENTER FILE NAME:";F$
270   PRINT D$;"OPEN"F$
280   PRINT D$;"CLOSE"F$
290   PRINT D$;"APPEND"F$
300   :
310   REM      DATA ENTRY ROUTINE
320   :
330   HOME
340   PRINT "TYPE 'STOP' WHEN ALL ITEMS ARE ENTERED."
350   PRINT
360   INPUT "ENTER ITEM DESCRIPTION:";N$
370   IF N$ = "STOP" THEN 570
380   IF  LEN (N$) = 0 THEN  PRINT : PRINT "PLEASE ENTER A DESCRIPTION OR _
      'STOP'": PRINT :  GOTO 360
390   IF  LEN (N$) > 20 THEN  PRINT : PRINT "PLEASE LIMIT DESCRIPTION TO 20
      CHARS.MAX.": PRINT :  GOTO 360
400   :
410   INPUT "ENTER QUANTITY:";Q
420   IF Q >  = 1 AND Q <  = 10 THEN 500
430   PRINT "YOU ENTERED A QUANTITY OF:";Q
440   INPUT "IS THAT WHAT YOU WANTED?";R$
450   IF  LEFT$ (R$,1) <  > "N" AND  LEFT$ (R$,1) <  > "Y" THEN  PRINT  CHR$
      (7);"PLEASE TYPE 'Y' FOR YES OR 'N' FOR NO.": PRINT :  GOTO 430
460   IF  LEFT$ (R$,1) = "N" THEN 410
470   :
480   REM      WRITE TO FILE ROUTINE
490   :
500   PRINT D$;"WRITE"F$
510   PRINT N$: PRINT Q
520   PRINT D$
530   GOTO 330
540   :
550   REM      CLOSE FILE
560   :
570   PRINT D$;"CLOSE"F$
580   PRINT : PRINT "NEW DATA APPENDED AND FILE CLOSED."
590   END
```

(a) Write the corresponding program line number(s) for each step listed below.

1. Open the file for the APPEND operation. _____

2. Enter and test the next dataset. _____

3. Write the dataset to the file. _____

4. Close the file. _____

5. What must the user enter to cause the close operation to take place?

_____

_ _ _ _ _ _ _ _ _ _ _ _ _ _ _

(a)   1.   290
      2.   310–460
      3.   480–530
      4.   570
      5.   STOP

Now enter and RUN the program-appending data to the file named GROCERY. Use the program to read GROCERY (Chapter 4 Self-Test, problem 2a) to verify the success of the APPEND procedure.

You can use another procedure to add data to the end of the sequential data file or to make changes in the contents of a file. (We'll show you how to do that later.) The success of this procedure depends on how much data the file contains and the amount of available memory in your computer. The procedure uses arrays. Follow these steps:

1.   OPEN the file
2.   READ the file contents into one or more arrays.
3.   Add to the array or change the items in the array.
4.   CLOSE the file, DELETE the file.
5.   OPEN the file.
6.   WRITE the current array contents to the file.
7.   CLOSE the file.

Use this procedure only if the file is rather small and the datasets are easy to manage (for example, when the data are all packed into one string variable). If these two circumstances are present, you are not likely to encounter errors. However, when files are large or data are placed into more than one array or into a two-dimensional array, then the probability increases that data will get lost or "forgotten," resulting in errors.

You will see this procedure used in program listings for computers other than the APPLE. For the APPLE, we recommend the APPEND procedure as illustrated in the grocery list program. It is clean and neat!

MAKING A FILE COPY

A very useful file utility program is one that makes a duplicate copy of your data file. Your APPLE system master disk is equipped with such a program. This allows you to make back-up copies of data files or copy a file from one disk to another. In this section, however, we will show you how to write such a program in BASIC. A file copy utility program in BASIC not only allows you to make back-up copies of data files, it can also be incorporated into later programs to change data in existing data files.

You now have the background to write a file copying program. Follow these steps:

1.   OPEN the source or original file. (Use the file named CUST created in the Chapter 4 Self-Test.)

2. OPEN the file that will become the copy. (Name this file CUST COPY.)
3. Test the source file for end-of-data using ONERR.
4. READ the first dataset.
5. Terminate the READ operation.
6. WRITE to the copy file.
7. Terminate the WRITE operation.
8. Return to step 3 above.
9. CLOSE both files.

Assume that you are going to copy a file that contains an unknown number of datasets, with each dataset containing two twenty-five-character strings and two numeric variables. Use the file named CUST created in the Chapter 4 Self-Test. Here is the introductory module and the initialization section. Fill in the blanks in lines 260, 290, and 320 to complete steps 1 and 2 of the outline.

(a)
```
100   REM      UTILITY PROGRAM TO COPY FILES
110   :
120   REM      VARIABLES USED
130   REM        A$, B$ = STRING VARIABLES
140   REM        A,B = NUMERIC VARIABLES
150   REM        D$ = CONTROL D
160   REM         F$ = USER ENTERED SOURCE FILE NAME
170   REM        F1$ = USER ENTERED COPY FILE NAME
180   :
190   REM      FILES USED
200   REM        SEQUENTIAL SOURCE FILE NAME: CUST (USER ENTERED)
210   REM        SEQ. COPY FILE NAME: CUST COPY (USER ENTERED)
220   REM        DATASET FORMAT:A$,B$,A,B
230   :
240   REM      INITIALIZATION
250   :
260
270   INPUT "ENTER SOURCE FILE NAME:";F$
280   INPUT "ENTER COPY FILE NAME:";F1$
290
300   PRINT D$;"OPEN"F1$
310   PRINT D$;"DELETE"F1$
320
330   :
```

- - - - - - - - - - - - - - - -

(a)
```
100   REM      UTILITY PROGRAM TO COPY FILES
110   :
120   REM      VARIABLES USED
130   REM        A$, B$ = STRING VARIABLES
140   REM        A,B = NUMERIC VARIABLES
150   REM        D$ = CONTROL D
160   REM         F$ = USER ENTERED SOURCE FILE NAME
170   REM        F1$ = USER ENTERED COPY FILE NAME
180   :
190   REM      FILES USED
200   REM        SEQUENTIAL SOURCE FILE NAME: CUST (USER ENTERED)
210   REM        SEQ. COPY FILE NAME: CUST COPY (USER ENTERED)
220   REM        DATASET FORMAT:A$,B$,A,B
230   :
240   REM      INITIALIZATION
250   :
260   LET D$ =   CHR$ (4)
270   INPUT "ENTER SOURCE FILE NAME:";F$
280   INPUT "ENTER COPY FILE NAME:";F1$
290   PRINT D$;"OPEN"F$
300   PRINT D$;"OPEN"F1$
310   PRINT D$;"DELETE"F1$
320   PRINT D$;"OPEN"F1$
330   :
```

The routine at lines 300, 310, and 320 is a good procedure to follow; always OPEN, then DELETE, a file to which you plan to WRITE, to avoid overprinting existing data (if any) and ending up with a possible mixture of new and old data in your file. The second OPEN statement at line 320 assures an empty OPEN file for the copy.

Here is the program module to READ from the source file and WRITE to the copy file. Fill in the blanks in lines 370, 380, 430, and 440 to complete steps 3, 4, 5, 6, 7, and 8 of the outline.

(a)
```
340   REM       READ FROM SOURCE FILE
350 :
360   ONERR   GOTO 500
370
380
390   PRINT D$
400 :
410   REM       WRITE TO COPY FILE
420 :
430
440
450   PRINT D$
460   GOTO 370
470 :
```

— — — — — — — — — — — — — — —

(a)
```
340   REM       READ FROM SOURCE FILE
350 :
360   ONERR   GOTO 500
370   PRINT D$;"READ"F$
380   INPUT A$,B$,A,B
390   PRINT D$
400 :
410   REM       WRITE TO COPY FILE
420 :
430   PRINT D$;"WRITE"F1$
440   PRINT A$: PRINT B$: PRINT A: PRINT B
450   PRINT D$
460   GOTO 370
470 :
```

And finally, the close file routine. Fill in the blank at line 490 to close both files with one CLOSE statement, completing step 9 of the outline.

(a)
```
480   REM     CLOSE FILES
490
500   IF  PEEK (222) (  ) 5 THEN  PRINT : PRINT "UNUSUAL ERROR PROGRAM
      TERMINATED.": PRINT : GOTO 510
510 :
520   END
```

— — — — — — — — — — — — — — —

(a)
```
480   REM     CLOSE FILES
490 :
500   IF  PEEK (222) (  ) 5 THEN  PRINT : PRINT "UNUSUAL ERROR PROGRAM
      TERMINATED.": PRINT : GOTO 510
510   PRINT D$;"CLOSE"
520   END
```

Here is a complete listing of the program you have just completed.

```
100   REM     UTILITY PROGRAM TO COPY FILES
110 :
120   REM       VARIABLES USED
130   REM         A$, B$ = STRING VARIABLES
140   REM         A,B = NUMERIC VARIABLES
150   REM         D$ = CONTROL D
160   REM          F$ = USER ENTERED SOURCE FILE NAME
170   REM         F1$ = USER ENTERED COPY FILE NAME
180 :
190   REM       FILES USED
200   REM         SEQUENTIAL SOURCE FILE NAME: CUST (USER ENTERED)
210   REM         SEQ. COPY FILE NAME: CUST COPY (USER ENTERED)
220   REM         DATASET FORMAT:A$,B$,A,B
230 :
240   REM       INITIALIZATION
250 :
260   LET D$ =  CHR$ (4)
270   INPUT "ENTER SOURCE FILE NAME:";F$
280   INPUT "ENTER COPY FILE NAME:";F1$
290   PRINT D$;"OPEN"F$
300   PRINT D$;"OPEN"F1$
310   PRINT D$;"DELETE"F1$
320   PRINT D$;"OPEN"F1$
330 :
340   REM       READ FROM SOURCE FILE
350 :
360   ONERR  GOTO 500
370   PRINT D$;"READ"F$
380   INPUT A$,B$,A,B
390   PRINT D$
400 :
410   REM     WRITE TO COPY FILE
420 :
430   PRINT D$;"WRITE"F1$
440   PRINT A$: PRINT B$: PRINT A: PRINT B
450   PRINT D$
460   GOTO 370
470 :
480   REM     CLOSE FILES
490 :
500   IF  PEEK (222) <  > 5 THEN  PRINT : PRINT "UNUSUAL ERROR PROGRAM
      TERMINATED.": PRINT : GOTO 510
510   PRINT D$;"CLOSE"
520   END
```

(a)   When you RUN this program, what appears on the screen?

_____

_____

_____

_____

_____

– – – – – – – – – – – – – – –

(a)   RUN

ENTER SOURCE FILE NAME:

ENTER COPY FILE NAME:

(CURSOR)

It can be unsettling to get no more than the above display from a program when so much internal activity is supposed to be taking place. The final flashing "cursor" is the only clue that your program completed its task. But you don't know for sure that it did. We have a suggestion.

Add a statement at line 505 that prints a message indicating that the job is complete. For example,

505 PRINT "COPY COMPLETED"

A statement such as this lets you know that the program did execute past the error trap at line 500. This will verify that at least that much was done. Then add line 515 PRINT "FILE CLOSED" to indicate to the user that the program has executed past the CLOSE operation.

The blank PRINT D$ in lines 390 and 450 were placed there to terminate the operation in progress before starting a new operation. In this case, however, the termination procedure was not necessary, as a new PRINT D$ of any type terminates the previous file operation. That is, the WRITE statement in line 430 would have automatically terminated the READ from line 370. We left the blank PRINT D$ statements in our program for clarity to the reader, and encourage you to do the same. Though not always necessary, the blank PRINT D$ to terminate a file operation makes your program much more readable and avoids the question, "Is this the time CTRL D is needed or not?"

You now have a complete file-copying utility program. You can use it to copy any sequential data file by simply changing the INPUT and PRINT statements to conform to the data format or datasets in the particular data file you want to copy. We encourage you to enter and RUN this program using the datafile named CUST with the corresponding dataset format that you created in the Chapter 4 Self-Test, problem 1a.

After you have created CUST COPY, modify the program you wrote for the Chapter 4 Self-Test, problem 1b, to read and display the contents of CUST COPY. Modify lines 240, 290, and 390 in the solution we provided for Chapter 4 Self-Test, problem 1b.

(a)   240 _____

      290 _____

      390 _____

- - - - - - - - - - - - - - - -


```
(a)   240   PRINT D$;"OPEN CUST COPY"
      290   PRINT D$;"READ CUST COPY"
      390   PRINT D$;"CLOSE CUST COPY"
```

CHANGING DATA IN A FILE

We implied earlier in this book that it is not easy to change data that are already located in a sequential data file, but it can be done. The procedure is straightforward: copy all unchanged data into a temporary file, make any changes by writing to the temporary file, and then either copy the temporary file back into the original file or use the RENAME statement. A few tricks will be explained, as you are guided in writing this program.

```
]RUN
ENTER FILE NAME:CREDIT
ENTER 'STOP' TO END DATA ENTRY.

ENTER CUSTOMER #:12345
PAUL ARMITICE CREDIT RATING: 4
ENTER NEW CREDIT RATING:5
RENAME COMPLETED
DO YOU HAVE MORE CREDIT RATING CHANGES?Y
ENTER 'STOP' TO END DATA ENTRY.

ENTER CUSTOMER #:12346
MISS PIGGY CREDIT RATING: 1
ENTER NEW CREDIT RATING:2
RENAME COMPLETED
DO YOU HAVE MORE CREDIT RATING CHANGES?NO

PROGRAM COMPLETED AS REQUESTED.
```

While the procedure outlined below is tailored to the particular dataset used in this example, the basic idea is easily adaptable to data files with different datasets.

1. OPEN the customer credit file. Use the file named CREDIT created in the Chapter 4 Self-Test.
2. OPEN a temporary file. Name this file TEMP.
3. Enter the customer number for the client whose credit rating is to be changed. Include data-entry tests and a "no more searches" option.
4. Check for end-of-data in credit file using ONERR. If end-of-data is found:
   a. display an error message indicating an unsuccessful search.
   b. CLOSE both files.
   c. return to step 1.
5. READ a complete dataset.
6. Test for wanted customer number.
7. PRINT rejected datasets to temporary file (those which are to be copied to the new file unchanged).
8. Display data; ask user to enter changes, with data entry test for the changes.
9. PRINT dataset with new data to temporary file.
10. PRINT remainder of credit file datasets (those with no changes) to temporary file.
11. CLOSE both files.
12. Copy temporary file to CREDIT file, or use the RENAME operation to make the temporary file the new corrected credit file.
13. Provide the user with the option of repeating the process.

The program will be developed one segment at a time, with blanks for you to fill in, as before. Below is the introductory module, which you should understand by now, followed by the first data entry routine with data entry checks. Read it over carefully to get the flow of the program. The first three steps of the outline are completed in this module.

```
100   REM       CREDIT FILE CHANGER
110   :
120   REM       VARIABLES USED
130   REM         F$ = FILE NAME
140   REM         C$ = CUST. #
150   REM         C1$ = CUST. #
160   REM         N$ = NAME
170   REM         R$ = ENTRY VARIABLE
180   REM         R,R1 = CREDIT RATING VALUE
190   REM         D$ = CONTROL D
200   :
210   REM       FILES USED
220   REM           SEQ.FILE NAME: CREDIT (USER ENTERED)
230   REM           TEMPORARY FILE NAME: TEMP
240   REM           DATSET FORMAT: C$,N$,R
250   :
260   REM       INITIALIZE
270   :
280   LET D$ =  CHR$ (4)
290   HOME : INPUT "ENTER FILE NAME:";F$
300   PRINT D$;"OPEN"F$
310   PRINT D$;"OPEN TEMP"
320   :
330   REM       DATA ENTRY ROUTINE
340   :
350   HOME
360   PRINT "ENTER 'STOP' TO END DATA ENTRY."
370   PRINT
380   INPUT "ENTER CUSTOMER #:";C$
390   IF C$ = "STOP" THEN 1070
400   IF  LEN (C$) = 0 THEN  PRINT "ENTER CUSTOMER NUMBER OR TYPE 'STOP'":
      GOTO 380
410   IF  LEN (C$) <  > 5 THEN  PRINT "ENTRY ERROR. REENTER WITH 5 DIGITS.":
      GOTO 380
420   IF  VAL (C$) = 0 THEN  PRINT "ENTRY ERROR.  NUMBERS ONLY.": GOTO 380
430   :
```

Now for the interesting part. The program must search through the data file for the customer number that the user entered.

(a) When searching the data file for the customer number and encountering the end of the file without finding the customer, what should the program do?

_____

_____

_____

(b) Before another search is made for a customer number in the file, what must be done to the file?

_____

_____

_____

– – – – – – – – – – – – – – –

(a) Print an error message indicating that the customer was not in the file (see the sample RUN shown earlier).

(b) CLOSE and reOPEN the files to reset the file pointer to the beginning of the data files. (Very important!)

(a) Fill in lines 470, 480, 490, 510, 520, and 530 below. These correspond to outline steps 5, 6, and 7.

```
440    REM        FILE SEARCH ROUTINE
450  :
460    ONERR   GOTO 550
470
480
490
500    IF C$ = C1$ THEN 630
510
520
530
540    GOTO 470
550    PRINT   CHR$ (7);"ERROR MESSAGE. WE CANNOT FIND"
560    PRINT "CUSTOMER # ";C$;" ON THE FILE."
570    PRINT "PLEASE CHECK YOUR NUMBER AND REENTER."
580    PRINT D$;"CLOSE"
590    GOTO 300
600  :
```

- - - - - - - - - - - - - - -

```
440    REM        FILE SEARCH ROUTINE
450  :
460    ONERR   GOTO 550
470    PRINT D$;"READ"F$
480    INPUT C1$,N$,R
490    PRINT D$
500    IF C$ = C1$ THEN 630
510    PRINT D$;"WRITE TEMP"
520    PRINT C1$: PRINT N$: PRINT R
530    PRINT D$
540    GOTO 470
550    PRINT   CHR$ (7);"ERROR MESSAGE. WE CANNOT FIND"
560    PRINT "CUSTOMER # ";C$;" ON THE FILE."
570    PRINT "PLEASE CHECK YOUR NUMBER AND REENTER."
580    PRINT D$;"CLOSE"
590    GOTO 300
600  :
```

(a) In the solution above, why was variable C1$ used instead of C$? in line 480? (See line 380.)

_____

_____

_____

(b) If you delete line 580 above, then RUN the program, what will happen if an incorrect customer number is entered at line 300 and then, after the error message at line 570, a correct customer number is entered?

_____

_____

- - - - - - - - - - - - - - -

(a) Two different assignments would have been made to C$, creating a program error. Note the error message at lines 550 to 570.

(b) The ONERR check in line 460 will detect the end of the file for both entries, and the error message will be printed after both entries. The second customer number may be valid, but since the pointer was not reset to the beginning of the file, the error message will reappear.

When the file has been searched and the correct customer found, the program prints the customer name on the screen (line 640) as a double check to the operator that the correction is being made for the right customer. Outline steps 8 and 9 are contained in this module.

```
610   REM      CUST # FOUND.   PROCEED W/ DATA ENTRY
620   :
630   HOME
640   PRINT N$;" CREDIT RATING: ";R
650   INPUT "ENTER NEW CREDIT RATING:";R$
660   IF  LEN (R$) <  > 1 THEN  PRINT "ONLY ONE DIGIT NUMBER IS
      ACCEPTABLE.": GOTO 650
670   IF  VAL (R$) < 1 OR  VAL (R$) > 5 THEN  PRINT "NUMBERS 1-5 ONLY,
      PLEASE.": GOTO 650
680   LET R1 =  VAL (R$)
690   :
700   REM     PRINT NEW INFO TO TEMP
710   :
720   PRINT D$;"WRITE TEMP"
730   PRINT C$: PRINT N$: PRINT R1
740   PRINT D$
750   :
```

In line 730, the new customer rating (R1) is written into the temporary file, along with the accompanying customer number and name. You have now completed the routines to search the original file and to place old and new data into the temporary file.

(a) Considering the location of the file pointer in the CREDIT file, what should the program do next?

- - - - - - - - - - - - - - -

(a)   Write the remainder of the CREDIT file to the temporary file.

Fill in all the blanks in the program segment below, including lines 790, 800, 810, 820, 830, 840, and 910, completing steps 10 and 11 of the outline.

```
(a)   760   REM      PRINT REMAINDER OF FILE TO TEMP
      770 :
      780   ONERR   GOTO 890
      790
      800
      810
      820
      830
      840
      850   GOTO 790
      860 :
      870   REM      CLOSE FILES
      880 :
      890   IF  PEEK (222) = 5 THEN 910
      900   PRINT : PRINT "UNUSUAL ERROR. PROGRAM TERMINATED.": PRINT
      910
      920 :
```

— — — — — — — — — — — — — — — —

```
(a)   760   REM      PRINT REMAINDER OF FILE TO TEMP
      770 :
      780   ONERR   GOTO 890
      790   PRINT D$;"READ"F$
      800   INPUT C$,N$,R
      810   PRINT D$
      820   PRINT D$;"WRITE TEMP"
      830   PRINT C$: PRINT N$: PRINT R
      840   PRINT D$
      850   GOTO 790
      860 :
      870   REM      CLOSE FILES
      880 :
      890   IF  PEEK (222) = 5 THEN 910
      900   PRINT : PRINT "UNUSUAL ERROR. PROGRAM TERMINATED.": PRINT
      910   PRINT D$;"CLOSE"
      920 :
```

The final program module should copy the complete temporary file back into the original credit file. We could use a file copy program like the one completed earlier in this chapter for that. However, your APPLE has a command that allows you to RENAME a program or file. It is quite easy to use:

```
100   PRINT D$;"RENAME OLD NAME,NEW NAME"
```

Or, if you are using files named in variables:

```
110   PRINT D$;"RENAME"F$,F1$
```

or

```
120   PRINT D$;"RENAME OLD NAME,"F1$
```

Note: The punctuation shown above (the comma) is very important.

Your files should be closed before you RENAME. If not, however, RENAME will close them first. There is one problem with RENAME: It does not bother to check whether there is already another program with the new name on your disk. It just moves ahead. This can result in two files on your disk with the same name — in which case you have a real problem. The solution we devised was to DELETE the old copy of the credit file before we RENAMEd the temporary file. Here is the final module of the program that completes the copy or RENAME operation, including steps 12 and 13 of our original procedure outline.

```
930  REM      DELETE/RENAME FILE
940  :
950  PRINT D$;"DELETE"F$
960  PRINT D$;"RENAME TEMP,"F$
970  PRINT "RENAME COMPLETED"
980  :
990  REM      CONTINUE REQUEST
1000 :
1010 INPUT "DO YOU HAVE MORE CREDIT RATING CHANGES?";R$
1020 IF  LEFT$ (R$,1) (  ) "Y" AND  LEFT$ (R$,1) (  ) "N" THEN  PRINT
     CHR$ (7);"ENTER 'Y' FOR YES OR 'N' FOR NO.": PRINT : GOTO 1010
1030 IF  LEFT$ (R$,1) = "Y" THEN 300
1040 PRINT : PRINT "PROGRAM COMPLETED AS REQUESTED."
1050 END
```

If you RUN this program with large files, each change will take considerable computer time. If you enter the data in the original file in customer number order, and also enter all changes in customer number order; the need to repeatedly execute the RENAME routine is eliminated, reducing the computer time between transactions.

Here is a complete listing of the credit file change program. You are encouraged to enter and RUN this program using the datafile named CREDIT that you created in the Chapter 4 Self-Test.

```
100   REM     CREDIT FILE CHANGER
110   :
120   REM     VARIABLES USED
130   REM       F$ = FILE NAME
140   REM       C$ = CUST. #
150   REM       C1$ = CUST. #
160   REM       N$ = NAME
170   REM       R$ = ENTRY VARIABLE
180   REM       R,R1 = CREDIT RATING VALUE
190   REM       D$ = CONTROL D
200   :
210   REM     FILES USED
220   REM       SEQ.FILE NAME: CREDIT (USER ENTERED)
230   REM       TEMPORARY FILE NAME: TEMP
240   REM       DATSET FORMAT: C$,N$,R
250   :
260   REM     INITIALIZE
270   :
280   LET D$ = CHR$ (4)
290   HOME : INPUT "ENTER FILE NAME:";F$
300   PRINT D$;"OPEN"F$
310   PRINT D$;"OPEN TEMP"
320   :
330   REM     DATA ENTRY ROUTINE
340   :
350   HOME
360   PRINT "ENTER 'STOP' TO END DATA ENTRY."
370   PRINT
380   INPUT "ENTER CUSTOMER #:";C$
390   IF C$ = "STOP" THEN 1080
400   IF LEN (C$) = 0 THEN  PRINT "ENTER CUSTOMER NUMBER OR TYPE 'STOP'":
      GOTO 380
410   IF LEN (C$) < > 5 THEN  PRINT "ENTRY ERROR. REENTER WITH 5 DIGITS.":
      GOTO 380
420   IF VAL (C$) = 0 THEN  PRINT "ENTRY ERROR.  NUMBERS ONLY.": GOTO 380
430   :
440   REM     FILE SEARCH ROUTINE
450   :
460   ONERR  GOTO 550
470   PRINT D$;"READ"F$
480   INPUT C1$,N$,R
490   PRINT D$
500   IF C$ = C1$ THEN 630
510   PRINT D$;"WRITE TEMP"
520   PRINT C1$: PRINT N$: PRINT R
530   PRINT D$
540   GOTO 470
550   PRINT  CHR$ (7);"ERROR MESSAGE. WE CANNOT FIND"
560   PRINT "CUSTOMER # ";C$;" ON THE FILE."
570   PRINT "PLEASE CHECK YOUR NUMBER AND REENTER."
580   PRINT D$;"CLOSE"
590   GOTO 300
600   :
610   REM     CUST # FOUND.  PROCEED W/ DATA ENTRY
620   :
630   HOME
640   PRINT N$;" CREDIT RATING: ";R
650   INPUT "ENTER NEW CREDIT RATING:";R$
660   IF LEN (R$) < > 1 THEN  PRINT "ONLY ONE DIGIT NUMBER IS
      ACCEPTABLE.": GOTO 650
670   IF VAL (R$) < 1 OR  VAL (R$) > 5 THEN  PRINT "NUMBERS 1-5 ONLY,
      PLEASE.": GOTO 650
680   LET R1 = VAL (R$)
690   :
700   REM     PRINT NEW INFO TO TEMP
710   :
720   PRINT D$;"WRITE TEMP"
730   PRINT C$: PRINT N$: PRINT R1
740   PRINT D$
750   :
```

```
760  REM      PRINT REMAINDER OF FILE TO TEMP
770  :
780  ONERR  GOTO 890
790  PRINT D$;"READ"F$
800  INPUT C$,N$,R
810  PRINT D$
820  PRINT D$;"WRITE TEMP"
830  PRINT C$: PRINT N$: PRINT R
840  PRINT D$
850  GOTO 790
860  :
870  REM      CLOSE FILES
880  :
890  IF  PEEK (222) = 5 THEN 910
900  PRINT : PRINT "UNUSUAL ERROR. PROGRAM TERMINATED.": PRINT
910  PRINT D$;"CLOSE"
920  :
930  REM      DELETE/RENAME FILE
940  :
950  PRINT D$;"DELETE"F$
960  PRINT D$;"RENAME TEMP,"F$
970  PRINT "RENAME COMPLETED"
980  :
990  REM      CONTINUE REQUEST
1000 :
1010 INPUT "DO YOU HAVE MORE CREDIT RATING CHANGES?";R$
1020 IF  LEFT$ (R$,1) < > "Y" AND  LEFT$ (R$,1) < > "N" THEN   PRINT
     CHR$ (7);"ENTER 'Y' FOR YES OR 'N' FOR NO.": PRINT : GOTO 1010
1030 IF  LEFT$ (R$,1) = "Y" THEN 300
1040 PRINT : PRINT "PROGRAM COMPLETED AS REQUESTED."
1050 END
```

(a) Write the corresponding program line number(s) for each step in the outline.

1. OPEN the credit file. _____

2. OPEN a temporary file. _____

3. Enter the customer number, the item to be searched (include data entry

    tests and a "no more searches" option). _____

4. Check for end-of-data in credit file. If end-of-data is found:

    a. display an error message indicating an unsuccessful search _____

    b. CLOSE both files. _____

    c. return to step 1. _____

5. READ a complete dataset. _____

6. Test for wanted customer number. _____

7. PRINT rejected datasets to temporary file. _____

8. Display needed information; ask user for changes with data entry test.

    _____

9. PRINT dataset with new data to temporary file. _____

10. PRINT remainder of credit file to temporary file. _____

11. CLOSE both files. _____

12. RENAME temporary file as credit file. _____

13. Provide the user with the option of repeating the process. _____

– – – – – – – – – – – – – – – –

(a)   1.   300
      2.   310
      3.   360–420
      4.   460
      1a. 550–570
      4b. 580
      4c. 590
      5.   470–490
      6.   500
      7.   510–530
      8.   640–680
      9.   720–740
     10.   780–850
     11.   910
     12.   950–970
     13.   1010–1040

EDITING, DELETING, AND INSERTING FILE DATA

Whenever we work extensively with files, we write a small utility program that lets us read through the file, one item at a time, to verify that everything is as it should be. A properly written data file editing program also lets you make changes in the file data as it reads through the file. We will start with a simple program to examine the contents of a file, one data item at a time. Our example will use the previous application – the CREDIT file. Remember the dataset consists of:

1. a five-digit customer number stored as a string
. 2. a twenty-character customer name
3. a credit rating, stored as a numeric value from 1 through 5

The first program below allows you to look at each dataset, one item at a time, with the prompt "PRESS RETURN TO CONTINUE." The PRESS RETURN TO CONTINUE technique is very popular for CRT screen-oriented systems. The program allows the user to review the data displayed for the length of time needed and then move to the next dataset. The program then refreshes, or clears, the screen to remove "screen clutter" before the next data are displayed, using the HOME instruction. Examine the program to see how the user INPUT statement is used in the PRESS RETURN TO CONTINUE technique.

```
100   REM     CREDIT FILE EDITOR (VERSION 1)
110   REM   THIS PROGRAM DEMONSTRATES
120   REM     PRESS 'RETURN' TO CONTINUE
130  :
140   REM     VARIABLES USED
150   REM        C$ = CUST # (5)
160   REM        N$ = CUST NAME (20)
170   REM        R = CREDIT RATING (1)
180   REM        R$ = USER RESPONSE
190   REM        F$ = FILE NAME
200   REM        D$ = CONTROL D
210  :
220   REM     FILES USED
230   REM        SEQ. FILE NAME: CREDIT (USER ENTERED)
240   REM           DATASET FORMAT: C$,N$,R
250  :
260   REM     INITIALIZATION
270  :
280   LET D$ = CHR$ (4)
290   INPUT "ENTER FILE NAME:";F$
300   PRINT D$;"OPEN"F$
310  :
320   REM     READ FILE AND DISPLAY
330  :
340   HOME
350   PRINT "PRESS 'RETURN' TO DISPLAY NEXT ITEM.": PRINT
360   ONERR  GOTO 510
370   PRINT D$;"READ"F$
380   INPUT C$,N$,R
390   PRINT D$
400   PRINT C$
410   INPUT "";R$
420   PRINT N$
430   INPUT "";R$
440   PRINT R
450   INPUT "";R$
460   PRINT
470   GOTO 340
480  :
490   REM     CLOSE FILE
500  :
510   IF  PEEK (222) = 5 THEN 530
520   PRINT : PRINT "UNUSUAL ERROR. PROGRAM TERMINATED."
530   PRINT D$;"CLOSE"
540   HOME
550   PRINT "JOB COMPLETED"
560   END
```

(a)   What is assigned to R$ in lines 410, 430, and 450?

_____

(b)   Since R$ acts as a dummy variable in the program above, what is the purpose of lines 410, 430, and 450?

_____

_____

_____

(c)   How often was the screen "refreshed" in the program above?

_____

– – – – – – – – – – – – – – –

_____

(a)   Nothing (a null string)
(b)   Keeps the data items on the CRT display until the user presses RETURN to continue (Program waits at INPUT statement until RETURN key is pressed, with or without any other entry.)
(c)   Before (or after) each complete dataset of three items was displayed

The next version of this program allows the user to change any data items as they are displayed on the screen, or accept data "as is" by pressing RETURN to continue. The procedure includes copying the credit data file to a temporary file "TEMPFIL" as you read through the file making changes. Here is the first part of the program, which includes the ability to change the customer number.

```
100   REM     CREDIT FILE EDITOR (VERSION 2)
110   REM     THIS PROGRAM DEMONSTRATES
120   REM     TYPE 'C' TO CHANGE ITEM, OR
130   REM     PRESS 'RETURN' TO CONTINUE.
140   :
150   REM        VARIABLES USED
160   REM          C$ = CUST # (5)
170   REM          N$ = CUST NAME (20)
180   REM          R = CREDIT RATING
190   REM          R$ = USER RESPONSE
200   REM          F$ = FILE NAME
210   REM          D$ = CONTROL D
220   :
230   REM        FILES USED
240   REM          SEQ. FILE NAME: CREDIT (USER ENTERED)
250   REM          SEQ. TEMPORARY FILE NAME: TEMPFIL
260   REM          DATASET FORMAT: C$,N$,R
270   :
280   REM        INITIALIZATION
290   :
300   LET D$ = CHR$ (4)
310   INPUT "ENTER FILE NAME:";F$
320   PRINT D$;"OPEN"F$
330   PRINT D$;"OPEN TEMPFIL"
340   PRINT D$;"DELETE TEMPFIL"
350   PRINT D$;"OPEN TEMPFIL"
360   :
370   REM        READ FILE AND DISPLAY
380   :
390   HOME
400   PRINT "TYPE 'C' TO CHANGE ITEM DISPLAYED."
410   PRINT "PRESS 'RETURN' TO CONTINUE WITHOUT CHANGES."
420   ONERR  GOTO 770
430   PRINT D$;"READ"F$
440   INPUT C$,N$,R
450   PRINT D$
460   :
470   REM     DISPLAY & CHANGE OPTION FOR CUST. #
480   :
490   PRINT : PRINT C$
500   INPUT "";R$
510   IF R$ < > "" AND R$ < > "C" THEN  PRINT  CHR$ (7);"ENTRY ERROR. TRY
      AGAIN " GOTO 500
520   IF  LEFT$ (R$,1) = "C" THEN  GOSUB 880
530   :
850   :
860   REM        CHANGE CUST # SUBROUTINE
870   :
880   INPUT "ENTER NEW CUST. #:";C$
890   IF  LEN (C$) = 0 THEN  PRINT "ENTER NUMBERS PLEASE.": GOTO 740
900   IF  LEN (C$) < > 5 THEN  PRINT "ENTRY ERROR.  REENTER WITH 5
      DIGITS.": GOTO 880
910   IF  VAL (C$) = 0 THEN  PRINT "ENTRY ERROR, NUMBERS ONLY.": GOTO 880
920   RETURN
930   :
```

Notice the few additions: the temporary file (lines 260 and 340); the instruction changes (lines 130 and 370); and the entry test (line 470). For reasons that will become apparent, a subroutine (lines 700 through 750) is used for entering the change to the customer number. The same data entry checks are used that were originally used in the credit file creating program. Caution: This program segment does not write the new customer number to TEMPFIL. In order to maintain identical files, use one statement to write the entire dataset into TEMPFIL as was originally done with the credit rating data file. If you are particularly sharp, you may have noted that the new customer number was assigned to C$, replacing the old customer number stored there. Can you look ahead and see why?

Now its your turn. Write a routine that will allow a change in the customer name. Use the subroutine format like that above. Fill in lines 960, 970, 980, and 990.

(a)
```
540   REM  DISPLAY AND CHANGE OPTION FOR NAME
550 :
560   PRINT : PRINT N$
570   INPUT "";R$
580   IF  LEFT$ (R$,1) ( ) "" AND  LEFT$ (R$,1) ( ) "C" THEN  PRINT :
      PRINT "PRESS 'RETURN' FOR NO CHANGE OR ENTER 'C' TO CHANGE NAME.":
      PRINT : GOTO 570
590   IF R$ = "C" THEN  GOSUB 960
600 :
940   REM     NAME CHANGE SUBROUTINE
950 :
960
970
980
990
1000 :
```

- - - - - - - - - - - - - - - -

(a)
```
540   REM  DISPLAY AND CHANGE OPTION FOR NAME
550 :
560   PRINT : PRINT N$
570   INPUT "";R$
580   IF  LEFT$ (R$,1) ( ) "" AND  LEFT$ (R$,1) ( ) "C" THEN  PRINT :
      PRINT "PRESS 'RETURN' FOR NO CHANGE OR ENTER 'C' TO CHANGE NAME.":
      PRINT : GOTO 570
590   IF R$ = "C" THEN  GOSUB 960
600 :
940   REM     NAME CHANGE SUBROUTINE
950 :
```
```
960   INPUT "ENTER NEW NAME:";N$
970   IF  LEN (N$) = 0 THEN  PRINT : PRINT "NO ENTRY MADE. PLEASE ENTER AS
      REQUESTED.": PRINT : GOTO 960
980   IF  LEN (N$) ) 20 THEN  PRINT : PRINT "ABBREVIATE NAME TO 20
      CHARACTERS OR LESS.": PRINT : GOTO 960
990   RETURN
1000 :
```

Nice work! Now, write a program segment that allows a change to be entered for the credit rating. Upon returning from the subroutine, have the program record the entire dataset, including changes, if any, to TEMPFIL. Fill in lines 700, 710, 720, 1030, 1040, 1050, and 1060.

(a)
```
610   REM   DISPLAY & CHANGE OPTION FOR RATING
620  :
630   PRINT : PRINT R
640   INPUT ""; R$
650   IF R$ <  > "" AND R$ <  > "C" THEN  PRINT : PRINT "PLEASE PRESS
      'RETURN' IF NO CHANGE, OR TYPE 'C' TO CHANGE RATING.": PRINT : GOTO 640
660   IF R$ = "C" THEN  GOSUB 1030
670  :
680   REM    WRITE ONE DATASET BACK TO FILE
690  :
700
710
720
730   GOTO 390
740  :
1010  REM    CREDIT RATING CHANGE SUBROUTINE
1020  :
1030
1040
1050
1060
1070  RETURN
1080  :
```

- - - - - - - - - - - - - - -

(a)
```
610   REM   DISPLAY & CHANGE OPTION FOR RATING
620  :
630   PRINT : PRINT R
640   INPUT ""; R$
650   IF R$ <  > "" AND R$ <  > "C" THEN  PRINT : PRINT "PLEASE PRESS
      'RETURN' IF NO CHANGE, OR TYPE 'C' TO CHANGE RATING.": PRINT : GOTO 640
660   IF R$ = "C" THEN  GOSUB 1030
670  :
680   REM    WRITE ONE DATASET BACK TO FILE
690  :
700   PRINT D$; "WRITE TEMPFIL"
710   PRINT C$: PRINT N$: PRINT R
720   PRINT D$
730   GOTO 390
740  :
1010  REM    CREDIT RATING CHANGE SUBROUTINE
1020  :
1030   INPUT "ENTER NEW CREDIT RATING:"; R$
1040   IF  LEN (R$) <  > 1 THEN  PRINT : PRINT "ENTER ONE DIGIT NUMBER ONLY,
       PLEASE.": PRINT : GOTO 1030
1050   IF  VAL (R$) < 1 OR  VAL (R$) > 5 THEN  PRINT : PRINT "ENTER DIGITS
       1 TO 5 ONLY.": PRINT : GOTO 1030
1060   LET R =  VAL (R$)
1070   RETURN
1080  :
```

Did you get line 710? Carefully planned, the routine that prints or writes to the file uses the same variables (C$, N$, and R) that can contain either new data or the original unchanged data items.

(a)   Describe the last routine needed to complete this program.

_____

- - - - - - - - - - - - - -

(a)   Close the files and RENAME TEMPFIL to F$.

The end of data error trap is already set up in line 420 to branch to line 770.

While experiencing a bit of *deja vu*, complete the final section to RENAME
TEMPFIL by filling in lines 770, 780, 800, 810, and 820.

(a)
```
750   REM    CLOSE FILES
760 :
770
780
790   HOME : PRINT "WORKING"
800
810
820
830   PRINT : PRINT "JOB COMPLETE."
840   END
850 :
```

- - - - - - - - - - - - - -

(a)
```
750   REM    CLOSE FILES
760 :      /
770   IF  PEEK (222) = 5 THEN 790
780   PRINT : PRINT "UNUSUAL ERROR. PROGRAM TERMINATED. READ AND DISPLAY
      FILE CONTENTS TO CHECK FOR ERRORS.": PRINT : GOTO 800
790   HOME : PRINT "WORKING"
800   PRINT D$;"CLOSE"
810   PRINT D$;"DELETE"F$
820   PRINT D$;"RENAME TEMPFIL,"F$
830   PRINT : PRINT "JOB COMPLETE."
840   END
850 :
```

Here is a complete listing of the second version of the credit file editor program.
Be sure to enter and RUN this program before continuing.

```
100   REM     CREDIT FILE EDITOR (VERSION 2)
110   REM     THIS PROGRAM DEMONSTRATES
120   REM     TYPE 'C' TO CHANGE ITEM, OR
130   REM     PRESS 'RETURN' TO CONTINUE.
140   :
150   REM        VARIABLES USED
160   REM          C$ = CUST # (5)
170   REM          N$ = CUST NAME (20)
180   REM          R = CREDIT RATING
190   REM          R$ = USER RESPONSE
200   REM          F$ = FILE NAME
210   REM          D$ = CONTROL D
220   :
230   REM        FILES USED
240   REM          SEQ. FILE NAME: CREDIT (USER ENTERED)
250   REM          SEQ. TEMPORARY FILE NAME: TEMPFIL
260   REM          DATASET FORMAT: C$,N$,R
270   :
280   REM       INITIALIZATION
290   :
300   LET D$ =   CHR$ (4)
310   INPUT "ENTER FILE NAME:";F$
320   PRINT D$;"OPEN"F$
330   PRINT D$;"OPEN TEMPFIL"
340   PRINT D$;"DELETE TEMPFIL"
350   PRINT D$;"OPEN TEMPFIL"
360   :
370   REM       READ FILE AND DISPLAY
380   :
390   HOME
400   PRINT "TYPE 'C' TO CHANGE ITEM DISPLAYED."
410   PRINT "PRESS 'RETURN' TO CONTINUE WITHOUT CHANGES."
420   ONERR  GOTO 770
430   PRINT D$;"READ"F$
440   INPUT C$,N$,R
450   PRINT D$
460   :
470   REM     DISPLAY & CHANGE OPTION FOR CUST. #
480   :
490   PRINT : PRINT C$
500   INPUT "";R$
510   IF R$ <  > "" AND R$ <  > "C" THEN  PRINT  CHR$ (7);"ENTRY ERROR. TRY
      AGAIN.": GOTO 500
520   IF  LEFT$ (R$,1) = "C" THEN  GOSUB 880
530   :
540   REM  DISPLAY AND CHANGE OPTION FOR NAME
550   :
560   PRINT : PRINT N$
570   INPUT "";R$
580   IF  LEFT$ (R$,1) <  > "" AND  LEFT$ (R$,1) <  > "C" THEN  PRINT :
      PRINT "PRESS 'RETURN' FOR NO CHANGE OR ENTER 'C' TO CHANGE NAME.":
      PRINT : GOTO 570
590   IF R$ = "C" THEN  GOSUB 960
600   :
610   REM   DISPLAY & CHANGE OPTION FOR RATING
620   :
630   PRINT : PRINT R
640   INPUT "";R$
650   IF R$ <  > "" AND R$ <  > "C" THEN  PRINT : PRINT "PLEASE PRESS
      'RETURN' IF NO CHANGE, OR TYPE'C' TO CHANGE RATING.": PRINT : GOTO 640
660   IF R$ = "C" THEN  GOSUB 1030
670   :
680   REM     WRITE ONE DATASET BACK TO FILE
690   :
700   PRINT D$;"WRITE TEMPFIL"
710   PRINT C$: PRINT N$: PRINT R
720   PRINT D$
730   GOTO 390
740   :
```

```
750   REM     CLOSE FILES
760 :
770   IF  PEEK (222) = 5 THEN 790
780   PRINT : PRINT "UNUSUAL ERROR. PROGRAM TERMINATED. READ AND DISPLAY
      FILE CONTENTS TO CHECK FOR ERRORS.": PRINT : GOTO 800
790   HOME : PRINT "WORKING"
800   PRINT D$;"CLOSE"
810   PRINT D$;"DELETE"F$
820   PRINT D$;"RENAME TEMPFIL,"F$
830   PRINT : PRINT "JOB COMPLETE."
840   END
850 :
860   REM     CHANGE CUST # SUBROUTINE
870 :
880   INPUT "ENTER NEW CUST. #:";C$
890   IF  LEN (C$) = 0 THEN  PRINT "ENTER NUMBERS PLEASE.": GOTO 740
900   IF  LEN (C$) <  > 5 THEN  PRINT "ENTRY ERROR.   REENTER WITH 5
      DIGITS.": GOTO 880
910   IF  VAL (C$) = 0 THEN  PRINT "ENTRY ERROR, NUMBERS ONLY.": GOTO 880
920   RETURN
930 :
940   REM     NAME CHANGE SUBROUTINE
950 :
960   INPUT "ENTER NEW NAME:";N$
970   IF  LEN (N$) = 0 THEN  PRINT : PRINT "NO ENTRY MADE. PLEASE ENTER AS
      REQUESTED.": PRINT : GOTO 960
980   IF  LEN (N$) > 20 THEN  PRINT : PRINT "ABBREVIATE NAME TO 20
      CHARACTERS OR LESS.": PRINT : GOTO 960
990   RETURN
1000 :
1010  REM     CREDIT RATING CHANGE SUBROUTINE
1020 :
1030  INPUT "ENTER NEW CREDIT RATING:";R$
1040  IF  LEN (R$) <  > 1 THEN  PRINT : PRINT "ENTER ONE DIGIT NUMBER ONLY,
      PLEASE.": PRINT : GOTO 1030
1050  IF  VAL (R$) < 1 OR  VAL (R$) > 5 THEN  PRINT : PRINT "ENTER DIGITS
      1 TO 5 ONLY.": PRINT : GOTO 1030
1060  LET R =  VAL (R$)
1070  RETURN
1080 :
```

Yet another desireable editing feature is the ability to delete a complete dataset from a data file. This is in addition to the program's ability to make changes in an existing dataset. To delete a dataset, have the program read the dataset from the file, but *not* copy it into TEMPFIL. Thus, the dataset "disappears." This editing option can be integrated into the existing program you have been developing. First, enter a statement to inform the user of the option to delete a dataset.

```
395  PRINT : PRINT "TYPE 'D' TO DELETE THIS ENTIRE DATASET FROM THE FILE."
```

(a)   Complete the change in the statement line that tests for legal user inputs.

_____

(b)   Write a statement to branch to line 390, thus never writing the current dataset if the user entered 'D'.
      [525]

(a)   510   IF R$ < > "" AND R$ < > "C" AND R$ < > "D" THEN PRINT : PRINT
            CHR$ (7);"ENTRY ERROR. READ THE INSTRUCTIONS AND TRY AGAIN.": PRINT :
            GOTO 500

(b)   525   IF R$ = "D" THEN 430

You now have a model for a file editor that allows for changes, deletions, or no changes. Another useful editing feature allows you to keep data in numerical or alphabetical order by insertion of a new dataset part way through an existing data file. After locating a certain dataset, the new dataset is inserted by using the subroutines used to make changes in the file. How's that for program efficiency. Following are some of the new statements needed, with space for you to complete lines 396, 510, and 526.

(a)   396

      510

      526

      841 :
      842   REM   SUBROUTINE TO WRITE CURRENT DATASET TO FILE UNCHANGED BEFORE NEW
            DATASET IS INSERTED
      843 :
      844   PRINT D$;"WRITE TEMPFIL"
      845   PRINT C$: PRINT N$: PRINT R
      846   PRINT D$
      847   RETURN
      848 :

- - - - - - - - - - - - - - - -

(a)   396   PRINT : PRINT "TYPE 'I' TO INSERT A NEW DATASET AFTER THE ONE
            DISPLAYED. CURRENT DATASET DISPLAYED WILL BE PLACED IN THE FILE
            UNCHANGED.": PRINT
      397 :
      398 :
      510   IF R$ < > "" AND R$ < > "C" AND R$ < > "D" AND R$ < > "I" THEN
            PRINT : PRINT CHR$(7);"ENTRY ERROR. READ DIRECTIONS AND ENTER
            ACCORDINGLY.": PRINT : GOTO 500
      511 :
      512 :
      526   IF R$ = "I" THEN GOSUB 844: GOSUB 880: GOSUB 960: GOSUB 1030: GOTO
            700
      527 :
      528 :
      841 :
      842   REM   SUBROUTINE TO WRITE CURRENT DATASET TO FILE UNCHANGED BEFORE
            NEW DATASET IS INSERTED
      843 :
      844   PRINT D$;"WRITE TEMPFIL"
      845   PRINT C$: PRINT N$: PRINT R
      846   PRINT D$
      847   RETURN
      848 :

To change, delete, or insert data in the CREDIT file gather together this data file editing utility program.

```
100   REM     CREDIT FILE EDITOR (VERSION 3)
110   REM     THIS PROGRAM ALLOWS CHANGES IN CURRENT DATA, DELETION OF
      DATASETS, AND
120   REM     INSERTION OF NEW DATASETS. IT ALSO ALLOWS YOU TO
130   REM     PRESS 'RETURN' TO CONTINUE DISPLAY OF DATA WITH NO CHANGES TO
      DATA ITEMS.
140   :
150   REM        VARIABLES USED
160   REM        C$ = CUST # (5)
170   REM        N$ = CUST NAME (20)
180   REM        R = CREDIT RATING
190   REM        R$ = USER RESPONSE
200   REM        F$ = FILE NAME
210   REM        D$ = CONTROL D
220   :
230   REM        FILES USED
240   REM        SEQ. FILE NAME: CREDIT (USER ENTERED)
250   REM        SEQ. TEMPORARY FILE NAME: TEMPFIL
260   REM        DATASET FORMAT: C$,N$,R
270   :
280   REM     INITIALIZATION
290   :
300   LET D$ =   CHR$ (4)
310   INPUT "ENTER FILE NAME:";F$
320   PRINT D$;"OPEN"F$
330   PRINT D$;"OPEN TEMPFIL"
340   PRINT D$;"DELETE TEMPFIL"
350   PRINT D$;"OPEN TEMPFIL"
360   :
370   REM     READ FILE AND DISPLAY
380   :
390   HOME
395   PRINT : PRINT "TYPE 'D' TO DELETE THIS ENTIRE DATASET FROM THE FILE."
396   PRINT : PRINT "TYPE 'I' TO INSERT A NEW DATASET AFTER THE ONE
      DISPLAYED. CURRENT DATASET DISPLAYED WILL BE PLACED IN THE FILE
      UNCHANGED.": PRINT
400   PRINT "TYPE 'C' TO CHANGE ITEM DISPLAYED.": PRINT
410   PRINT "PRESS 'RETURN' TO CONTINUE WITHOUT CHANGES."
420   ONERR  GOTO 770
430   PRINT D$;"READ"F$
440   INPUT C$,N$,R
450   PRINT D$
460   :
470   REM     DISPLAY & CHANGE OPTION FOR CUST. #
480   :
490   PRINT : PRINT C$
500   INPUT "";R$
510   IF R$ <  > "" AND R$ <  > "C" AND R$ <  > "D" AND R$ <  > "I" THEN
      PRINT : PRINT  CHR$(7);"ENTRY ERROR. READ DIRECTIONS AND ENTER
      ACCORDINGLY.": PRINT : GOTO 500
520   IF  LEFT$ (R$,1) = "C" THEN  GOSUB 880
525   IF R$ = "D" THEN  430
526   IF R$ = "I" THEN  GOSUB 844: GOSUB 880: GOSUB 960: GOSUB 1030: GOTO
      700
530   :
540   REM  DISPLAY AND CHANGE OPTION FOR NAME
550   :
560   PRINT : PRINT N$
570   INPUT "";R$
580   IF  LEFT$ (R$,1) <  > "" AND  LEFT$ (R$,1) <  > "C" THEN  PRINT :
      PRINT "PRESS 'RETURN' FOR NO CHANGE OR ENTER 'C' TO CHANGE NAME.":
      PRINT : GOTO 570
590   IF R$ = "C" THEN  GOSUB 960
600   :
610   REM     DISPLAY & CHANGE OPTION FOR RATING
620   :
630   PRINT : PRINT R
640   INPUT "";R$
650   IF R$ <  > "" AND R$ <  > "C" THEN  PRINT : PRINT "PLEASE PRESS
      'RETURN' IF NO CHANGE, OR TYPE'C' TO CHANGE RATING.": PRINT :
      GOTO 640
660   IF R$ = "C" THEN  GOSUB 1030
670   :
```

continued on next page

```
680   REM     WRITE ONE DATASET BACK TO FILE
690   :
700   PRINT D$;"WRITE TEMPFIL"
710   PRINT C$: PRINT N$: PRINT R
720   PRINT D$
730   GOTO 390
740   :
750   REM     CLOSE FILES
760   :
770   IF  PEEK (222) = 5 THEN 790
780   PRINT : PRINT "UNUSUAL ERROR. PROGRAM TERMINATED. READ AND DISPLAY
      FILE CONTENTS TO CHECK FOR ERRORS.": PRINT : GOTO 800
790   HOME : PRINT "WORKING"
800   PRINT D$;"CLOSE"
810   PRINT D$;"DELETE"F$
820   PRINT D$;"RENAME TEMPFIL,"F$
830   PRINT : PRINT "JOB COMPLETE."
840   END
841   :
842   REM     SUBROUTINE TO WRITE CURRENT DATASET TO FILE UNCHANGED BEFORE
      NEW DATASET IS INSERTED
843   :
844   PRINT D$;"WRITE TEMPFIL"
845   PRINT C$: PRINT N$: PRINT R
846   PRINT D$
847   RETURN
850   :
860   REM        CHANGE CUST # SUBROUTINE
870   :
880   INPUT "ENTER NEW CUST. #:";C$
890   IF  LEN (C$) = 0 THEN  PRINT "ENTER NUMBERS PLEASE.": GOTO 740
900   IF  LEN (C$) <  > 5 THEN  PRINT "ENTRY ERROR.   REENTER WITH 5
      DIGITS.": GOTO 880
910   IF  VAL (C$) = 0 THEN  PRINT "ENTRY ERROR, NUMBERS ONLY.": GOTO 880
920   RETURN
930   :
940   REM       NAME CHANGE SUBROUTINE
950   :
960   INPUT "ENTER NEW NAME:";N$
970   IF  LEN (N$) = 0 THEN  PRINT : PRINT "NO ENTRY MADE. PLEASE ENTER AS
      REQUESTED.": PRINT : GOTO 960
980   IF  LEN (N$) > 20 THEN  PRINT : PRINT "ABBREVIATE NAME TO 20
      CHARACTERS OR LESS.": PRINT : GOTO 960
990   RETURN
1000  :
1010  REM     CREDIT RATING CHANGE SUBROUTINE
1020  :
1030  INPUT "ENTER NEW CREDIT RATING:";R$
1040  IF  LEN (R$) <  > 1 THEN  PRINT : PRINT "ENTER ONE DIGIT NUMBER ONLY,
      :PLEASE.": PRINT GOTO 1030
1050  IF  VAL (R$) < 1 OR  VAL (R$) > 5 THEN  PRINT : PRINT "ENTER DIGITS
      :1 TO 5 ONLY.": PRINT GOTO 1030
1060  LET R =  VAL (R$)
1070  RETURN
1080  :
```

The following outline for the final version of the program allows for insertion, deletion, or changes of data in the file.

(1) Open the source file.
(2) Open the temporary file.
(3) Display a "menu" for the user to select changes to be made, including a "no changes" option.
(4) Set ONERR for end-of-file detection.
(5) Read the entire dataset from the file and display the first data *item* (not dataset) in the current dataset.
(6) Allow the user to enter a selection from the "menu" and test for the legal selection possibilities.
(7) If user entered "C" for change:
     (a) Allow user to enter change with data entry checks.

    (b)   Display next data item from current dataset (if any items remain in this dataset).

    (c)   User entered option for another change and test selection.

    (d)   User entered change with data entry checks.

    (e)   Repeat (7) (b), (c), and (d) until all items in a dataset have been through the change option.

    (f)   Print the dataset (with any changes) to the temporary file.

    (g)   Go to step (3).

(8)   If user entered "I" for insert:

    (a)   Print the dataset to the temporary file.

    (b)   User enters new dataset with data entry checks.

    (c)   Print the newly entered data to the temporary file.

    (d)   Go to step (3).

(9)   If user entered "D" for delete, go to step (5).

(10) If the user entered no response (just pressed the RETURN key), go to steps (7) (b) to (g).

(11) Close both files.

(12) RENAME TEMPFIL to source file name.

(a)   Write the corresponding program line number(s) for each step in the outline below, except for item (10), where you are to fill in the blanks in the parentheses.

    (1)   Open the source file. _____

    (2)   Open the temporary file. _____

    (3)   Display a "menu" for the user to select changes to be made, including a "no changes" option. _____

    (4)   Set ONERR for end-of-file detection. _____

    (5)   Read the entire dataset from the file and display the first data *item* (not dataset) in the current dataset. _____

    (6)   Allow the user to enter a selection from the "menu" and test for the legal selection possibilities. _____

    (7)   If user entered "C" for change:

        (a)   Allow user to enter change with data entry checks. _____
            _____

        (b)   Display next data item from current dataset (if any items remain in this dataset). _____

        (c)   User entered option for another change and test selection. _____
            _____

(d) User entered change with data entry checks. _____

_____

(e) Repeat (7) (b), (c), and (d) until all items in a dataset have been through the change option. _____

(f) Print the dataset (with any changes) to the temporary file. _____

(g) Go to step (3). _____

(8) If user entered "I" for insert:

(a) Print the dataset to the temporary file. _____

(b) User enters new dataset with data entry checks. _____

_____

(c) Print the newly entered data to the temporary file. _____

(d) Go to step (3). _____

(9) If user entered "D" for delete, go to step (5). _____

(10) If the user entered no response (just pressed the RETURN key), go to steps (__) (__) to (__) (__). (Fill in the blanks.)

(11) Close both files. _____

(12) RENAME TEMPFIL to source file name. _____

_____

- - - - - - - - - - - - - - -

(a)　(1)　line 320
　　(2)　lines 330 to 350
　　(3)　lines 390 to 410
　　(4)　line 420
　　(5)　lines 430 to 490
　　(6)　lines 500 to 526
　　(7)　(a)　lines 880 to 920
　　　　(b)　line 560
　　　　(c)　lines 570 to 590
　　　　(d)　lines 880 to 920
　　　　(e)　lines 560 to 590, 880 to 920
　　　　(f)　lines 700 to 720
　　　　(g)　line 730
　　(8)　(a)　lines 844 to 847
　　　　(b)　lines 880 to 920, 960 to 990, and 1030 to 1070.

        (c)   lines 700 to 720

        (d)   line 730

  (9)   line 525

 (10)   steps (7) (b) to (7) (g)

 (11)   line 800

 (12)   lines 810 and 820

Enter and RUN the program; put it through its paces. Test all of the possible change options that this program makes available, and verify that the changes were actually made to the file.

MERGING THE CONTENTS OF FILE

In many business applications of computers, information in data files is maintained in alphabetic or numeric order. This can be done by customer number, customer name, product number, or some other key to filing. It is often necessary or desirable to merge the contents of two data files, both already in some order, to a make a third data file with the same order or sequence. A utility program to merge files also allows you to learn some new file programming techniques with wider applications.

    Follow these steps to merge two data files into one.

(1)   Open the two files to be merged (#1 and #2).

(2)   Open, delete, and reopen the file (#3) that will contain the merged data.

(3)   Use ONERR to branch to step (10) if end-of-file is encountered for either file #1 or file #2.

(4)   Read the first dataset from file #1.

(5)   Read the first dataset from file #2.

(6)   Test datasets to see which file dataset (#1 or #2) is to be copied or printed to the merge file (#3).

(7)   Print the selected dataset to file #3; this requires two separate routines:

    (a)   One if file #1 dataset is selected, or

    (b)   Another if file #2 dataset is selected.

(8)   Read another dataset from whichever file's dataset was printed to file #3 in step (7). Again, two separate routines are needed:

    (a)   Read another dataset from file #1, or

    (b)   Read another dataset from file #2.

(9)   Again, separate routines are needed to "dump" or transfer the remaining data in file #1 or #2 to file #3:

    (a)   If file #1 comes to end-of-file first, copy the remaining datasets in file #2 to file #3, or

    (b)   If file #2 comes to end-of-file first, copy the remaining datasets in file #1 to file #3.

(10) Close all files.

(11) Optional routine to display merged data files for confirmation of a successful merge.

The model program merges two transaction files into a third larger file that combines the other two. In the example, each transaction produces a dataset as shown below.

Account number = five characters
Transaction code = two characters (for a bank, 1 = check, 2 = deposit, etc.)
Amount = seven characters

This data is contained in the files named TRANSACTION-1 and TRANS-ACTION-2. Assume that the datasets are stored in two data files each in ascending numerical order by account number (problem 3 in the Chapter 4 Self-Test). The goal is to produce a third file named TRANSACTION-MERGE that combines the data in the first two files, but maintains the numerical order when the file merging is complete. Also assume that more than one dataset can have the same account number in either or both data files.

This last assumption requires a decision. When merging, if two datasets have the same account number, the program will copy the dataset from file #1 first, then the dataset with the same number from file #2.

FILE #1	FILE #2
10762	10761
18102	18203
43611	43611
43611	80111
43611	80772
80223	80772
98702	89012

File #3 (files #1 and #2 merged into one)

```
10761
10762
18102
18203
43611
43611
43611
43611
80111
80223
80772
80772
89102
98702
```

(Note: Only the account numbers are shown here; the complete datasets also include transaction codes and amounts.)

While the outline provides the logic, structure, and flow of the program, the summary of the program modules is given below to further aid your understanding of what may seem, at first, to be a very complicated program. The modules are:

Introduction
Initialize
Read first dataset from file #1
Read first dataset from file #2
Compare datasets
Print one dataset from file #1 to merged file
Read subsequent dataset from file #1
Print one dataset from file #2 to merged file
Read subsequent dataset from file #2
Copy leftover datasets from file #1 to merged file
Copy leftover datasets from file #2 to merged file
Close files
Open, display all datasets and close merged file

This program is called Merge. It gets tricky, so read the text and program segments carefully. The initializing process is familiar; you should have no trouble completing steps 1 and 2 of the outline.

```
100   REM     MERGE FILES UTILITY PROGRAM
110   :
120   REM     VARIABLES USED
130   REM     F1$,F2$,F3$ = USER ENTERED FILE NAMES
140   REM     A1$,A2$ = ACC'T NUMBER(5 CHAR.)
150   REM     T1$,T2$ = TRANSACTION CODE(1 CHAR.)
160   REM     C1$,C2$ = CASH AM'T(9999.99 OR 7 CHAR. MAX.)
170   REM     X = FOR NEXT LOOP CONTROL VARIABLE
180   REM     D$ = CONTROL D
190   :
200   REM     FILES USED
210   REM       SEQ. FILE NAMES: TRANSACTION-1, TRANSACTION-2,
      TRANSACTION-MERGE (ALL USER ENTERED)
220   REM       DATASET FORMAT: A$,T$,C$
230   :
240   REM     INITIALIZE
250   :
260   LET D$ =  CHR$ (4)
270   INPUT "ENTER SOURCE FILE 1:";F1$
280   INPUT "ENTER SOURCE FILE 2:";F2$
290   INPUT "ENTER OUTPUT (MERGED) FILE NAME:";F3$
300   HOME : PRINT "WORKING"
310   :
320   PRINT D$;"OPEN"F1$
330   PRINT D$;"OPEN"F2$
340   PRINT D$;"OPEN"F3$
350   PRINT D$;"DELETE"F3$
360   PRINT D$;"OPEN"F3$
370   :
```

(a)   Why is the OPEN–DELETE–OPEN sequence used for the F3$ file?

_____

_____

_____

(a)   The other two files are source files. F3$ (the merged file) is the only one to be written to, and this section of the program makes certain no extraneous data are in the file to begin with.

Next, the first dataset is read from file #1. Notice that the end-of-file error test is made before the first dataset is read, just in case the file has no data. This corresponds to steps 3 and 4 of the outline. If file #1 is empty to begin with, GOTO 1010.

```
380   REM      READ SOURCE 1
390 :
400   ONERR  GOTO 1010
410   PRINT D$;"READ"F1$
420   INPUT A1$,T1$,C1$
430   PRINT D$
440   LET A1 =  VAL (A1$)
450 :
```

Line 440 coverts the string that contains the account number into a numeric value. Now write the next segment corresponding to step 5 in the outline. The program should read the first data item from file #2. Fill in lines 490, 500, 510, and 520.

(a)
```
460   REM      READ SOURCE 2
470 :
480   ONERR  GOTO 900
490
500
510
520
530 :
```

- - - - - - - - - - - - - - - - -

(a)
```
460   REM      READ SOURCE 2
470 :
480   ONERR  GOTO 900
490   PRINT D$;"READ"F2$
500   INPUT A2$,T2$,C2$
510   PRINT D$
520   LET A2 =  VAL (A2$)
530 :
```

The next decision is which dataset — that from file #1 or that from file #2 — will be copied into file #3 first? This corresponds to step 6 in the outline.

```
540   REM      MERGE TESTING
550 :
560   IF A1 = A2 THEN 620
570   IF A1 < A2 THEN 620
580   GOTO 740
590 :
```

The program so far, as shown below, provides only for input of the first dataset from each of the two files to be merged, and compares the numeric values of the account numbers.

```
100   REM      MERGE FILES UTILITY PROGRAM
110   :
120   REM      VARIABLES USED
130   REM       F1$,F2$,F3$ = USER ENTERED FILE NAMES
140   REM       A1$,A2$ = ACC'T NUMBER(5 CHAR.)
150   REM       T1$,T2$ = TRANSACTION CODE(1 CHAR.)
160   REM       C1$,C2$ = CASH AM'T(9999.99 OR 7 CHAR. MAX.)
170   REM       X = FOR NEXT LOOP CONTROL VARIABLE
180   REM       D$ = CONTROL D
190   :
200   REM      FILES USED
210   REM        SEQ. FILE NAMES: TRANSACTION-1, TRANSACTION-2,
      TRANSACTION-MERGE (ALL USER ENTERED)
220   REM        DATASET FORMAT: A$,T$,C$
230   :
240   REM      INITIALIZE
250   :
260   LET D$ =  CHR$ (4)
270   INPUT "ENTER SOURCE FILE 1:";F1$
280   INPUT "ENTER SOURCE FILE 2:";F2$
290   INPUT "ENTER OUTPUT (MERGED) FILE NAME:";F3$
300   HOME : PRINT "WORKING"
310   :
320   PRINT D$;"OPEN"F1$
330   PRINT D$;"OPEN"F2$
340   PRINT D$;"OPEN"F3$
350   PRINT D$;"DELETE"F3$
360   PRINT D$;"OPEN"F3$
370   :
380   REM      READ SOURCE 1
390   :
400   ONERR  GOTO 1010
410   PRINT D$;"READ"F1$
420   INPUT A1$,T1$,C1$
430   PRINT D$
440   LET A1 =  VAL (A1$)
450   :
460   REM      READ SOURCE 2
470   :
480   ONERR  GOTO 900
490   PRINT D$;"READ"F2$
500   INPUT A2$,T2$,C2$
510   PRINT D$
520   LET A2 =  VAL (A2$)
530   :
540   REM      MERGE TESTING
550   :
560   IF A1 = A2 THEN 620
570   IF A1 < A2 THEN 620
580   GOTO 740
590   :
```

(a)   Look at lines 560 and 570. What should happen in the program routine that starts at line 620?

_____

(b)   The program tests for equality in line 560. In line 570, the test was for A1 less than A2. If both tests are false, what is the relationship of A1 to A2?

_____

(c)   What should happen in the program routine at line 740 that line 580 branches to?

_____

(a)   The dataset from source file #1 is copied.
(b)   A1 is greater than A2.
(c)   The dataset from source file #2 to file #3 is printed.

Continue with the file copying segment for copying a dataset from file #1 to file #3 (outline step 7a).

```
600   REM     PRINT #1 TO #3, READ #1
610   :
620   PRINT D$;"WRITE"F3$
630   PRINT A1$: PRINT T1$: PRINT C1$
640   PRINT D$
```

(a)   After executing the above segment, the program should now read another dataset from file #1. You might want to have the program branch back to the routine at line 410 and continue executing from there. Why would this result in a program error?

_____

_____

_____

– – – – – – – – – – – – – – – –

(a)   The routine at line 410 reads from file #1, but then continues to read another dataset from file #2, replacing the dataset already assigned to A2$, T2$, and C2$ without copying them to file #3.

The rest of this program segment is used for reading the next data item from file #1. This corresponds to outline step 8a.

```
600   REM     PRINT #1 TO #3, READ #1
610   :
620   PRINT D$;"WRITE"F3$
630   PRINT A1$: PRINT T1$: PRINT C1$
640   PRINT D$
650   ONERR  GOTO 1010
660   PRINT D$;"READ"F1$
670   INPUT A1$,T1$,C1$
680   PRINT D$
690   LET A1 =  VAL (A1$)
700   GOTO 560
710   :
```

(a)   When the program finds the end of file #1, it branches to line 1010. Think ahead: What should happen in the routine at line 1010?

_____

_____

– – – – – – – – – – – – – –

(a)   Since all datasets have been read from file #1 and copied to file #3, all the remaining data from file #2 should be copied into file #3 (you'll see this routine soon).

Here is the routine we need to copy a dataset from file #2 to file #3, and to read a new dataset from file #2. This corresponds to outline steps 7b and 8b.

```
720   REM      PRINT #2 TO #3, READ #2
730   :
740   PRINT D$;"WRITE"F3$
750   PRINT A2$: PRINT T2$: PRINT C2$
760   PRINT D$
770   ONERR  GOTO 900
780   PRINT D$;"READ"F2$
790   INPUT A2$,T2$,C2$
800   PRINT D$
810   LET A2 =   VAL (A2$)
820   GOTO 560
830   :
```

Notice how carefully you must think through these file utility programs. You are nearing the end; only a few more "clean up" routines are needed. Two similar routines are needed to copy or dump the remainders of file #2 to file #3, and file #1 to file #3. First, here are the program instructions that correspond to the outline, step 9a.

```
950   REM      DUMP #2 TO #3
960   :
1010  PRINT D$;"WRITE"F3$
1020  PRINT A2$: PRINT T2$: PRINT C2$
1030  PRINT D$
1040  GOTO 970
1050  :
```

Line 1010 is branched to from lines 400 or 650 on end of file checks for file #1.

The rest is easy. Here is the complete routine. Check file #2 for end of file and, if encountered, dump any remaining file #2 datasets to file #3.

```
950   REM      DUMP #2 TO #3
960   :
970   ONERR  GOTO 1080
980   PRINT D$;"READ"F2$
990   INPUT A2$,T2$,C2$
1000  PRINT D$
1010  PRINT D$;"WRITE"F3$
1020  PRINT A2$: PRINT T2$: PRINT C2$
1030  PRINT D$
1040  GOTO 970
1050  :
```

Write the corresponding routine to dump file #1 to file #3. The end of data error statement should branch to line 1080. Complete lines 860, 870, 880, 890, 900, 910, and 920.

(a)
```
840   REM       DUMP #1 TO #3
850 :
860
870
880
890
900
910
920
930   GOTO 860
940 :
```

(b)   The ONERR trap in lines 860 and 970 both branch to line 1080. What final routine should appear there?

_ _ _ _ _ _ _ _ _ _ _ _ _ _ _

(a)
```
840   REM       DUMP #1 TO #3
850 :
860   ONERR  GOTO 1080
870   PRINT D$;"READ"F1$
880   INPUT A1$,T1$,C1$
890   PRINT D$
900   PRINT D$;"WRITE"F3$
910   PRINT A1$: PRINT T1$: PRINT C1$
920   PRINT D$
930   GOTO 860
940 :
```

(b)   Close all files, since all data have been copied and merged.

Once the files are closed, the program gives the user the option to display the contents of the merged files to verify that it did happen and to judge whether the program works properly. In Merge all the activity takes place between the computer memory and the disk with no evidence of the action appearing on the CRT screen. You only see RUN, so did it really happen? The routine included at the end of the complete listing of Merge lets you be sure (see 1150 through 1330).

```
100   REM        MERGE FILES UTILITY PROGRAM
110   :
120   REM        VARIABLES USED
130   REM        F1$,F2$,F3$ = USER ENTERED FILE NAMES
140   REM        A1$,A2$ = ACC'T NUMBER(5 CHAR.)
150   REM        T1$,T2$ = TRANSACTION CODE(1 CHAR.)
160   REM        C1$,C2$ = CASH AM'T(9999.99 OR 7 CHAR. MAX.)
170   REM        X = FOR NEXT LOOP CONTROL VARIABLE
180   REM        D$ = CONTROL D
190   :
200   REM        FILES USED
210   REM          SEQ. FILE NAMES: TRANSACTION-1, TRANSACTION-2,
      TRANSACTION-MERGE (ALL USER ENTERED)
220   REM          DATASET FORMAT: A$,T$,C$
230   :
240   REM        INITIALIZE
250   :
260   LET D$ =  CHR$ (4)
270   INPUT "ENTER SOURCE FILE 1:";F1$
280   INPUT "ENTER SOURCE FILE 2:";F2$
290   INPUT "ENTER OUTPUT (MERGED) FILE NAME:";F3$
300   HOME : PRINT "WORKING"
310   :
320   PRINT D$;"OPEN"F1$
330   PRINT D$;"OPEN"F2$
340   PRINT D$;"OPEN"F3$
350   PRINT D$;"DELETE"F3$
360   PRINT D$;"OPEN"F3$
370   :
380   REM        READ SOURCE 1
390   :
400   ONERR  GOTO 1010
410   PRINT D$;"READ"F1$
420   INPUT A1$,T1$,C1$
430   PRINT D$
440   LET A1 =  VAL (A1$)
450   :
460   REM        READ SOURCE 2
470   :
480   ONERR  GOTO 900
490   PRINT D$;"READ"F2$
500   INPUT A2$,T2$,C2$
510   PRINT D$
520   LET A2 =  VAL (A2$)
530   :
540   REM        MERGE TESTING
550   :
560   IF A1 = A2 THEN 620
570   IF A1 < A2 THEN 620
580   GOTO 740
590   :
600   REM        PRINT #1 TO #3, READ #1
610   :
620   PRINT D$;"WRITE"F3$
630   PRINT A1$: PRINT T1$: PRINT C1$
640   PRINT D$
650   ONERR  GOTO 1010
660   PRINT D$;"READ"F1$
670   INPUT A1$,T1$,C1$
680   PRINT D$
690   LET A1 =  VAL (A1$)
700   GOTO 560
710   :
720   REM        PRINT #2 TO #3, READ #2
730   :
740   PRINT D$;"WRITE"F3$
750   PRINT A2$: PRINT T2$: PRINT C2$
760   PRINT D$
770   ONERR  GOTO 900
780   PRINT D$;"READ"F2$
790   INPUT A2$,T2$,C2$
800   PRINT D$
810   LET A2 =  VAL (A2$)
820   GOTO 560
830   :
```

continued on next page

```
840  REM      DUMP #1 TO #3
850  :
860  ONERR  GOTO 1080
870  PRINT D$;"READ"F1$
880  INPUT A1$,T1$,C1$
890  PRINT D$
900  PRINT D$;"WRITE"F3$
910  PRINT A1$: PRINT T1$: PRINT C1$
920  PRINT D$
930  GOTO 860
940  :
950  REM      DUMP #2 TO #3
960  :
970  ONERR  GOTO 1080
980  PRINT D$;"READ"F2$
990  INPUT A2$,T2$,C2$
1000  PRINT D$
1010  PRINT D$;"WRITE"F3$
1020  PRINT A2$: PRINT T2$: PRINT C2$
1030  PRINT D$
1040  GOTO 970
1050  :
1060  REM      CLOSE FILES
1070  :
1080  IF  PEEK (222) = 5 THEN 1100
1090  PRINT : PRINT  CHR$ (7);"UNUSUAL ERROR. PROGRAM TERMINATED."
1100  PRINT D$;"CLOSE"
1110  PRINT : PRINT "JOB COMPLETED."
1120  :
1130  REM    REQUEST TO DISPLAY MERGED FILES
1140  :
1150  PRINT : INPUT "DO YOU WANT TO SEE THE MERGED DATA?";R$
1160  IF  LEFT$ (R$,1) <  > "N" AND  LEFT$ (R$,1) <  > "Y" THEN  PRINT :
      PRINT "ENTER 'Y' FOR YES OR 'N' FOR NO.": PRINT : GOTO 1150
1170  IF R$ = "Y" THEN 1220
1180  IF R$ = "N" THEN 1330
1190  :
1200  REM      PRINT CONTENTS OF MERGED FILE
1210  :
1220  PRINT D$;"OPEN"F3$
1230  ONERR  GOTO 1320
1240  PRINT D$;"READ"F3$
1250  INPUT A$,T$,C$
1260  PRINT D$
1270  PRINT A$,T$,C$
1280  GOTO 1240
1290  :
1300  REM      CLOSE FILE
1310  :
1320  PRINT D$;"CLOSE"
1330  END
```

(a)   Write the corresponding program line number(s) for each step of the following outline.

(1)   Open the two files to be merged (#1 and #2).

_____

(2)   Open, delete, and reopen the file (#3) that will contain the merged data.

_____

(3)   Use ONERR to branch to step (9) if end-of-file is encountered for either file #1 or file #2. _____

(4)   Read the first dataset from file #1. _____

(5)   Read the first dataset from file #2. _____

(6) Test datasets to see which file dataset (#1 or #2) is to be copied or printed to the merge file (#3). _____

(7) Print the selected dataset to file #3; this requires two separate routines:

    (a) One if file #1 dataset is selected, _____ or

    (b) Another if file #2 dataset is selected. _____

(8) Read another dataset from whichever file's dataset was printed in file #3 in step (7). Again, two separate routines are needed:

    (a) Read another dataset from file #1, _____

    _____ or

    (b) Read another dataset from file #2. _____

    _____

(9) Again, separate routines are needed to "dump" or transfer the remaining data in file #1 or #2 to file #3:

    (a) If file #1 comes to end-of-file first, copy the remaining datasets in file #2 to file #3, _____ or

    (b) If file #2 comes to end-of-file first, copy the remaining datasets in file #1 to file #3. _____

(10) Close all files. _____

(11) Optional routine to display merged data files for confirmation of a successful merge. _____

— — — — — — — — — — — — — — — —

(a) (1) lines 320 and 330   (8) (a) lines 660 to 680
    (2) lines 340 to 360   (b) lines 780 to 800
    (3) lines 400 and 480   (9) (a) lines 970 to 1040
    (4) lines 410 to 430   (b) lines 860 to 930
    (5) lines 490 to 510   (10) line 1100
    (6) lines 560 to 580   (11) lines 1150 to 1330
    (7) (a) lines 620 to 640
         (b) lines 740 to 760

Enter and RUN the program, using the two data files named TRANSACTION-1 and TRANSACTION-2 that you created in the Chapter 4 Self-Test, problem 4a.

PROBLEMS WITH SEQUENTIAL DATA FILES

You should be aware of some frequent errors made in using sequential files and some programming techniques used for successful programs accessing data files.

The most frequent programming error is failing to keep track of the file pointers. Each time you use a file INPUT statement in a program, ask yourself how the file pointer is affected and where it is located before and after executing the statement.

(a)   How can you reset the datafile pointer to the beginning of a file? _____

_____

– – – – – – – – – – – – – – – –

(a)   Close the file. Pointer is at beginning of file when file is reopened.

Another frequent error occurs when a program sequentially searches through a data file for a particular dataset or data item. Let's say you have a data file of names arranged alphabetically by last names. After you enter the name to be searched, the program searches through the file until it finds the name and then prints the information on your printer for that person. Then you enter a second name. When writing the program, ask yourself where the file pointer will be located after the first search. Assume the first name searched and located is DORIAN SCHMIDT and the second name is HAMILTON ANDERSON. The data file search for the second name takes up where the search for the first name left off. The second name obviously will not be found before you reach the end-of-file. If the data file pointer was not reset to the beginning of the file after the first search, ANDERSON will never be found because the file was in alphabetical order and the search for the second name started at SCHMIDT. The solution, of course, is to make sure the program resets the pointer to the beginning of the file after every search, by using a CLOSE followed by an OPEN statement.

(a)   When a file has been partially read through during a data search, why must the file pointer be reset to the beginning of the file before a new search of the file commences?

_____

_____

_____

– – – – – – – – – – – – – – – –

(a)   Because if the pointer is midway in the file and the new datum searched for is near the beginning of the file, the search would not find the datum.

Errors can also occur when the contents of arrays are copied into a data file, a topic mentioned earlier. The contents of a one- or two-dimensional array can be copied into a file or read from a file back into an array, provided you use the correct programming techniques. Such data manipulation has many uses. There is a tendency to think of array data as something that is used up or consumed, but storing array data in a file gives it permanence.

To load array data into a data file from a one-dimensional array:

P	(1)	1761
	(2)	18
	(3)	1942
	(4)	24
	(5)	8209
	(6)	2

The correct procedure:

```
200   PRINT D$;"WRITE FILENAME"
210   FOR X = 1 TO 6
220   PRINT P(X)
230   NEXT X
240   PRINT D$
```

Similarly, to load array data into a data file from a two-dimensional array:

C	(1,1)	(1,2)	(1,3)
(1,1)	A	C	P
(2,1)	N	M	S
(3,1)	G	H	T
(4,1)	B	D	E

The correct procedure:

```
300   PRINT D$;"WRITE FILENAME"
310   FOR X = 1 TO 4
320   FOR Y = 1 TO 3
330   PRINT C(X,Y)
340   NEXT Y
350   NEXT X
360   PRINT D$
```

(a)   To read data into (or out of) an array from (or to) a data file, what programming technique is used? _____

— — — — — — — — — — — — — —

(a)   FOR NEXT loop

Another useful technique deals with applications where data are to be added to a file. Let's say a client number needs to be assigned to a new client or customer as part of a new dataset. In a business environment, the new client number might be assigned by data preparation personnel or the data entry person, relying on a list or on their knowledge of what number was last used. However, if you let the computer do it you can avoid "human error" commonly mislabeled "computer error." In the data file and after any copy made for modification of the file, reserve the very first file data position for the next available client number. Then when new clients are added to the file, follow these steps.

1. Read the first data item (next available client number) = N.
2. Assign N to the next client.
3. Increment N by 1 (or perhaps by +2 or +5 or +10 to leave room for future client data to be squeezed in) = N1.
4. Then have the program place N1 as the first item in the temporary file.
5. Copy the rest of the old file to the temporary file.
6. Place the new client data in the temporary file.
7. Copy the temporary file (including N1) back to the old file.
8. Repeat from step 1 for each new client.

Using the first part of a data file to hold information needed by the program, followed by the regular data, is a broadly useful technique. For example, the contents of an array could be placed at the head or beginning of a file, followed by the main datasets that make up the file. This procedure prevents using a separate data file for array data that are a part of the file. Just don't forget how the data file is set up, or some rather horrific file input errors could ensue. Such information should be included in the documentation prepared for each program and its corresponding data files. We recommend including the dataset format in the introductory module of all programs that deal with data files.

A LETTER–WRITING PROGRAM

The next sequential file application example is a letter-writing program you may find useful in your home or business. This application presents some new techniques and reviews others.

Assume that you did the Chapter 4 Self-Test and have three form letters stored in data files called LETTER1, LETTER2, and LETTER3. When these letters are printed, you want the program to put the inside address and salutation in the letter from data located in yet another sequential data file called ADDRESS. The file ADDRESS contains the names and addresses in the mailing list. The data have the format shown below, with each dataset containing five items in fields within one string.

```
                                          55
/1                   20/21           40/41    50/12/53        57/
        name              address        city   state    zip code
```

The salutation for each letter will be:

Dear resident of   (name of city)

To print the letters on your line printer, be sure to turn the printer on by using PR#1 or PR#2. See your system's reference material for details if you are unfamiliar with these instructions.

The program uses the CRT screen to enter which form letter (1, 2, or 3) you want to send to each name on the mailing list. This program, then, uses four data files (only two data files at a time), a line printer, and a CRT screen. If you don't have a line printer, the program is easily adapted to have all the program output displayed on a CRT screen. Some interesting techniques can be learned from this example.

Follow these steps for this particular program.

(1) Open the ADDRESS data file.
(2) Use ONERR to check for end-of-file for ADDRESS and if found, close all files and end the program.
(3) Input the address dataset and display the name.
(4) User entry option to select the form letter to this address (or to skip this address), with data entry checks. If skipped, go to step (2).
(5) Open selected form letter file.
(6) Print inside heading address.
(7) Print salutation with addressee's last name.
(8) Use ONERR to check for end-of-file for letter file and if found,
    (a) close that form letter file, and
    (b) repeat from step (2).
(9) Input a dataset (one line of text from the letter file) and print it.
(10) Repeat steps (8) and (9).

Look at the introductory module of the program. The ADDRESS file is opened and, as indicated in the line 290 remark, the LETTER files are user selected and opened when selected.

```
100  REM     LETTER WRITING PROGRAM
110  :
120  REM     VARIABLES USED
130  REM     N$ = FIELDED ADDRESS STRING
140  REM     R$ = USER RESPONSE
150  REM     T$ = LETTER FILE TEXT STRING
160  REM     F$ = FILE NAME
170  REM     D$ = CONTROL D
180  REM     FILES USED
190  REM     SEQ.FILE NAME: ADDRESS
200  REM     DATASET FORMAT: ONE FIELDED STRING
210  REM     SEQ.FILE NAMES: LETTER1, LETTER2, LETTER2 (NUMBER FOR FILE
             NAME IS USER SELECTED)
220  REM     DATASET FORMAT: ONE OR MORE LONG STRINGS
230  :
240  REM     INITIALIZATION
250  :
260  LET D$ =  CHR$ (4)
270  PRINT D$;"OPEN ADDRESS"
280  :
290  REM     LETTER FILE IS USER SELECTED AND OPENED WHEN NEEDED
300  :
310  REM     READ NAME/ADDRESS
320  :
330  ONERR  GOTO 850
340  PRINT D$;"READ ADDRESS"
350  INPUT N$
360  PRINT D$
370  :
```

The program assigns the first name and address dataset string to variable N$ in line 350. Notice that the program tests for the end of file marker *before* the first datum is read from the file. Always include this ONERR strategy in your programs dealing with sequential data files.

Now it's your turn. Have the program display the party's name on the CRT, and then ask the user to select the letter to be printed to this party. Fill in lines 410, 440, and 450.

(a)
```
380   REM      DISPLAY NAME/LETTER REQUEST
390   :
400   HOME
410
420   PRINT "ENTER 1, 2, OR 3 TO SELECT LETTER1, LETTER2, OR LETTER3 FOR
      ABOVE ADRESSEE."
430   INPUT "ENTER '9' TO SKIP ABOVE ADDRESS:";R$
440
450
460   :
```

- - - - - - - - - - - - - - -

(a)
```
380   REM      DISPLAY NAME/LETTER REQUEST
390   :
400   HOME
410   PRINT  LEFT$ (N$,20): PRINT
420   PRINT "ENTER 1, 2, OR 3 TO SELECT LETTER1, LETTER2, OR LETTER3 FOR
      ABOVE ADDRESSEE."
430   INPUT "ENTER '9' TO SKIP ABOVE ADDRESS:";R$
440   IF R$ = "9" THEN 340
450   IF  VAL (R$) < 1 OR  VAL (R$) > 3 THEN  PRINT "ERROR.  LETTERS 1-3
      ONLY.": GOTO 420
460   :
```

Examine the following routine for creating the name of an existing data file.

```
470   REM      INITIALIZE LETTER FILE
480   :
490   LET F$ = "LETTER" + R$
500   PRINT D$;"OPEN"F$
510   :
```

(a)   If the user enters 2 in response to line 430, what file name is created and assigned to F$?

_____

- - - - - - - - - - - - - - -

(a)   LETTER2 (Note the string concatenation in line 000)

_____

Write the inside address printing statements (to be printed by the line printer). Fill in lines 560, 570, and 580.

(a)
```
520   REM      PRINT INSIDE ADDRESS"
530  :
540   PRINT D$;"PR#1"
550   PRINT : PRINT : PRINT
560
570
580
590  :
```

– – – – – – – – – – – – – – –

(a)
```
520   REM      PRINT INSIDE ADDRESS"
530  :
540   PRINT D$;"PR#1"
550   PRINT : PRINT : PRINT
560   PRINT  LEFT$ (N$,20)
570   PRINT  MID$ (N$,21,20)
580   PRINT  MID$ (N$,41,10), MID$ (N$,51,2), RIGHT$ (N$,5)
590  :
```

This next routine prints the salutation. Notice how the city name is extracted from N$ in line 630.

```
600   REM      PRINT SALUTATION
610  :
620   PRINT : PRINT
630   PRINT "DEAR RESIDENT OF "; MID$ (N$,41,10)
640  :
```

(a)   For practice, write a BASIC statement that would print this alternate salutation: HELLO THERE ALL YOU FOLKS AT (street address)

– – – – – – – – – – – – – – –

(a)   `630  PRINT "HELLO THERE ALL YOU FOLKS AT "; MID$ (N$,21,20)`

The next routine to print the text of the letter is fairly straightforward. The data input loop continues until that file data are exhausted. Assume that all line feeds and carriage returns are included with the text in the data file.

```
650   REM       PRINT TEXT OF LETTER
660   :
670   ONERR  GOTO 780
680   PRINT D$;"PR#0"
690   PRINT D$;"READ"F$
700   INPUT T$
710   PRINT D$
720   PRINT D$;"PR#1"
730   PRINT T$
740   GOTO 680
750   :
760   REM       CLOSE LETTER FILE AND RETURN FOR NEXT ADDRESS
770   :
780   PRINT D$;"CLOSE"F$
790   IF  PEEK (222) = 5 THEN 810
800   PRINT : PRINT  CHR$ (7);"UNUSUAL ERROR. PROGRAM TERMINATED.": PRINT :
      GOTO 850
810   GOTO 330
```

(a)   Give two reasons for closing the letter file in line 780.

_____

_____

(b)   Without checking back, what happens in the routine starting at line 330, which is branched to from line 810 GOTO 330?

_____

_____

– – – – – – – – – – – – – – – –

(a)   Resets the pointer so that the letter can be used again, and only one OPEN statement is needed for all letter files

(b)   End-of-data tests and next name and address data set are read.

And now, you write the last routine necessary to properly complete this program by completing line 850.

(a)
```
830   REM       CLOSE ADDRESS FILE
840   :
850
860   PRINT "JOB COMPLETED"
```

– – – – – – – – – – – – – – – –

(a)
```
830   REM       CLOSE ADDRESS FILE
840   :
850   PRINT D$;"CLOSE"
860   PRINT "JOB COMPLETED"
```

Following is a complete listing of the letter-writing program.

```
100   REM      LETTER WRITING PROGRAM
110   :
120   REM      VARIABLES USED
130   REM      N$ = FIELDED ADDRESS STRING
140   REM      R$ = USER RESPONSE
150   REM      T$ = LETTER FILE TEXT STRING
160   REM      F$ = FILE NAME
170   REM      D$ = CONTROL D
180   REM      FILES USED
190   REM       SEQ.FILE NAME: ADDRESS
200   REM       DATASET FORMAT: ONE FIELDED STRING
210   REM       SEQ.FILE NAMES: LETTER1, LETTER2, LETTER2 (NUMBER FOR FILE
      NAME IS USER SELECTED)
220   REM       DATASET FORMAT: ONE OR MORE LONG STRINGS
230   :
240   REM      INITIALIZATION
250   :
260   LET D$ =  CHR$ (4)
270   PRINT D$;"OPEN ADDRESS"
280   :
290   REM      LETTER FILE IS USER SELECTED AND OPENED WHEN NEEDED
300   :
310   REM      READ NAME/ADDRESS
320   :
330   ONERR  GOTO 850
340   PRINT D$;"READ ADDRESS"
350   INPUT N$
360   PRINT D$
370   :
380   REM      DISPLAY NAME/LETTER REQUEST
390   :
400   HOME
410   PRINT  LEFT$ (N$,20): PRINT
420   PRINT "ENTER 1, 2, OR 3 TO SELECT LETTER1, LETTER2, OR LETTER3 FOR
      ABOVE ADDRESSEE."
430   INPUT "ENTER '9' TO SKIP ABOVE ADDRESS:";R$
440   IF R$ = "9" THEN 340
450   IF  VAL (R$) < 1 OR  VAL (R$) > 3 THEN  PRINT "ERROR.  LETTERS 1-3
      ONLY.": GOTO 420
460   :
470   REM      INITIALIZE LETTER FILE
480   :
490   LET F$ = "LETTER" + R$
500   PRINT D$;"OPEN"F$
510   :
520   REM      PRINT INSIDE ADDRESS"
530   :
540   PRINT D$;"PR#1"
550   PRINT : PRINT : PRINT
560   PRINT  LEFT$ (N$,20)
570   PRINT  MID$ (N$,21,20)
580   PRINT  MID$ (N$,41,10), MID$ (N$,51,2), RIGHT$ (N$,5)
590   :
600   REM      PRINT SALUTATION
610   :
620   PRINT : PRINT
630   PRINT "DEAR RESIDENT OF "; MID$ (N$,41,10)
640   :
650   REM      PRINT TEXT OF LETTER
660   :
670   ONERR  GOTO 780
680   PRINT D$;"PR#0"
690   PRINT D$;"READ"F$
700   INPUT T$
710   PRINT D$
720   PRINT D$;"PR#1"
730   PRINT T$
740   GOTO 680
750   :
```

continued on next page

```
760   REM      CLOSE LETTER FILE AND RETURN FOR NEXT ADDRESS
770   :
780   PRINT D$;"CLOSE"F$
790   IF  PEEK (222) = 5 THEN 810
800   PRINT : PRINT  CHR$ (7);"UNUSUAL ERROR. PROGRAM TERMINATED.": PRINT :
      GOTO 850
810   GOTO 330
820   :
830   REM      CLOSE ADDRESS FILE
840   :
850   PRINT D$;"CLOSE"
860   PRINT "JOB COMPLETED"
```

Enter and RUN the program. If you are not using a printer, modify lines 540, 680, and 720. Be sure the disks with the ADDRESS and LETTER files are in the disk drive.

CHAPTER 5 SELF-TEST

1. Write a program to make a copy of the ADDRESS file that you created in the Chapter 4 Self-Test, problem 5, and that you used in the letter-writing program. Name the copy file ADDRESS COPY. Include a routine to display the contents of ADDRESS COPY to verify a successful copy.

```
100   REM     COPY PROGRAM FOR 'ADDRESS'
110   REM        VARIABLES USED
120   REM          N$ = CONCATENATED DATASET
130   REM          R$ = USER RESPONSE
140   REM          D$ = CONTROL D
150   REM        FILES USED
160   REM          SEQ. FILE NAMES: ADDRESS, ADDRESS COPY
170   REM          DATASET FORMAT: N$ (BOTH FILES)
```

2a.   Write a program that you can use to create a sequential data file whose items are the titles of computer magazines. Use the program to create two separate files, named MAGLIST1 and MAGLIST2, using the titles given below. Maintain alphabetical order of the data items within each file.

File One:
BYTE Magazine
Compute
Dr. Dobbs Journal
Kilobaud Microcomputing
Recreational computing

File Two:
Creative Computing
DATAMATION
Interface Age
ON Computing
Personal Computing

```
100   REM     CREATE MAGAZINE TITLE FILES
110 :
120   REM     VARIABLES USED
130   REM     M$ = MAGAZINE TITLE
140   REM     F$ = USER SELECTED FILE NAME
150   REM     D$ = CONTROL D
160   REM     FILES USED
170   REM       SEQ. FILE NAMES: MAGLIST1, MAGLIST2 (USER SELECTED AND
                ENTERED)
180   REM       DATASET FORMAT: M$ (ONE STRING FOR TITLE)
190 :
```

_____

_____

_____

_____

_____

_____

_____

_____

_____

_____

_____

_____

_____

_____

_____

_____

_____

_____

_____

2b. Write a program that can display the contents of the user-selected file of
magazine titles, including either MAGLIST1 or MAGLIST2. Use the program
to verify the contents of the files mentioned.

```
100   REM     READ/DISPLAY MAGLIST FILES
110 :
120   REM     VARIABLES USED
130   REM     M$ = MAGAZINE TITLE
140   REM     F$ = USER SELECTED FILE NAME
150   REM     D$ = CONTROL D
160   REM     FILES USED
170   REM       SEQ. FILE NAMES: MAGLIST1, MAGLIST2 (USER SELECTED AND
                ENTERED)
180   REM       DATASET FORMAT: M$ (ONE STRING FOR TITLE)
190 :
```

2c.   Write a program to merge into one alphabetically organized sequential data file
the contents of MAGLIST1 and MAGLIST2. These two files should have their
own data organized alphabetically within each file. Name the merged file
MAGLISTMERGE. Include a routine at the end of this program (similar to the
program from Chapter 5, Self-Test question 2b) to automatically display
MAGLISTMERGE to verify a successful and complete merge. Refer back to
this chapter for guidelines to organizing your program.

```
100  REM     SOLUTION TO CH5 SELFTEST PROB 2C
110  :
120  REM     VARIBLES USED
130  REM       M1$, M2$ = MAGAZINE TITLES
140  REM       D$ = CONTROL D
150  REM     FILES USED
160  REM       SEQ. FILE NAMES:MAGLIST1, MAGLIST2, MAGLISTMERGE
170  REM       DATASET FORMAT: M$ (ONE STRING DATASET, ALL FILES)
180  :
190  REM     INITIALIZE
200  :
```

_____

_____

_____

_____

_____

_____

_____

_____

_____

_____

_____

_____

_____

_____

_____

_____

_____

_____

_____

_____

3. Write a program that allows you to enter a list of household maintenance tasks
    to be done into a sequential data file, and allows you to add to or delete from
    the data file using a temporary file for the updates. Name the source file
    WORK REMINDER and the temporary file TEMPFILE.

```
100   REM    SOLUTION CH5 SELFTEST PROB 3
110  :
120   REM    VARIABLES USED
130   REM       A$ = WORK DESCRIPTION
140   REM       R$ = RESPONSE VARIABLE
150   REM       D$ = CONTROL D
160   REM    FILES USED
170   REM     SEQ. FILE NAMES: WORK REMINDER, TEMPFILE
180  :
190   REM       DATASET FORMATS: A$ (ONE STRING, SAME FOR BOTH FILES)
200  :
```

Answer Key

1.

```
100   REM     COPY PROGRAM FOR 'ADDRESS'
110   REM       VARIABLES USED
120   REM         N$ = CONCATENATED DATASET
130   REM         R$ = USER RESPONSE
140   REM         D$ = CONTROL D
150   REM       FILES USED
160   REM         SEQ. FILE NAMES: ADDRESS, ADDRESS COPY
170   REM         DATASET FORMAT: N$ (BOTH FILES)
180   :
190   REM     INITIALIZE
200   :
210   HOME : PRINT
220   PRINT "FILE COPYING IN PROGRESS."
230   LET D$ =  CHR$ (4)
240   PRINT D$;"OPEN ADDRESS COPY"
250   PRINT D$;"DELETE ADDRESS COPY"
260   PRINT D$"OPEN ADDRESS COPY"
270   PRINT D$;"OPEN ADDRESS"
280   ONERR  GOTO 420
290   :
300   REM     COPYING ROUTINE
310   :
320   PRINT D$;"READ ADDRESS"
330   INPUT N$
340   PRINT D$
350   PRINT D$;"WRITE ADDRESS COPY"
360   PRINT N$
370   PRINT D$
380   GOTO 320
390   :
400   REM     CLOSE FILES
410   :
420   PRINT D$;"CLOSE"
430   PRINT "FILE COPIED AND CLOSED."
440   :
450   REM     DISPLAY OPTION
460   :
470   PRINT
480   INPUT "WOULD YOU LIKE TO SEE THE COPIED FILE (Y OR N)?";R$
490   IF R$ <  > "Y" AND R$ <  > "N" THEN  PRINT  CHR$ (7);"TYPE 'Y' FOR YES
      OR 'N' FOR NO.": PRINT : GOTO 480
500   IF R$ = "N" THEN 610
510   ONERR  GOTO 590
520   PRINT
530   PRINT D$;"OPEN ADDRESS COPY"
540   PRINT D$;"READ ADDRESS COPY"
550   INPUT N$
560   PRINT D$
570   PRINT N$
580   PRINT : GOTO 540
590   PRINT D$;"CLOSE"
600   PRINT "END OF COPIED FILE"
610   END
```

```
2a.  100   REM     CREATE MAGAZINE TITLE FILES
     110 :
     120   REM     VARIABLES USED
     130   REM     M$ = MAGAZINE TITLE
     140   REM     F$ = USER SELECTED FILE NAME
     150   REM     D$ = CONTROL D
     160   REM     FILES USED
     170   REM        SEQ. FILE NAMES: MAGLIST1, MAGLIST2 (USER SELECTED AND
                      ENTERED)
     180   REM        DATASET FORMAT: M$ (ONE STRING FOR TITLE)
     190 :
     200   REM     INITIALIZE
     210 :
     220   LET D$ =  CHR$ (4)
     230   INPUT "ENTER FILE NAME:";F$
     240   PRINT D$;"OPEN"F$
     250 :
     260   REM     DATA ENTRY ROUTINE
     270 :
     280   HOME
     290   PRINT "ENTER '9' IF NO MORE TITLES."
     300   INPUT "ENTER TITLE:";M$
     310   IF  LEN (M$) = 0 THEN  PRINT :  PRINT  CHR$ (7);"PLEASE ENTER AS
           REQUESTED.":  PRINT :  GOTO 300
     320   IF M$ = "9" THEN 430
     330 :
     340   REM     WRITE TO FILE ROUTINE
     350 :
     360   PRINT D$;"WRITE"F$
     370   PRINT M$
     380   PRINT D$
     390   GOTO 280
     400 :
     410   REM     CLOSE FILE
     420 :
     430   PRINT D$;"CLOSE"F$
     440   PRINT "FILE CLOSED"


2b.  100   REM     READ/DISPLAY MAGLIST FILES
     110 :
     120   REM     VARIABLES USED
     130   REM     M$ = MAGAZINE TITLE
     140   REM     F$ = USER SELECTED FILE NAME
     150   REM     D$ = CONTROL D
     160   REM     FILES USED
     170   REM        SEQ. FILE NAMES: MAGLIST1, MAGLIST2 (USER SELECTED AND
                      ENTERED)
     180   REM        DATASET FORMAT: M$ (ONE STRING FOR TITLE)
     190 :
     200   REM     INITIALIZE
     210 :
     220   LET D$ =  CHR$ (4)
     230   INPUT "ENTER FILE NAME:";F$
     240   PRINT D$;"OPEN"F$
     250 :
     260   REM     READ/DISPLAY ROUTINE
     270 :
     280   PRINT
     290   ONERR  GOTO 380
     300   PRINT D$;"READ"F$
     310   INPUT M$
     320   PRINT D$
     330   PRINT M$
     340   GOTO 300
     350 :
     360   REM     CLOSE FILE
     370 :
     380   IF  PEEK (222) = 5 THEN 400
     390   PRINT :  PRINT  CHR$ (7);"UNUSUAL ERROR. PROGRAM TERMINATED."
     400   PRINT D$;"CLOSE"F$
     410   PRINT :  PRINT "FILE CLOSED"
```

```
2c.   100   REM      SOLUTION TO CH5 SELFTEST PROB 2C
      110   :
      120   REM      VARIBLES USED
      130   REM        M1$, M2$ = MAGAZINE TITLES
      140   REM        D$ = CONTROL D
      150   REM      FILES USED
      160   REM        SEQ. FILE NAMES:MAGLIST1, MAGLIST2, MAGLISTMERGE
      170   REM        DATASET FORMAT: M$ (ONE STRING DATASET, ALL FILES)
      180   :
      190   REM      INITIALIZE
      200   :
      210   HOME : PRINT : PRINT "WORKING"
      220   LET D$ =  CHR$ (4)
      230   PRINT D$;"OPEN MAGLIST1"
      240   PRINT D$;"OPEN MAGLIST2"
      250   PRINT D$;"OPEN MAGLISTMERGE"
      260   PRINT D$;"DELETE MAGLISTMERGE"
      270   PRINT D$;"OPEN MAGLISTMERGE"
      280   :
      290   REM      READ DATASET FROM FILE 1
      300   :
      310   ONERR  GOTO 870
      320   PRINT D$;"READ MAGLIST1"
      330   INPUT M1$
      340   PRINT D$
      350   :
      360   REM      READ DATASET FROM FILE 2
      370   :
      380   ONERR  GOTO 770
      390   PRINT D$;"READ MAGLIST2"
      400   INPUT M2$
      410   PRINT D$
      420   :
      430   REM      COMPARE FOR ALPHABETICAL ORDER
      440   :
      450   IF M1$ < M2$ THEN 510
      460   IF M1$ > M2$ THEN 620
      470   GOTO 510
      480   :
      490   REM      WRITE FILE 1 ITEM TO MERGE, THEN READ FILE 1
      500   :
      510   PRINT D$;"WRITE MAGLISTMERGE"
      520   PRINT M1$
      530   PRINT D$
      540   ONERR  GOTO 880
      550   PRINT D$;"READ MAGLIST1"
      560   INPUT M1$
      570   PRINT D$
      580   GOTO 450
      590   :
      600   REM      WRITE FILE 2 ITEM TO MERGE, THEN READ FILE 1
      610   :
      620   PRINT D$;"WRITE MAGLISTMERGE"
      630   PRINT M2$
      640   PRINT D$
      650   ONERR  GOTO 770
      660   PRINT D$;"READ MAGLIST2"
      670   INPUT M2$
      680   PRINT D$
      690   GOTO 450
      700   :
      710   REM      DUMP REMAINING FILE 1 TO MERGE
      720   :
      730   ONERR  GOTO 950
      740   PRINT D$;"READ MAGLIST1"
      750   INPUT M1$
      760   PRINT D$
      770   PRINT D$;"WRITE MAGLISTMERGE"
      78C   PRINT M1$
      790   PRINT D$
      800   GOTO 730
      810   :
```

continued on next page

```
820    REM    DUMP REMAINING FILE 2 TO MERGE
830    :
840    ONERR   GOTO 950
850    PRINT D$;"READ MAGLIST2"
860    INPUT M2$
870    PRINT D$
880    PRINT D$;"WRITE MAGLISTMERGE"
890    PRINT M2$
900    PRINT D$
910    GOTO 840
920    :
930    REM     CLOSE FILES
940    :
950    PRINT D$;"CLOSE MAGLIST1"
960    PRINT D$;"CLOSE MAGLIST2"
970    PRINT D$;"CLOSE MAGLISTMERGE"
980    :
990    REM     DISPLAY MERGED DATA
1000   :
1010   PRINT
1020   ONERR   GOTO 1090
1030   PRINT D$;"OPEN MAGLISTMERGE"
1040   PRINT D$;"READ MAGLISTMERGE"
1050   INPUT M$
1060   PRINT D$
1070   PRINT M$
1080   GOTO 1040
1090   PRINT D$;"CLOSE MAGLISTMERGE"
1100   PRINT : PRINT "FILE DISPLAYED AND CLOSED."
```

```
3. 100   REM     SOLUTION CH5 SELFTEST PROB 3
   110   :
   120   REM     VARIABLES USED
   130   REM         A$ = WORK DESCRIPTION
   140   REM         R$ = RESPONSE VARIABLE
   150   REM         D$ = CONTROL D
   160   REM     FILES USED
   170   REM        SEQ. FILE NAMES: WORK REMINDER, TEMPFILE
   180   :
   190   REM        DATASET FORMATS: A$ (ONE STRING, SAME FOR BOTH FILES)
   200   :
   210   REM        INITIALIZE
   220   :
   230   LET D$ =  CHR$ (4)
   240   PRINT D$;"OPEN WORK REMINDER"
   250   PRINT D$;"OPEN TEMPFILE"
   260   PRINT D$;"CLOSE TEMPFILE"
   270   PRINT D$;"OPEN TEMPFILE"
   280   :
   290   REM     READ/DISPLAY FILE DATA
   300   :
   310   HOME
   320   PRINT "TYPE 'D' TO DELETE AN ITEM"
   330   PRINT "PRESS 'RETURN' TO DISPLAY NEXT ITEM."
   340   ONERR  GOTO 540
   350   PRINT D$;"READ WORK REMINDER"
   360   INPUT A$
   370   PRINT D$
   380   PRINT A$
   390   INPUT "";B$
   400   IF B$ <  > "" AND B$ <  > "D" THEN  PRINT  CHR$ (7);"PLEASE TYPE 'D'
         TO DELETE THE ITEM DISPLAYED ABOVE, OR PRESS 'RETURN' TO DISPLAY THE
         NEXT ITEM.": GOTO 390
   410   IF B$ = "D" THEN  PRINT A$;" REMOVED FROM LIST.": PRINT : GOTO 350
   420   :
   430   REM     ROUTINE TO RETAIN DATA ITEM
   440   :
   450   PRINT D$;"WRITE TEMPFILE"
   460   PRINT A$
   470   PRINT D$
   480   GOTO 350
   490   :
   500   REM     ROUTINE TO ADD ITEMS TO FILE
   510   IF  PEEK (222) = 5 THEN 530
   520   PRINT : PRINT  CHR$ (7);"UNUSUAL ERROR. PROGRAM TERMINATED.": PRINT :
         GOTO 660
   530   HOME
   540   HOME : PRINT
   550   INPUT "DO YOU WISH TO ADD ANOTHER ITEM (Y OR N)?";R$
   560   IF R$ <  > "Y" AND R$ <  > "N" THEN  PRINT  CHR$ (7);"PLEASE TYPE 'Y'
         FOR YES OR 'N' FOR NO.": GOTO 550
   570   IF R$ = "N" THEN 670
   580   PRINT
   590   INPUT "ENTER NEW ITEM:";A$
   600   PRINT D$;"WRITE TEMPFILE"
   610   PRINT A$
   620   PRINT D$
   630   GOTO 540
   640   :
   650   REM     CLOSE FILES, RENAME TEMPFILE
   660   :
   670   PRINT D$;"CLOSE TEMPFILE"
   680   PRINT D$;"CLOSE WORK REMINDER"
   690   PRINT D$;"DELETE WORK REMINDER"
   700   PRINT D$;"RENAME TEMPFILE,WORK REMINDER"
   710   PRINT : PRINT "FILE CLOSED"
```

CHAPTER SIX
Random Access Data Files

Objectives: When you complete this chapter, you will be able to create, verify, copy, and change random access disk data files. You will also be able to convert sequential files to random access files. The random access file manipulating statements you will use are similar to those used with sequential files and, therefore, should be familiar to you.

WHAT IS A RANDOM ACCESS FILE?

A random access data file is a disk file divided into sections called records. Each record can contain one complete dataset. The typical random access data file format of placing only one entire dataset into each record makes finding and changing data easy. The structure also allows for fast access of data, whether located in the first or last record in the file. These two strengths of random access files are the greatest weakness of sequential data files.

Random access files use the same BASIC file manipulation statements as sequential files. The only difference in statement formats is the provision for the record number and the length of the record. Random access files on your APPLE computer use what is called a variable length record. This means that the programmer determines how long, in bytes, the records for the file will be. Once established, each record in the file has the same length.

The length of the record is dependent on the amount of data in the dataset being written to the file. In Chapter 4 we discussed the storage requirements of data that are placed in the file. With random access files it is imperative that you plan your file structure based on storage requirements or you will experience file errors. To review, the storage requirement for string information is one byte per character in the string, plus one byte for "overhead." If you include a twenty-character name in each dataset, then each name will occupy, at most, twenty-one bytes of storage. Numeric information works the same way: one byte per character in the number, plus one byte for "overhead." A numeric integer value of 1 through 999 takes a maximum of four bytes in a random access file: three for the number, plus one for "overhead." A value such as 542.45 has 6 characters (counting the decimal point), and will take seven bytes, including "overhead."

(a)   In a random access file application that uses a twenty-character name, a twenty-character address, and a twelve-character phone number string, how large will the record need to be in bytes? _____

_ _ _ _ _ _ _ _ _ _ _ _ _ _

(a)   55 bytes

For each random access file, you will need to compute the record size based on the dataset that is used for that file. It is important that you indicate the record size in the introductory module of your program so that the record size is permanently recorded somewhere. Once a file program is written, there is no instruction that will help you find the record size. You should include the record size in the introductory module of the program, and in any other documentation you prepare. This is as important as documenting the dataset formats; it should not be taken lightly.

The variable-size record available in APPLESOFT BASIC means that the use of diskette space is very efficient. Other computers use a fixed-size record length of 256 bytes. In those systems, if the dataset only uses fifty bytes, the remaining 206 bytes in the record are wasted, and much valuable disk storage space goes unused. This will not be the case in your APPLESOFT programs where you will tailor the record size to the dataset used in each random access file.

Random access files require more planning and more carefully designed systems for organizing and using data. Once planned, random access files may require much less programming to accomplish the same activities as sequential files. Random access files are best used when the data in the files will change frequently. This might be the case with a customer charge account file or when you have a large data base, such as a credit information file that will be accessed in no particular order (randomly). For large scale applications, you may find yourself designing systems that use both sequential files and some random access files.

(a)   What are two advantages of random access files over sequential files?

_____

_____

_____

_ _ _ _ _ _ _ _ _ _ _ _ _ _

(a)   Fast access to all datasets (records), regardless of position within the file, and ease of changing data within a particular dataset or record.

INITIALIZING RANDOM ACCESS FILES

For random access files, the OPEN statement serves the same purpose of opening the file and assigning the buffer. In addition, the OPEN statement indicates the length of the file records in bytes. The format of the OPEN statement for random access files is as follows:

```
120   PRINT D$;"OPEN FILENAME,L50"

130   PRINT D$;"OPEN"F$",L50"
```

Notice the unusual punctuation in line 130 above. The comma is an integral and essential part of the OPEN statement. Therefore, it must be included inside the quotation marks, as shown in lines 120 and 130. You will NOT get an error message if you use an incorrect format in the OPEN statement. However, you will not open the file the way you intended either, so enter these statements carefully. Notice how a file name assigned to a string variable (F$) is outside the quotations that enclose "OPEN" and ",L50" in line 130.

(a)   What is the record length in the OPEN statements above? _____

_ _ _ _ _ _ _ _ _ _ _ _ _ _ _ _

(a)   Fifty bytes

SIMPLE READ AND WRITE OPERATIONS TO RANDOM ACCESS FILES

Our first random access file application is to create an inventory of repair parts. The dataset includes a six-digit product number entered as a string, a product description of twenty characters, and a numeric quantity that will be no larger than 999, with no fractional amount.

(a)   What is the record size needed for this application? _____

(b)   Here is the introductory module. Complete the OPEN statement by filling in line 310.

```
2 :
100   REM       INVENTORY RANDOM FILE
110   :
120   REM       VARIABLES USED
130   REM          N$ = PRODUCT NUMBER (6)
140   REM          P$ = PROD. DESCRIPTION (20)
150   REM          Q =QUANTITY (<=999)
160   REM          D$ = CONTROL D
170   REM          R1 = RECORD COUNT
180   REM          R$ = USER RESPONSE
190   :
200   REM       FILES USED
210   REM          RANDOM ACCESS FILE NAME: INVEN
220   REM          RECORD SIZE: 32 BYTES
230   REM          DATASET FORMAT:N$,P$,Q
240   :
250   REM       INITIALIZE
260   :
270   LET R1 = 1
280   LET D$ =   CHR$ (4)
290   PRINT D$;"OPEN INVEN"
300   PRINT D$;"DELETE INVEN"
310
320   :
```

- - - - - - - - - - - - - -

(a)   32 bytes. six + one for the product number, twenty + one for the description and three + one for the quantity.

(b)   `310   PRINT D$;"OPEN INVEN,L32"`

In line 270 in problem (b) we initialized the variable R1 to one (1). This variable is used to keep track of the file record count in this program. Dataset number one is in record number one, dataset number two is in record number two, etc.

Here is the data entry module for this application. We have left out the data entry tests so that the structure of the program is more clearly revealed in the program listings. By now, you know how to design good data entry error traps, and your completed programs should include them. You will see how difficult accurate data entry can be if you use the "bare bones" program listed below.

```
330   REM       DATA ENTRY MODULE
340   :
350   HOME
360   INPUT "ENTER PRODUCT NUMBER (6):";N$
370   REM       DATA ENTRY TESTS
380   INPUT "ENTER PROD. DESCRIPT.(20 CHAR):";P$
390   REM       DATA ENTRY TESTS
400   INPUT "ENTER QUANTITY:";Q
410   REM       DATA ENTRY TESTS
420   :
```

The file is OPEN; the data are entered. The next operation is to print the data to the file in the first record. The file WRITE instruction for random access files is similar to the sequential file instruction, but now also includes the record number of the random access record to be printed:

```
240  PRINT D$;"WRITE FILENAME,R51"

250  PRINT D$;"WRITE"F$",R"R1
```

In line 240 above, the WRITE statement moves the file pointer to record number 51, where the next PRINT statements will write the information to the file. Notice in line 250 how all variables are placed outside of the quotation marks. Notice, too, the similarity in format to the random access OPEN statement, where the L, for length of file, and the comma that precedes it are always within quotation marks. In random access file READ and WRITE statements, the R for Record and the comma that precedes it must be enclosed in quotation marks.

(a)   What record will be printed by the WRITE statement in line 250 above? _____

_____

_____

- - - - - - - - - - - - - - -

(a)   Whatever record value is assigned to variable R1. (In our example program, the record number is 1, for the first dataset.)

The PRINT statements for random access files use the same format as the statements used with sequential files. You must turn the WRITE operation *on,* PRINT the dataset to the file, and turn the WRITE operation *off.*

(a)   Here is the next part of our inventory program. Fill in the blank lines at 450, 460, and 470.

```
430  REM     PRINT TO FILE
440  :
450
460
470
480  :
490  INPUT "MORE ENTRIES?";R$
500  IF  LEFT$ (R$,1) (  ) "Y" AND  LEFT$ (R$,1) (  ) "N" THEN  PRINT :
     PRINT  CHR$ (7);"TYPE 'Y' FOR YES OR 'N' FOR NO.": PRINT : GOTO 490
510  IF  LEFT$ (R$,1) = "N" THEN 600
520  :
530  REM     INCREASE RECORD COUNT
540  :
550  LET R1 = R1 + 1
560  GOTO 350
570  :
```

(b)   What is the purpose of line 550? _____

_____

- - - - - - - - - - - - - - -

(a)
```
430   REM     PRINT TO FILE
440   :
450   PRINT D$;"WRITE INVEN, R";R1
460   PRINT N$: PRINT P$: PRINT Q
470   PRINT D$
480   :
490   INPUT "MORE ENTRIES?";R$
500   IF  LEFT$ (R$,1) (   ) "Y" AND  LEFT$ (R$,1) (   ) "N" THEN  PRINT :
      PRINT  CHR$ (7);"TYPE 'Y' FOR YES OR 'N' FOR NO.": PRINT : GOTO 490
510   IF  LEFT$ (R$,1) = "N" THEN 600
520   :
530   REM     INCREASE RECORD COUNT
540   :
550   LET R1 = R1 + 1
560   GOTO 350
570   :
```

(b)   Increments the record number by one so that if another dataset is entered, it will
      be recorded in the next random access record.

The final program module is the file close routine. The format of the random
access CLOSE statement is the same as that used with sequential files.

```
580   REM     CLOSE FILE
590   :
600   PRINT D$;"CLOSE INVEN"
610   PRINT "FILE CLOSED"
620   END
```

Here is the complete listing of our random access file printing inventory application.

```
100   REM       INVENTORY RANDOM FILE
110   :
120   REM       VARIABLES USED
130   REM         N$ = PRODUCT NUMBER (6)
140   REM         P$ = PROD. DESCRIPTION (20)
150   REM         Q =QUANTITY ((=999)
160   REM         D$ = CONTROL D
170   REM         R1 = RECORD COUNT
180   REM         R$ = USER RESPONSE
190   :
200   REM       FILES USED
210   REM          RANDOM ACCESS FILE NAME: INVEN
220   REM          RECORD SIZE: 32 BYTES
230   REM          DATASET FORMAT:N$,P$,Q
240   :
250   REM       INITIALIZE
260   :
270   LET R1 = 1
280   LET D$ =  CHR$ (4)
290   PRINT D$;"OPEN INVEN"
300   PRINT D$;"DELETE INVEN"
310   PRINT D$;"OPEN INVEN, L32"
320   :
330   REM       DATA ENTRY MODULE
340   :
350   HOME
360   INPUT "ENTER PRODUCT NUMBER (6):";N$
370   REM         DATA ENTRY TESTS
380   INPUT "ENTER PROD. DESCRIPT.(20 CHAR):";P$
390   REM         DATA ENTRY TESTS
400   INPUT "ENTER QUANTITY:";Q
410   REM         DATA ENTRY TESTS
420   :
430   REM     PRINT TO FILE
440   :
450   PRINT D$;"WRITE INVEN, R";R1
460   PRINT N$: PRINT P$: PRINT Q
470   PRINT D$
480   :
490   INPUT "MORE ENTRIES?";R$
500   IF  LEFT$ (R$,1) (  ) "Y" AND  LEFT$ (R$,1) (  ) "N" THEN  PRINT :
      PRINT  CHR$ (7);"TYPE 'Y' FOR YES OR 'N' FOR NO.": PRINT : GOTO 490
510   IF  LEFT$ (R$,1) = "N" THEN 600
520   :
530   REM     INCREASE RECORD COUNT
540   :
550   LET R1 = R1 + 1
560   GOTO 350
570   :
580   REM       CLOSE FILE
590   :
600   PRINT D$;"CLOSE INVEN"
610   PRINT "FILE CLOSED"
620   END
```

Many uses of random access files require that the BASIC program accessing the file know where the file ends or how many datasets (records) exist in the file. As no system command is available in APPLESOFT to count or display the number of records in a file, your programs to create and use random access files should provide a counting variable to keep track of the total number of records that are used in the file. This process is used often in programming applications.

The numbering of random access file records actually begins at zero, so the very first record in a random access file is record zero (R0). This record is sometimes used to keep "housekeeping" information. One item of data that could be saved in R0 is the record number for the last filled record in the file. Then, when you want to add data to the file, you would follow these steps:

1. OPEN the file.
2. READ R0 to find the record number for the last filled record.
3. Increment the last record by one (1).
4. Enter data.
5. PRINT to the file.
6. Ask for more entries.
6a. If yes, increment the record counter by one and return for more data.
6b. If no, PRINT the current record counter value to R0, so that the record number for the last filled record is available the next time it is needed.
7. CLOSE the file.

When creating a random access file, a counting statement such as LET R1 = R1 + 1 can be used. The placement of the counting statement within a program is crucial for counting accuracy. Only datasets actually entered must be counted, so the counting statement is usually after the dataset PRINT statement. In this way, if no more data are forthcoming, the record number will not have already been increased.

Notice where the record counting statement is placed in the previous program. The logic in this case is to increase the record counting variable by one after the user responds "yes" to the question, MORE ENTRIES?

In the example program to create the INVEN file, no provision is made to store the record count for the future reference or use by BASIC programs that access the file. Our strategy is to store the record count in R0, the first record in the file. This record is accessed by using R0 in a READ or WRITE statement.

```
470   PRINT D$;"READ FILENAME, R0"

980   PRINT D$;"WRITE FILENAME, R0"
```

Caution: Don't accidentally type the letter O (oh) for the number zero.

(a) Modify the program that creates the INVEN file so that the total number of records containing data (record count) is placed in R0. This routine should be included in the Close File Module.

_____

_____

_____

_____

_____

_____

_____

‒ ‒ ‒ ‒ ‒ ‒ ‒ ‒ ‒ ‒ ‒ ‒ ‒ ‒ ‒ ‒

```
(a)  580   REM       CLOSE FILE
     590   :
     600   PRINT D$;"WRITE INVEN, R0"
     610   PRINT R1
     620   PRINT D$
     630   PRINT D$;"CLOSE INVEN"
     640   PRINT "FILE CLOSED"
     650   END
```

Enter and RUN the modified program. Create the file INVEN for use in this section, as well as later programs.

Now let's write a separate program to display the contents of this random access file. Here is the introductory module and initialization module.

```
     100   REM       INVEN READ/PRINT
     110   :
     120   REM       VARIABLES USED
     130   REM         N$ = PRODUCT NUMBER (8)
     140   REM         P$ = PROD. DESCRIPTION (20)
     150   REM         Q  =QUANTITY (<=999)
     160   REM         D$ = CONTROL D
     170   REM         R1 = RECORD #
     180   :
     190   REM       FILES USED
     200   REM         R.A.FILE NAME: INVEN
     210   REM         RECORD LENGTH: 32 BYTES
     220   REM         DATASET FORMAT:N$,P$,Q
     230   :
     240   REM       INITIALIZE
     250   :
     260   LET R1 = 1
     270   LET D$ =  CHR$ (4)
     280   PRINT D$;"OPEN INVEN, L32"
     290   :
```

(a)   What is the purpose of line 260 above? _____

_____

(b)   What does the L32 in line 280 represent? _____

‒ ‒ ‒ ‒ ‒ ‒ ‒ ‒ ‒ ‒ ‒ ‒ ‒ ‒ ‒ ‒

(a)   Assigns the number one (1) to R1 to initialize the record counting variable
(b)   The record length of thirty-two bytes

The random access READ statement follows the same format as the WRITE statement, in that it requires a record number be included in the statement.

```
     250   PRINT D$;"READ FILENAME,R"R1
```

Here is the file read and report printing module of the inventory reading program.

```
300  REM      PRINT HEADING
310  :
320  PRINT "PROD #"; TAB( 10);"PROD DESCR"; TAB( 26);"QUANTITY"
330  :
340  REM      FILE READ/PRINT
350  :
360  ONERR  GOTO 460
370  PRINT D$;"READ INVEN,R";R1
380  INPUT N$,P$,Q
390  PRINT D$
400  PRINT N$; TAB( 10);P$; TAB( 31);Q
410  LET R1 = R1 + 1
420  GOTO 370
430  :
440  REM      CLOSE FILES
450  :
460  PRINT D$;"CLOSE"
470  END
```

The INPUT statement at line 380 has the same format as that used with sequential files. The ONERR statement at line 360 works the same way as with sequential files. The only real difference between a sequential file program and this one is the READ statement format and the addition of line 410.

(a)   What is the purpose of line 410 above?

_____

_____

— — — — — — — — — — — — — — — —

(a)   Increments the record number variable by one so that the next record in the file will be read.

Next, let's make use of the record count, instead of depending on ONERR to determine the end of the file. You can do this using a FOR NEXT loop to read only the number of datasets (records) that contain information. Notice how important this makes the accuracy of the record count. An "extra" count will lead to an OUT OF DATA error message if the program tries to read a nonexistent record. On the other hand, if the count is one short, one dataset will be left inaccessible.

First the record count is accessed and assigned to variable R1.

```
310  PRINT D$;"READ INVEN,R0"
320  INPUT R1
330  PRINT D$
```

Next, the value of R1 is used to tell the FOR NEXT loop how many datasets to read, and the FOR NEXT loop control variable X is used to count off the records.

```
340   FOR X = 1 TO R1
350   PRINT D$;"READ INVEN,R"X
360   INPUT N$,P$,Q
370   PRINT D$
380   PRINT N$; TAB( 10);P$; TAB( 31);Q
390   NEXT X
```

(a)   In which line is the record number to INPUT determined? _____

(b)   What is the record number of the first dataset accessed? _____

(c)   How many records will have been accessed when the FOR NEXT loop finishes execution? _____

- - - - - - - - - - - - - - -

(a)   line 350 (value of FOR NEXT loop control variable, X)
(b)   one
(c)   equal to value of R1

Below is another version of the program. Enter the program (and the first version if you wish) and display the contents of the INVEN file on your screen.

```
100   REM       INVEN READ/PRINT
110   :
120   REM       VARIABLES USED
130   REM         N$ = PRODUCT NUMBER (6)
140   REM         P$ = PROD. DESCRIPTION (20)
150   REM         Q =QUANTITY (<=999)
160   REM         D$ = CONTROL D
170   REM         R1 = RECORD #
180   :
190   REM       FILES USED
200   REM           R.A.FILE NAME: INVEN
210   REM           RECORD LENGTH: 32 BYTES
220   REM           DATASET FORMAT:N$,P$,Q
230   :
240   REM       INITIALIZE
250   :
260   LET D$ =   CHR$ (4)
270   PRINT D$;"OPEN INVEN, L32"
280   :
290   REM       PRINT HEADING
300   :
310   PRINT "PROD #"; TAB( 10);"PROD DESCR"; TAB( 26);"QUANTITY": PRINT
320   :
330   REM       FILE READ/PRINT
340   :
350   PRINT D$;"READ INVEN,R0"
360   INPUT R1
370   PRINT D$
380   FOR X = 1 TO R1
390   PRINT D$;"READ INVEN,R"X
400   INPUT N$,P$,Q
410   PRINT D$
420   PRINT N$; TAB( 10);P$; TAB( 31);Q
430   NEXT X
440   :
450   REM       CLOSE FILES
460   :
470   PRINT D$;"CLOSE"
480   END
```

ADDING DATA TO THE END OF A RANDOM ACCESS FILE

In the next application we want a program to add new datasets to an already existing random access file. To make it easy, we will add data to the current end of an existing file, rather than insert new records into the middle of the file.

First, create the random access file to which you will later be asked to add or change data. Name the file PHONE. The program should keep track of the number of records used in the file and place this information in record R0 before closing the file. The dataset has the following items entered as strings:

customer number (five characters)
customer name (twenty-character maximum)
customer phone number (eight characters, e.g., 999–9999)

Here is the introductory module. You complete the program.

```
(a)   100   REM     CREATE FILE NAMED 'PHONE'
      110   :
      120   REM     VARIABLES USED
      130   REM       N$ = CUSTOMER # (5 CHAR.)
      140   REM       C$ = CUST. NAME (20 CHAR. MAX.)
      150   REM       P$ = PHONE NUMBER (XXX-XXXX OR 8 CHAR.)
      160   REM       R$ = USER RESONSE
      170   REM       D$ = CONTROL D
      180   REM     FILE USED
      190   REM       R-A FILE NAME: PHONE
      200   REM       RECORD LENGTH: 36 BYTES
      210   REM       DATASET FORMAT: N$,C$,P$
      220   :
```

```
(a)  100   REM      CREATE FILE NAMED 'PHONE'
     110   :
     120   REM      VARIABLES USED
     130   REM        N$ = CUSTOMER # (5 CHAR.)
     140   REM        C$ = CUST. NAME (20 CHAR. MAX.)
     150   REM        P$ = PHONE NUMBER (XXX-XXXX OR 8 CHAR.)
     160   REM        R$ = USER RESONSE
     170   REM        D$ = CONTROL D
     180   REM      FILE USED
     190   REM        R-A FILE NAME: PHONE
     200   REM        RECORD LENGTH: 38 BYTES
     210   REM        DATASET FORMAT: N$,C$,P$
     220   :
     230   REM      INITIALIZE
     240   :
     250   LET D$ =  CHR$ (4)
     260   PRINT D$;"OPEN PHONE, L38"
     270   LET R1 = 0
     280   :
     290   REM      DATA ENTRY MODULE
     300   :
     310   HOME
     320   INPUT "ENTER 'STOP' OR CUSTOMER NUMBER (5 CHAR.)";N$
     330   IF N$ = "STOP" THEN 520
     340   LET R1 = R1 + 1
     350   :
     360   REM      DATA ENTRY TESTS
     370   :
     380   INPUT "ENTER CUSTOMER NAME (20 CHAR. MAX.):";C$
     390   REM      DATA ENTRY TESTS
     400   INPUT "ENTER PHONE NUMBER:";P$
     410   REM      DATA ENTRY TESTS
     420   :
     430   REM      WRITE TO FILE
     440   :
     450   PRINT D$;"WRITE PHONE,R";R1
     460   PRINT N$: PRINT C$: PRINT P$
     470   PRINT D$
     480   GOTO 320
     490   :
     500   REM      CLOSE FILE
     510   :
     520   PRINT D$;"WRITE PHONE,R0"
     530   PRINT R1
     540   PRINT D$;"CLOSE"
     550   PRINT : PRINT "FILE CLOSED"
```

Next, write a companion program that will display the contents of PHONE, using the FOR NEXT loop technique to cycle through the records in the file.

(a) _____

_____

_____

_____

_____

_____

_____

_____

_____

_____

_____

```
(a)  100  REM      CREATE FILE NAMED 'PHONE'
     110  :
     120  REM      VARIABLES USED
     130  REM         N$ = CUSTOMER # (5 CHAR.)
     140  REM         C$ = CUST. NAME (20 CHAR. MAX.)
     150  REM         P$ = PHONE NUMBER (XXX-XXXX OR 8 CHAR.)
     160  REM         R$ = USER RESONSE
     170  REM         D$ = CONTROL D
     180  REM      FILE USED
     190  REM         R-A FILE NAME: PHONE
     200  REM         RECORD LENGTH: 36 BYTES
     210  REM         DATASET FORMAT: N$,C$,P$
     220  :
     230  REM      INITIALIZE
     240  :
     250  LET D$ =  CHR$ (4)
     260  PRINT D$;"OPEN PHONE, L36"
     270  :
     280  REM      READ RECORD 0
     290  :
     300  HOME
     310  PRINT D$;"READ PHONE, R0"
     320  INPUT R1
     330  PRINT D$
     340  IF R1 = 0 THEN  PRINT "FILE EMPTY": GOTO 470
     350  :
     360  REM      READ/DISPLAY ROUTINE
     370  :
     380  FOR X = 1 TO R1
     390  PRINT D$;"READ PHONE,R";X
     400  INPUT N$,C$,P$
     410  PRINT D$
     420  PRINT N$;C$;P$
     430  NEXT X
     440  :
     450  REM      CLOSE FILE
     460  :
     470  PRINT D$;"CLOSE"
     480  PRINT : PRINT "FILE DISPLAYED AND CLOSED."
```

Our random access file is a customer list entered by customer number. The dataset includes the customer number, name, and phone number. To add new datasets to the file we must follow these steps:

1. Initialize and OPEN the file.
2. Ascertain the number of records in the file containing information.
3. Enter new data.
4. WRITE new data to the file.
5. Increment record count.
6. Return to step 3.
7. Write the new record count to R0 and CLOSE the file.

Here is the introductory module and initialization module. (Nothing really new here!)

```
100   REM      ADDING TO R-A FILE NAMED PHONE
110   :
120   REM      VARIABLES USED
130   REM        N$ = CUST. NUMBER (5)
140   REM        C$ = CUST. NAME (20)
150   REM        P$ = PHONE NUMBER (10)
160   REM        R1 = RECORD COUNTER
170   REM        D$ = CONTROL D
180   :
190   REM      FILES USED
200   REM      RANDOM ACCESS FILE NAME: PHONE
210   REM      RECORD LENGTH: 36 BYTES
220   REM      DATASET FORMAT: N$,C$,P$
230   :
240   REM      INITIALIZATION
250   :
260   LET D$ =  CHR$ (4)
270   PRINT D$;"OPEN PHONE,L36"
280   :
```

The next program module ascertains the end of file location by reading record R0. Complete lines 310, 320, and 330.

```
(a)   290   REM      LOCATE LAST FULL RECORD
      300   :
      310
      320
      330
      340   PRINT : PRINT "RECORD COUNT: ";R1: PRINT
      350   :
```

```
(a)   290   REM      LOCATE LAST FULL RECORD
      300   :
      310   PRINT D$;"READ PHONE,R0"
      320   INPUT R1
      330   PRINT D$
      340   PRINT : PRINT "RECORD COUNT: ";R1: PRINT
      350   :
```

Next comes the data entry module and the file WRITE module. Fill in lines 480, 490, 500, and 540 below. (You may also wish to construct the data entry checks now.)

(a)
```
350   REM       DATA ENTRY MODULE
370 :
380   LET R1 = R1 + 1
390   INPUT "ENTER CUST. #:";N$
400   REM       DATA ENTRY TESTS
410   INPUT "ENTER CUST. NAME:";C$
420   REM       DATA ENTRY TEST
430   INPUT "ENTER PHONE #:";P$
440   REM       DATA ENTRY TESTS
450 :
460 : REM       WRITE TO FILE ROUTINE
470 :
480
490
500
510   INPUT "MORE ENTRIES?";R$
520   IF  LEFT$ (R$,1) (  ) "Y" AND  LEFT$ (R$,1) (  ) "N" THEN  PRINT :
      PRINT  CHR$ (7);"ENTER 'Y' FOR YES OR 'N' FOR NO": PRINT : GOTO 510
530   IF  LEFT$ (R$,1) = "N" THEN 580
540
550 :
```

— — — — — — — — — — — — — — — —

(a)
```
360   REM       DATA ENTRY MODULE
370 :
380   LET R1 = R1 + 1
390   INPUT "ENTER CUST. #:";N$
400   REM       DATA ENTRY TESTS
410   INPUT "ENTER CUST. NAME:";C$
420   REM       DATA ENTRY TEST
430   INPUT "ENTER PHONE }:";P$
440   REM       DATA ENTRY TESTS
450 :
460 : REM       WRITE TO FILE ROUTINE
470 :
480   PRINT D$;"WRITE PHONE, R";R1
490   PRINT N$: PRINT C$: PRINT P$
500   PRINT D$
510   INPUT "MORE ENTRIES?";R$
520   IF  LEFT$ (R$,1) (  ) "Y" AND  LEFT$ (R$,1) (  ) "N" THEN  PRINT :
      PRINT  CHR$ (7);"ENTER 'Y' FOR YES OR 'N' FOR NO": PRINT : GOTO 510
530   IF  LEFT$ (R$,1) = "N" THEN 580
540   GOTO 380
550 :
```

The final program segment shown below closes the file and posts the record count to record zero.

```
560   REM       CLOSE FILE
570 :
580   PRINT D$;"WRITE PHONE, R0"
590   PRINT R1
600   PRINT D$
610   PRINT D$;"CLOSE PHONE"
620   PRINT : PRINT "FILE CLOSED"
630   PRINT : PRINT "NEW RECORD COUNT: ";R1
```

Here is the complete listing of the program to add data to an existing random access file program

```
100   REM      ADDING TO R-A FILE NAMED PHONE
110   :
120   REM      VARIABLES USED
130   REM      N$ = CUST. NUMBER (5)
140   REM      C$ = CUST. NAME (20)
150   REM      P$ = PHONE NUMBER (10)
160   REM      R1 = RECORD COUNTER
170   REM      D$ = CONTROL D
180   :
190   REM      FILES USED
200   REM      RANDOM ACCESS FILE NAME: PHONE
210   REM      RECORD LENGTH: 36 BYTES
220   REM      DATASET FORMAT: N$,C$,P$
230   :
240   REM      INITIALIZATION
250   :
260   LET D$ = CHR$ (4)
270   PRINT D$;"OPEN PHONE,L36"
280   :
290   REM      LOCATE LAST FULL RECORD
300   :
310   PRINT D$;"READ PHONE,R0"
320   INPUT R1
330   PRINT D$
340   PRINT : PRINT "RECORD COUNT: ";R1: PRINT
350   :
360   REM      DATA ENTRY MODULE
370   :
380   LET R1 = R1 + 1
390   INPUT "ENTER CUST. #:";N$
400   REM      DATA ENTRY TESTS
410   INPUT "ENTER CUST. NAME:";C$
420   REM      DATA ENTRY TEST
430   INPUT "ENTER PHONE #:";P$
440   REM      DATA ENTRY TESTS
450   :
460   : REM      WRITE TO FILE ROUTINE
470   :
480   PRINT D$;"WRITE PHONE, R";R1
490   PRINT N$: PRINT C$: PRINT P$
500   PRINT D$
510   INPUT "MORE ENTRIES?";R$
520   IF LEFT$ (R$,1) < > "Y" AND LEFT$ (R$,1) < > "N" THEN PRINT :
      PRINT CHR$ (7);"ENTER 'Y' FOR YES OR 'N' FOR NO": PRINT : GOTO 510
530   IF LEFT$ (R$,1) = "N" THEN 580
540   GOTO 380
550   :
560   REM      CLOSE FILE
570   :
580   PRINT D$;"WRITE PHONE, R0"
590   PRINT R1
600   PRINT D$
610   PRINT D$;"CLOSE PHONE"
620   PRINT : PRINT "FILE CLOSED"
630   PRINT : PRINT "NEW RECORD COUNT: ";R1
```

Enter the program and add data to PHONE. Then use the previously written program that reads and displays PHONE to verify that the additions are now in the file.

RANDOM ACCESS FILE UTILITY PROGRAMS

Having covered the essentials of using random access files, let's write two file utility programs to further your understanding and provide models for similar programs you can write. The first program simply copies the data from one random access file into another random access file, record for record. The data are both alphabetic and numeric.

Write a program to create a random access file named MASTER. This file will be used later in this section by a file utility program that makes a copy of a random access file. You can decide what information corresponds to the variables listed in the introductory module given below. Use your imagination!

(a)
```
100   REM      CREATE FILE NAMED MASTER
110   :
120   REM      VARIABLES USED
130   REM        C$=20 CHAR. MAX.
140   REM        S=8 CHAR. MAX.
150   REM        Q=4 CHAR. MAX.
160   REM        M$=30 CHAR. MAX.
170   REM        R1=RECORD NUMBER
180   REM        D$=CONTROL D
190   :
200   REM      FILES USED
210   REM        R-A SOURCE FILE NAME: MASTER
215   REM          RECORD LENGTH: 66 BYTES
216   REM          DATASET FORMAT: C$,S,Q,M$
230   :
```

_____

_____

_____

_____

_____

_____

_____

_____

_____

_____

_____

_____

_____

_____

_____

_____

_____

_____

_____

_____

_____

_____

_____

_____

_____

_____

_____

_____

_____

- - - - - - - - - - - - - - -

(a)
```
230 :
240 REM    INITIALIZE
250 :
260 LET D$ =  CHR$ (4)
270 LET R1 = 1
280 PRINT D$;"OPEN MASTER,L66"
290 :
300 REM    DATA ENTRY ROUTINE
310 :
320 INPUT "ENTER STRING DATA (20 CHAR.MAX.):";G$
330 REM      DATA ENTRY TESTS GO HERE
340 INPUT "ENTER NUMERIC VALUE (8 CHAR.MAX.):";S
350 REM      DATA ENTRY TESTS GO HERE
360 INPUT "ENTER NUMERIC VALUE (4 CHAR.MAX.):";Q
370 REM      DATA ENTRY TESTS GO HERE
380 INPUT "ENTER STRING DATA (30 CHAR.MAX.):";M$
390 REM      DATA ENTRY TESTS GO HERE
400 :
410 REM    WRITE DATASET TO FILE
420 :
430 PRINT D$;"WRITE MASTER,R"R1
440 PRINT G$: PRINT S: PRINT Q: PRINT M$
450 PRINT D$
460 INPUT "MORE DATA TO ENTER(Y OR N)?";R$
470 REM    USER RESPONSE DATA ENTRY TESTS GO HERE
480 IF R$ = "N" THEN 500
485 LET R1 = R1 + 1
486 HOME
487 GOTO 320
490 REM    CLOSE FILE
500 PRINT D$;"WRITE MASTER,R0"
510 PRINT R1
520 PRINT D$
530 PRINT D$;"CLOSE"
```

Now write a companion program to read and display the contents of MASTER. Allow the user to enter the file name. Include a "PRESS RETURN TO DISPLAY NEXT DATASET" routine inside the read/display loop.

(a)

```
100   REM     READ AND DISPLAY MASTER FILE
110   :
120   REM     VARIABLES USED
130   REM        C$ = 30 CHAR. MAX.
140   REM        S = 8 CHAR. MAX.
150   REM        Q = 4 CHAR. MAX.
160   REM        M$ = 50 CHAR. MAX.
170   REM        D$ = CONTROL D
180   REM        R1 = RECORD COUNTER
190   REM         R$ = USER RESPONSE VARIABLE
200   REM        F$ = USER ENTERED FILE NAME (MASTER)
210   REM     FILES USED
220   REM        R-A FILE NAME: MASTER
230   REM        DATASET FORMAT: C$,S,Q,M$
240   REM        RECORD LENGTH: 66
250   :
```

_____

_____

_____

_____

_____

_____

_____

_____

_____

_____

_____

_____

_____

_____

_____

_____

_____

_____

_____

_____

_____

_____

_____

_____

_____

_____

(a)
```
250 :
260 REM      INITIALIZE
270 :
280 LET D$ = CHR$ (4)
290 INPUT "ENTER NAME OF FILE:";F$
300 REM     DATA ENTRY TESTS GO HERE
310 PRINT
320 PRINT D$;"OPEN"F$",L66"
330 :
340 REM     DATA ENTRY MODULE
350 :
360 PRINT D$;"READ"F$",R0"
370 INPUT R1
380 PRINT D$
390 FOR X = 1 TO R1
400 PRINT D$;"READ"F$",R"X
410 INPUT G$,S,Q,M$
420 PRINT D$
430 PRINT G$: PRINT S: PRINT Q: PRINT M$
440 PRINT : INPUT "PRESS 'RETURN' TO DISPLAY NEXT DATASET";R$: PRINT
450 HOME
460 NEXT X
470 :
480 REM     CLOSE FILE
490 :
500 PRINT D$;"CLOSE"
510 PRINT : PRINT "FILE DISPLAYED AND CLOSED"
520 END
```

Follow these steps to create a random access file copying program:

1. OPEN the source file.
2. OPEN and clear the copy file.
3. Determine record count.
4. READ source file record.
5. WRITE copy file.
6. Return to step 4 until end of file.
7. CLOSE the files after posting record count in copy file.

We will now help you write a program that will make a copy of MASTER. The copy file is named STORE1. Here is the introductory module:

```
100 REM      PROGRAM TO MAKE A COPY OF R-A FILE 'MASTER'
110 :
120 REM      VARIABLES USED
130 REM        G$ = (20)
140 REM        S  = (8)
150 REM        Q  = (4)
160 REM        M$ = (30)
170 REM        R1 = RECORD COUNTER
180 REM        D$ = CONTROL D
190 :
200 REM      FILES USED
210 REM        R-A SOURCE FILE NAME: MASTER
220 REM        R-A COPY FILE NAME: STORE1
230 REM        RECORD LENGTH: 66 BYTES
240 REM        DATASET FORMAT: G$,S,Q,M$
250 :
```

Notice that we have only indicated the length of the variables; what data they represent is not important and has been left to your discretion and imagination.

As with sequential files, we recommend the OPEN-DELETE-OPEN sequence to clear a file of any previous data, thus preventing the accidental appearance at the end of the file of data left over from any previous version of STORE1. Complete the following segment to initialize the two files. Fill in lines 310, 320, 330, and 340.

(a)
```
260   REM       INITIALIZE
270 :
280   HOME : PRINT "WORKING"
290   LET D$ =  CHR$ (4)
300   LET R1 = 1
310
320
330
340
350 :
```

_ _ _ _ _ _ _ _ _ _ _ _ _ _ _

(a)
```
260   REM       INITIALIZE
270 :
280   HOME : PRINT "WORKING"
290   LET D$ =  CHR$ (4)
300   LET R1 = 1
310   PRINT D$;"OPEN MASTER, L66"
320   PRINT D$;"OPEN STORE1"
330   PRINT D$;"DELETE STORE1"
340   PRINT D$;"OPEN STORE1, L66"
350 :
```

The next section reads from the source file and writes to the copy file. Fill in the blanks in lines 380, 390, 400, 420, 430, 440, 480, 490, and 500.

(a)
```
360   REM       READ SOURCE FILE
370 :
380 :
390
400
410   FOR X = 1 TO R1
420
430
440
450 :
460   REM       PRINT COPY FILE
470 :
480
490
500
510   NEXT X
520 :
```

_ _ _ _ _ _ _ _ _ _ _ _ _ _ _

(a)
```
360   REM      READ SOURCE FILE
370   :
380   PRINT D$;"READ MASTER,R0"
390   INPUT R1
400   PRINT D$
410   FOR X = 1 TO R1
420   PRINT D$;"READ MASTER,R"X
430   INPUT G$,S,Q,M$
440   PRINT D$
450   :
460   REM      PRINT COPY FILE
470   :
480   PRINT D$;"WRITE STORE1,R"X
490   PRINT G$: PRINT S: PRINT Q: PRINT M$
500   PRINT D$
510   NEXT X
520   :
```

You probably found completing that program easy. Random access files are easy to manipulate, once you get the hang of it.

Here is a complete copy of the program.

```
100   REM      PROGRAM TO MAKE A COPY OF R-A FILE 'MASTER'
110   :
120   REM      VARIABLES USED
130   REM       G$ = (20)
140   REM       S  = (8)
150   REM       Q  = (4)
160   REM       M$ = (30)
170   REM       R1 = RECORD COUNTER
180   REM       D$ = CONTROL D
190   :
200   REM      FILES USED
210   REM       R-A SOURCE FILE NAME: MASTER
220   REM       R-A COPY FILE NAME: STORE1
230   REM       RECORD LENGTH: 66 BYTES
240   REM       DATASET FORMAT: G$,S,Q,M$
250   :
260   REM      INITIALIZE
270   :
280   HOME : PRINT "WORKING"
290   LET D$ = CHR$ (4)
300   LET R1 = 1
310   PRINT D$;"OPEN MASTER, L66"
320   PRINT D$;"OPEN STORE1"
330   PRINT D$;"DELETE STORE1"
340   PRINT D$;"OPEN STORE1, L66"
350   :
360   REM      READ SOURCE FILE
370   :
380   PRINT D$;"READ MASTER,R0"
390   INPUT R1
400   PRINT D$
410   FOR X = 1 TO R1
420   PRINT D$;"READ MASTER,R"X
430   INPUT G$,S,Q,M$
440   PRINT D$
450   :
460   REM      PRINT COPY FILE
470   :
480   PRINT D$;"WRITE STORE1,R"X
490   PRINT G$: PRINT S: PRINT Q: PRINT M$
500   PRINT D$
510   NEXT X
520   :
530   REM      CLOSE FILES
540   :
550   PRINT D$;"WRITE STORE1,R0"
560   PRINT R1
570   PRINT D$
580   PRINT D$;"CLOSE"
590   PRINT : PRINT "FILE COPY COMPLETE"
600   END
```

(a)   Check your understanding of the file copying program by filling in the corre-
        sponding program line number(s) for each step in the following outline.

1.   OPEN the source file. _____

2.   OPEN and clear the copy file. _____

3.   Determine record count _____

4.   READ source file record. _____

5.   WRITE copy file. _____

6.   Return to step 4 until end-of-file. _____

7.   CLOSE the file after posting the record count in copy file. _____

_ _ _ _ _ _ _ _ _ _ _ _ _ _ _

(a)   1. line 310
        2. lines 320 to 340
        3. lines 380 to 400
        4. lines 420 to 440
        5. lines 480 to 500
        6. lines 410 to 510
        7. lines 550 to 580

CHANGING DATA IN AN EXISTING RANDOM ACCESS FILE

So far, you have learned how to add data to a random access file and how to make a copy
of a random access file. Next, let's consider a versatile utility program that allows a number of options for changing the data in a random access file. We will be using the INVEN
file you created earlier in this chapter. We will use the complete dataset with product
code number, product description, quantity available, and record count stored in R0.
You want your program to display the datasets in the file, one record at a time, and allow
the user the following options:

1.   Change all data items.
2.   Change the code number only.
3.   Change the description only.
4.   Change the quantity only.
5.   No change to this record.

Follow these steps:

1.   OPEN the file.
2.   Determine record count.
3.   READ a dataset.
4.   Display the dataset.

5. Display the "menu" of choices.
6. Request and test choice.
7. Branch to appropriate subroutines according to choice made.
8. Return to step 3 above.
9. CLOSE the file.

Here is the complete program:

```
100   REM       INVEN FILE EDITOR
110   :
120   REM       VARIABLES USED
130   REM         C$ = PART NO. (6)
140   REM         P$ = DESCRIPTION (20)
150   REM         Q = QUANTITY (3)
160   REM         D$ = CONTROL D
170   REM         R1 = RECORD NUMBER
180   :
190   REM       FILES USED
200   REM         R-A FILE NAME: INVEN
210   REM         RECORD LENGTH: 32 BYTES
220   REM         DATASET FORMAT: C$,P$,Q
230   :
240   REM       INITIALIZE
250   :
260   LET D$ = CHR$ (4)
270   PRINT D$;"OPEN INVEN, L32"
280   :
290   REM       READ ONE RECORD
300   :
310   PRINT D$;"READ INVEN,R0"
320   INPUT R1
330   PRINT D$
340   FOR X = 1 TO R1
350   PRINT D$;"READ INVEN,R"X
360   INPUT C$,P$,Q
370   PRINT D$
380   :
390   REM       DISPLAY DATASET AND OPTIONS
400   :
410   HOME
420   PRINT "PROD #:";C$
430   PRINT "DESCRIPT:";P$
440   PRINT "QUANTITY:";Q
450   PRINT
460   PRINT "ENTER ONE OF THESE OPTIONS:"
470   PRINT "   1.   CHANGE ALL"
480   PRINT "   2.   CHANGE NUMBER ONLY"
490   PRINT "   3.   CHANGE DESCRIPTION ONLY"
500   PRINT "   4.   CHANGE QUANTITY ONLY"
510   PRINT "   5.   NO CHANGE FOR THIS DATA"
520   PRINT
530   :
540   INPUT "ENTER YOUR CHOICE:";R$
550   IF  LEN (R$) = 0 THEN  PRINT : PRINT  CHR$ (7);"PLEASE MAKE A CHOICE
      FROM THE MENU": PRINT : GOTO 540
560   LET R2 =  VAL (R$)
570   IF R2 < 1 OR R2 > 5 THEN  PRINT "ENTER NUMBER 1-5 ONLY, PLEASE": GOTO
      540
580   IF R2 = 1 THEN  GOSUB 680: GOSUB 720: GOSUB 760: GOSUB 810: GOTO 630
590   IF R2 = 2 THEN  GOSUB 680: GOSUB 810: GOTO 630
600   IF R2 = 3 THEN  GOSUB 720: GOSUB 810: GOTO 630
610   IF R2 = 4 THEN  GOSUB 760: GOSUB 810: GOTO 630
620   IF R2 = 5 THEN  GOSUB 810
630   NEXT X
640   GOTO 880
650   :
660   REM       DATA ENTRY SUBROUTINES
670   :
680   INPUT "ENTER NEW PRODUCT CODE:";C$
690   REM       DATA ENTRY TESTS
700   RETURN
710   :
720   INPUT "ENTER NEW DESCRIPTION:";P$
730   REM       DATA ENTRY TESTS
740   RETURN
750   :
760   INPUT "ENTER NEW QUANTITY:";Q
770   REM       DATA ENTRY TESTS
780   RETURN
790   :
800   REM       FILE PRINT SUBROUTINE
810   PRINT D$;"WRITE INVEN,R";X
820   PRINT C$: PRINT P$: PRINT Q
830   PRINT D$
840   RETURN
850   :
860   REM       CLOSE FILE
870   :
880   PRINT D$;"CLOSE"
890   END
```

(a)   Study the program carefully and write the corresponding line numbers for each step in the outline shown below.

1.   OPEN the file. _____

2.   Determine record count. _____

3.   READ a dataset. _____

4.   Display the dataset. _____

5.   Display the "menu" of choices. _____

6.   Request and test choice. _____

7.   Branch to appropriate subroutines according to choice made. _____

8.   Return to step 3 above. _____

9.   CLOSE the file. _____

- - - - - - - - - - - - - - - - -

(a)   1. line 270
      2. lines 310 to 330
      3. lines 350 to 370
      4. lines 420 to 440
      5. lines 460 to 510
      6. lines 540 to 570
      7. lines 580 to 620
      8. line 640
      9. line 880

Now enter and RUN the program, testing out all change options available. Then use the final version of your program that reads and displays INVEN to verify corrections or changes made in the file.

CONVERTING SEQUENTIAL FILES TO RANDOM ACCESS FILES

Another useful file utility program is one that converts a sequential file to a random access file. The procedure involves making a copy of the sequential file and placing one dataset from the sequential file into one record in a random access file. If at some point you want to standardize your entire software collection or system into random access file format, a program modeled on the one you are about to write would do the job.

The example is a small business-type application where a sequential file contains data in this format:

customer number = five-character string

customer name = twenty-character string

credit status code = single-digit number, one to five . One-character
   numeric value.

You may recognize this as the format of the customer credit file named CREDIT, a sequential file you created in Chapter 4 Self Test, problem 3. It is the same file you used in Chapter 5 for file editing application programs. The task is to copy a sequential data file into a random access file, one dataset (as described above) per record. The outline of steps is as follows:

1.   OPEN the sequential file.
2.   OPEN the random access file.
3.   End-of-file trap for the sequential file.
4.   READ one dataset from sequential file.
5.   WRITE to the random access file.
6.   Increment the record counter by one.
7.   Return to step 4 above.
8.   CLOSE the files after posting record count to random access file.

Here are the introductory and initializing modules. Read them over carefully.

```
100  REM    COPY SEQ FILE TO RA FILE
110  :
120  REM       VARIABLES USED
130  REM       N$ = CUSTOMER NUMBER (5 CHAR)
140  REM       C$ = CUST.NAME(20 CHAR.MAX.)
150  REM       R = CREDIT RATING (1 CHAR)
160  REM       D$ = CONTROL D
170  REM       R1 = RECORD COUNT
180  :
190  REM       FILES USED
200  REM       SEQ FILE NAME: CREDIT
210  REM       R-A FILE NAME: R-A CREDIT
220  REM       RECORD LENGTH: 29 BYTES
230  :
240  REM       INITIALIZE
250  :
260  HOME
270  PRINT "WORKING"
280  LET D$ =   CHR$ (4)
290  LET R1 = 0
300  PRINT D$;"OPEN CREDIT"
310  PRINT D$;"OPEN R-A CREDIT,L29"
320  :
```

(a)   What is the length of the random access file record? _____

(b)   Which will be the first record to be filled by the program? _____

_ _ _ _ _ _ _ _ _ _ _ _ _ _ _

(a)   twenty-nine bytes (L29 in line 310)

(b)   R1 (R1 = 1)

Here is the rest of the program. Fill in the blanks on lines 360, 370, 380, 420, 430, 440, 450, 500, 510, and 520.

(a)
```
330   REM       READ SEQ FILE
340 :
350   ONERR  GOTO 500
360
370
380
390 :
400   REM       WRITE RA FILE
410 :
420
430
440
450
460   GOTO 360
470 :
480   REM       CLOSE FILES
490 :
500
510
520
530   PRINT D$;"CLOSE"
540   PRINT : PRINT "FILE COPY COMPLETE."
550   END
```

— — — — — — — — — — — — — —

(a)
```
330   REM       READ SEQ FILE
340 :
350   ONERR  GOTO 500
360   PRINT D$;"READ CREDIT"
370   INPUT N$,C$,R
380   PRINT D$
390 :
400   REM       WRITE RA FILE
410 :
420   LET R1 = R1 + 1
430   PRINT D$;"WRITE R-A CREDIT,R"R1
440   PRINT N$: PRINT C$: PRINT R
450   PRINT D$
460   GOTO 360
470 :
480   REM       CLOSE FILES
490 :
500   PRINT D$;"WRITE R-A CRDEIT,R0"
510   PRINT R1
520   PRINT D$
530   PRINT D$;"CLOSE"
540   PRINT : PRINT "FILE COPY COMPLETE."
550   END
```

Here is the complete file conversion program. Look it over and complete the outline that follows with corresponding line numbers from the program.

```
(a)   100   REM     COPY SEQ FILE TO RA FILE
      110   :
      120   REM        VARIABLES USED
      130   REM        N$ = CUSTOMER NUMBER (5 CHAR)
      140   REM        C$ = CUST.NAME(20 CHAR.MAX.)
      150   REM        R = CREDIT RATING (1 CHAR)
      160   REM        D$ = CONTROL D
      170   REM        R1 = RECORD COUNT
      180   :
      190   REM        FILES USED
      200   REM        SEQ FILE NAME: CREDIT
      210   REM        R-A FILE NAME: R-A CREDIT
      220   REM        RECORD LENGTH: 29 BYTES
      230   :
      240   REM        INITIALIZE
      250   :
      260   HOME
      270   PRINT "WORKING"
      280   LET D$ = CHR$ (4)
      290   LET R1 = 0
      300   PRINT D$;"OPEN CREDIT"
      310   PRINT D$;"OPEN R-A CREDIT,L29"
      320   :
      330   REM        READ SEQ FILE
      340   :
      350   ONERR  GOTO 500
      360   PRINT D$;"READ CREDIT"
      370   INPUT N$,C$,R
      380   PRINT D$
      390   :
      400   REM     WRITE RA FILE
      410   :
      420   LET R1 = R1 + 1
      430   PRINT D$;"WRITE R-A CREDIT,R"R1
      440   PRINT N$: PRINT C$: PRINT R
      450   PRINT D$
      460   GOTO 360
      470   :
      48C   REM        CLOSE FILES
      490   :
      500   PRINT D$;"WRITE R-A CREDIT,R0"
      510   PRINT R1
      520   PRINT D$
      530   PRINT D$;"CLOSE"
      540   PRINT : PRINT "FILE COPY COMPLETE."
      550   END
```

1.   OPEN the sequential file. _____

2.   OPEN the random access file. _____

3.   Test for end-of-file of the sequential file._____

4.   READ one dataset from sequential file. _____

5.   Increment the record counter by one._____

6.   WRITE to the random access file._____

7.   Return to step 4 above._____

8.   Post the record count to the random access file and CLOSE the files.

_____

(a) 1. line 300
2. line 310
3. line 350
4. lines 360 to 380
5. line 420
6. lines 430 to 450
7. line 460
8. lines 500 to 530

Write a program to display the random access CREDIT file.

```
(a)  100  REM      DISPLAY R-A FILE NAMED R-A CREDIT
     110  :
     120  REM      VARIABLES USED
     130  REM        F$ = USER ENTERED FILE NAME
     140  REM        C$ = CUST. #
     150  REM        N$ = CUST. NAME
     160  REM        R = CREDIT RATING
     170  REM        D$ = CONTROL D
     180  REM        R1 = RECORD COUNT
     190  REM        X =FOR NEXT LOOP VARIABLE
     200  :
     210  REM      FILES USED
     220  REM        R-A FILE NAME: R-A CREDIT (USER ENTERED)
     230  REM        DATASET FORMAT: C$,N$,R
     240  REM        RECORD LENGTH: 29 BYTES
     250  :
```

(a)
```
260   REM       INITIALIZE
270   :
280   LET D$ =  CHR$ (4)
290   HOME
300   INPUT "ENTER FILE NAME:";F$
310   PRINT D$;"OPEN"F$",L29"
320   :
330   REM       READ/PRINT FILE
340   :
350   PRINT D$;"READ"F$",R0"
360   INPUT R1
370   PRINT D$
380   FOR X = 1 TO R1
390   PRINT D$;"READ"F$",R"X
400   INPUT C$,N$,R
410   PRINT D$
420   PRINT C$: PRINT N$: PRINT R: PRINT
430   NEXT X
440   :
450   REM       CLOSE FILE
460   :
470   PRINT D$;"CLOSE"
480   PRINT " ALL DATA DISPLAYED AND FILE CLOSED"
490   END
```

CHAPTER 6 SELF-TEST

1a. Write a program to create a random access data file that contains the inventory of products carried by an imaginary business. Each random access record contains the following data for one item of inventory in the order shown below. Numbers in parentheses indicate maximum character counts. Name this file BUSINESS INVENTORY. Create the file with your program.

N$ = product number (4)
P$ = description of inventory item (20)
S$ = supplier (20)
L = reorder point (how low the stock of item can be before reordering) (3)
Y = reorder quantity (4)
Q = quantity available (currently in stock) (4)
C = cost (from supplier) (6)
U = unit selling price (what the item is sold for) (6)

Here is the introductory module and a sample RUN.

```
100   REM    SOLUTION, CH6 SELFTEST PROB 1A
110   :
120   REM    VARIABLES USED
130   REM     N$=PROD.NUMBER(4)
140   REM     P$=DESCRIPTION(20)
150   REM     S$=SUPPLIER(20)
160   REM     L=REORDER POINT(3)
170   REM     Y=REORDER QUANTITY(4)
180   REM     Q=QUANTITY IN STOCK(4)
190   REM     C=COST(TO RETAILER)(6)
200   REM     U=UNIT(RETAIL)PRICE(6)
210   REM     R$=USER RESPONSE
220   REM     D$=CONTROL D
230   REM     R1=RECORD COUNT
240   REM    FILES USED
250   REM     RA FILE NAME: BUSINESS INVENTORY
260   REM     RECORD LENGTH: 75 BYTES
270   REM     DATASET FORMAT:N$,P$,S$,L,Y,Q,C,U
280   :

]RUN
ENTER PRODUCT NUMBER(4 DIGITS): 1234
ENTER PRODUCT DESCRIPTION(20 CHAR.MAX.):SAMPLE DATA
ENTER NAME OF SUPPLIER(20 CHAR.MAX.):SOULE SOURCE
REORDER POINT:12
REORDER QUANTITY:24
QUANTITY NOW IN STOCK:36
WHOLESALE COST:.55
UNIT SELLING PRICE:1.10
MORE DATA(TYPE 'Y' FOR YES OR 'N' FOR NO)?N

1 TOTAL DATASETS. FILE CLOSED.
```

_____

_____

_____

_____

_____

_____

_____

_____

_____

_____

_____

_____

_____

_____

_____

1b.   Using the program from self test problem (1a), create a random access file named
      BUSINESS INVENTORY. Make up your own data for at least 5 records (inven-
      tory items) and enter them into the file. This file will be used in Chapter 7
      examples and activities. Write a program to display the contents of BUSINESS
      INVENTORY, including the record count.

1c. Write a program to create a sequential (not random access) file called POINTER that contains the following two items in each dataset:

1) Account numbers from BUSINESS INVENTORY file (a four-character string).

2) The record number (a numeric value) corresponding to the record location of each account number.

The program should read the first data item from each record in BUSINESS INVENTORY and write the account number (4 character string) and the record count number for that record into the sequential file called POINTER

```
100   REM   CREATE SEQ POINTER FILE FROM BUSINESS INVENTORY R-A FILE
110   :
120   REM     VARIABLES USED
130   REM       D$=CONTROL D
140   REM       N$=PRODUCT #(4 CHAR.)
160   REM       R1=RECORD COUNT
170   REM       X=FOR-NEXT CONTROL VARIABLE
180   REM     FILES USED
190   REM       R-A FILE NAME:BUSINESS INVENTORY
195   REM       FILE LENGTH:75 BYTES
200   REM       SEQ FILE NAME:POINTER
210   REM       DATASET FORMAT:N$,X
220   :
```

_____

_____

_____

_____

_____

_____

_____

_____

_____

_____

_____

_____

_____

_____

_____

_____

_____

_____

_____

1d.   Write a program to read and display the data items in POINTER.

2.   Write a program to make a copy of the random access file named R-A CREDIT
that you transferred from a sequential file in the last example program in Chapter 6. The copy should be another random access file named R-A CREDIT
COPY.

Here is the introductory module:

```
100   REM     SOLUTION CH6 SELFTEST PROB 2
110   :
120   REM       VARIABLES USED:
130   REM         N$=CUSTOMER NUMBER(5 CHAR)
140   REM         C$=CUST. NAME (20 CHAR.MAX.)
150   REM         R=CREDIT RATING
160   REM         D$=CONTROL D
170   REM         X=FOR NEXT LOOP VARIABLE
180   REM         R1=RECORD COUNTER VARIABLE
190   REM       FILES USED
200   REM         R-A SOURCE FILE NAME: R-A CREDIT
210   REM         R-A COPY FILE NAME: R-A CREDIT COPY
220   REM         RECORD LENGTH: 29
230   REM         DATASET FORMATS: N$,C$,R
240   :
```

3.   Write a program to display the contents of the original data file and the copy in
     the previous problem (2), for verification of the completeness and accuracy of
     the copy. The program should display the data in record 1 of the original file,
     and then the data from record 1 in the file copy, then the data from record 2 in
     the original file, followed by the data from record 2 in the copy, and so on to
     the end of the files.

```
100   REM      SOLUTION, CH6 SELFTEST PROB 3
110   REM      READ & DISPLAY TWO R-A FILES
120  :
130   REM       VARIABLES USED
140   REM         N$,N1$=CUST.#(5 CHAR)
150   REM         C$,C1$=CUST.NAME(20 CHAR.MAX.)
160   REM         C,C1=CREDIT RATING(1 CHAR)
170   REM         R,R1=RECORD COUNTS
180   REM         X=FOR NEXT LOOP VARIABLE
190   REM         D$=CONTROL D
200  :
210   REM       FILES USED
220   REM         R-A FILE NAMES: R-A CREDIT, R-A CREDIT COPY
230   REM         RECORD LENGTH: 29 BYTES
240   REM         DATASET FORMAT: N$,C$,C
250  :


]RUN
ORIGINAL FILE REPORTS 3 RECORDS.
COPY FILE REPORTS 3 RECORDS.

ORIG: 12345PAUL ARMITIGE5
COPY: 12345PAUL ARMITIGE5

PRESS 'RETURN' TO DISPLAY NEXT DATASETS.
ORIG: 12346MISS PIGGY1
COPY: 12346MISS PIGGY1

PRESS 'RETURN' TO DISPLAY NEXT DATASETS.
ORIG: 12347SIR GALAHAD3
COPY: 12347SIR GALAHAD3

PRESS 'RETURN' TO DISPLAY NEXT DATASETS.

COMPARISON COMPLETE.
```


Answer Key

1a.

```
100  REM    SOLUTION, CH6 SELFTEST PROB 1A
110  :
120  REM     VARIABLES USED
130  REM      N$=PROD.NUMBER(4)
140  REM      P$=DESCRIPTION(20)
150  REM      S$=SUPPLIER(20)
160  REM      L=REORDER POINT(3)
170  REM      Y=REORDER QUANTITY(4)
180  REM      Q=QUANTITY IN STOCK(4)
190  REM      C=COST(TO RETAILER)(6)
200  REM      U=UNIT(RETAIL)PRICE(6)
210  REM      R$=USER RESPONSE
220  REM      D$=CONTROL D
230  REM      R1=RECORD COUNT
240  REM     FILES USED
250  REM      RA FILE NAME: BUSINESS INVENTORY
260  REM       RECORD LENGTH: 75 BYTES
270  REM        DATASET FORMAT:N$,P$,S$,L,Y,Q,C,U
280  :
290  REM     INITIALIZE
300  :
310  LET D$ =  CHR$ (4)
320  LET R1 = 1
330  PRINT D$;"OPEN BUSINESS INVENTORY,L75"
340  :
350  REM    DATA ENTRY MODULE-DATA ENTRY TESTS OMITTED
360  :
370  INPUT "ENTER PRODUCT NUMBER(4 DIGITS):";N$
380  REM -DATA ENTRY TESTS GO HERE
390  INPUT "ENTER PRODUCT DESCRIPTION(20 CHAR.MAX.):";P$
400  REM -DATA ENTRY TESTS GO HERE
410  INPUT "ENTER NAME OF SUPPLIER(20 CHAR.MAX.):";S$
420  REM -DATA ENTRY TESTS GO HERE
430  INPUT "REORDER POINT:";L
440  REM -DATA ENTRY TESTS GO HERE
450  INPUT "REORDER QUANTITY:";Y
460  REM -DATA ENTRY TESTS GO HERE
470  INPUT "QUANTITY NOW IN STOCK:";Q
480  REM -DATA ENTRY TESTS GO HERE
490  INPUT "WHOLESALE COST:";C
500  REM -DATA ENTRY TESTS GO HERE
510  INPUT "UNIT SELLING PRICE:";U
520  REM -DATA ENTRY TESTS GO HERE
530  :
540  REM    WRITE DATASET TO FILE
550  :
560  PRINT D$;"WRITE BUSINESS INVENTORY,R"R1
570  PRINT N$: PRINT P$: PRINT S$: PRINT L: PRINT Y: PRINT Q: PRINT C:
     PRINT U
580  PRINT D$
590  :
600  REM    MORE DATA REQUEST
610  :
620  INPUT "MORE DATA(TYPE 'Y' FOR YES OR 'N' FOR NO)?";R$
630  REM -Y OR N ENTRY TEST
640  IF R$ = "Y" THEN R1 = R1 + 1: HOME : GOTO 370
650  :
660  REM -PRINT RECORD COUNTER VALUE & CLOSE FILE
670  :
680  PRINT D$;"WRITE BUSINESS INVENTORY,R0"
690  PRINT R1
700  PRINT D$
710  PRINT D$;"CLOSE"
720  PRINT : PRINT R1;" TOTAL DATASETS. FILE CLOSED."
730  END
```

1b.

```
100   REM     BUSINESS INVENTORY READER
110   :
120   REM     VARIABLES USED
130   REM      N$=PROD.NUMBER(4)
140   REM      P$=DESCRIPTION(20)
150   REM      S$=SUPPLIER(20)
160   REM      L=REORDER POINT(3)
170   REM      Y=REORDER QUANTITY(4)
180   REM      Q=QUANTITY IN STOCK(4)
190   REM      C=COST(TO RETAILER)(6)
200   REM      U=UNIT(RETAIL)PRICE(6)
210   REM      R$=USER RESPONSE
220   REM      D$=CONTROL D
230   REM      R1=RECORD COUNT
240   REM     FILES USED
250   REM      RA FILE NAME: BUSINESS INVENTORY
260   REM         RECORD LENGTH: 75 BYTES
270   REM         DATASET FORMAT:N$,P$,S$,L,Y,Q,C,U
280   :
290   REM     INITIALIZE
300   :
310   D$ =  CHR$ (4)
320    PRINT D$;"OPEN BUSINESS INVENTORY,L75"
330    PRINT D$;"READ BUSINESS INVENTORY,R0"
340    INPUT R1
350    PRINT D$
360    PRINT R1;" TOTAL DATASETS.": PRINT
370   :
380   REM     READ AND DISPLAY
390   :
400    FOR X = 1 TO R1
410    PRINT D$;"READ BUSINESS INVENTORY,R"X
420    INPUT N$,P$,S$,L,Y,Q,C,U
430    PRINT D$
440    PRINT N$: PRINT P$: PRINT S$: PRINT L: PRINT Y: PRINT Q: PRINT C:
       PRINT U: PRINT
450    PRINT : INPUT "PRESS RETURN FOR NEXT DISPLAY.";R$
460    HOME
470    NEXT X
480   :
490   REM     CLOSE FILE
500   :
510    PRINT D$;"CLOSE"
520    PRINT : PRINT "ALL DATASETS DISPLAYED."
```

1c.
```
100   REM     CREATE SEQ POINTER FILE FROM BUSINESS INVENTORY R-A FILE
110   :
120   REM        VARIABLES USED
130   REM          D$=CONTROL D
140   REM          N$=PRODUCT #(4 CHAR.)
160   REM          R1=RECORD COUNT
170   REM          X=FOR-NEXT CONTROL VARIABLE
180   REM        FILES USED
190   REM          R-A FILE NAME:BUSINESS INVENTORY
195   REM           FILE LENGTH:75 BYTES
200   REM          SEQ FILE NAME:POINTER
210   REM           DATASET FORMAT:N$,X
220   :
230   REM      INITIALIZE
240   :
245   HOME : PRINT "WORKING"
250   LET D$ =  CHR$ (4)
260   PRINT D$;"OPEN BUSINESS INVENTORY,L75"
270   PRINT D$;"OPEN POINTER"
280   :
290   REM     READ FIRST DATA ITEM FROM R-A FILE AND WRITE THAT ITEM+RECORD
      COUNT TO SEQ. FILE

300   :
310   PRINT D$;"READ BUSINESS INVENTORY,R0"
320   INPUT R1
325   PRINT D$
330   FOR X = 1 TO R1
340   PRINT D$;"READ BUSINESS INVENTORY,R"X
350   INPUT N$
360   PRINT D$
380   PRINT D$;"WRITE POINTER"
390   PRINT N$: PRINT X
400   PRINT D$
410   NEXT X
420   :
430   REM       CLOSE FILES
440   :
450   PRINT D$;"CLOSE"
460   PRINT : PRINT "FILES CLOSED."
470   END
```

1d.
```
100   REM      POINTER FILE READER
110   :
120   REM        VARIABLES USED
130   REM          D$=CONTROL D
140   REM          N$=ACCOUNT #
150   REM          R1=RECORD COUNT
160   REM          R$=USER RESPONSE VARIABLE
170   REM        FILE USED
180   REM          SEQ. FILE NAME: POINTER
190   REM          DATASET FORMAT: N$,R1
200   :
210   REM        INITIALIZE
220   :
230   LET D$ =  CHR$ (4)
240   PRINT D$;"OPEN POINTER"
250   :
260   REM      READ AND DISPLAY
270   :
280   ONERR  GOTO 400
290   PRINT D$;"READ POINTER"
300   INPUT N$,R1
310   PRINT D$
320   PRINT N$,R1
330   PRINT
340   INPUT "PRESS RETURN KEY TO DISPLAY NEXT DATA.";R$
350   PRINT
360   GOTO 290
370   :
380   REM      CLOSE FILE
390   :
400   PRINT D$;"CLOSE"
410   PRINT : PRINT "CONTENTS DISPLAYED & FILE CLOSED."
420   END
```

```
2.    100   REM    SOLUTION CH6 SELFTEST PROB 2
      110   :
      120   REM      VARIABLES USED:
      130   REM        N$=CUSTOMER NUMBER(5 CHAR)
      140   REM        C$=CUST. NAME (20 CHAR.MAX.)
      150   REM        R=CREDIT RATING
      160   REM      ' D$=CONTROL D
      170   REM        X=FOR NEXT LOOP VARIABLE
      180   REM        R1=RECORD COUNTER VARIABLE
      190   REM      FILES USED
      200   REM        R-A SOURCE FILE NAME: R-A CREDIT
      210   REM        R-A COPY FILE NAME: R-A CREDIT COPY
      220   REM        RECORD LENGTH: 29
      230   REM        DATASET FORMATS: N$,C$,R
      240   :
      250   REM      INITIALIZE
      260   :
      270   HOME
      280   PRINT "WORKING"
      290   LET D$ =  CHR$ (4)
      300   PRINT D$;"OPEN R-A CREDIT,L29"
      310   PRINT D$;"OPEN R-A CREDIT COPY,L29"
      320   PRINT D$;"DELETE R-A CREDIT COPY"
      330   PRINT D$;"OPEN R-A CREDIT COPY,L29"
      340   :
      350   REM      COPY ROUTINE
      360   :
      370   PRINT D$;"READ R-A CREDIT,R0"
      380   INPUT R1
      390   PRINT D$
      400   FOR X = 1 TO R1
      410   PRINT D$;"READ R-A CREDIT,R"X
      420   INPUT N$,C$,R
      430   PRINT D$
      440   PRINT D$;"WRITE R-A CREDIT COPY,R"X
      450   PRINT N$: PRINT C$: PRINT R
      460   PRINT D$
      470   NEXT X
      480   :
      490   REM     WRITE RECORD COUNT & CLOSE
      500   :
      510   PRINT D$;"WRITE R-A CREDIT COPY,R0"
      520   PRINT R1
      530   PRINT D$;"CLOSE"
      540   PRINT : PRINT "FILE DUPLICATED AND CLOSED."
      550   END
```

3.

```
100   REM      SOLUTION, CH6 SELFTEST PROB 3
110   REM      READ & DISPLAY TWO R-A FILES
120   :
130   REM       VARIABLES USED
140   REM        N$,N1$=CUST.#(5 CHAR)
150   REM        C$,C1$=CUST.NAME(20 CHAR.MAX.)
160   REM        C,C1=CREDIT RATING(1 CHAR)
170   REM        R,R1=RECORD COUNTS
180   REM        X=FOR NEXT LOOP VARIABLE
190   REM        D$=CONTROL D
200   :
210   REM       FILES USED
220   REM        R-A FILE NAMES: R-A CREDIT, R-A CREDIT COPY
230   REM        RECORD LENGTH: 29 BYTES
240   REM        DATASET FORMAT: N$,C$,C
250   :
260   REM      INITIALIZE
270   :
280   LET D$ =   CHR$ (4)
290   PRINT D$;"OPEN R-A CREDIT,L29"
300   PRINT D$;"OPEN R-A CREDIT COPY,L29"
310   :
320   REM      READ & DISPLAY RECORD COUNTS
330   :
340   PRINT D$;"READ R-A CREDIT,R0"
350   INPUT R
360   PRINT D$
370   PRINT D$;"READ R-A CREDIT COPY,R0"
380   INPUT R1
390   PRINT D$
400   PRINT "ORIGINAL FILE REPORTS ";R;" RECORDS."
410   PRINT "COPY FILE REPORTS ";R1;" RECORDS."
415   PRINT
420   :
430   REM      READ & DISPLAY ONE DATASET AT A TIME FROM EACH FILE
440   :
450   FOR X = 1 TO R
460   PRINT D$;"READ R-A CREDIT,R"X
470   INPUT N$,C$,C
480   PRINT D$
490   PRINT D$;"READ R-A CREDIT COPY,R"X
500   INPUT N1$,C1$,C1
510   PRINT D$
520   PRINT "ORIG: ";N$;C$;C
530   PRINT "COPY: ";N1$;C1$;C1
540   PRINT
550   INPUT "PRESS 'RETURN' TO DISPLAY NEXT DATASETS.";R$
560   HOME
570   NEXT X
580   :
590   REM      CLOSE FILES
600   :
610   PRINT D$;"CLOSE"
620   PRINT : PRINT "COMPARISON COMPLETE."
630   END
```

CHAPTER SEVEN
Random Access File Applications

Objectives: In this chapter you will learn expanded techniques for random access data file applications and how to use sequential "pointer" data files as an index for a random access data file.

SEQUENTIAL POINTER FILES FOR RANDOM ACCESS FILES

Two file applications are designed to be somewhat typical of the programs you might encounter as you design your own computer software systems and write your own programs. The programs are not really long, as you might expect, but they are only one component of a larger software system composed of many programs.

The first exercise is an inventory control application that uses both a sequential file and a random access file in the same program. The objective is to show how to use a sequential "pointer" file and how to change data located in a random access file record. The application could as well have been a mailing list, a credit information file, or any sort of master file application. While a pointer file may be superfluous in our simple example, the technique may be valuable in more complex software systems.

In this case, all the data regarding the inventory of products carried are stored in a random access file named BUSINESS INVENTORY. Each random access record contains the following data for one item of inventory in the order shown below:

```
N$ = PROD # (4)
P$ = DESCRIPTION (20)
S$ = SUPPLIER (20)
L  = REORDER POINT (3)
Y  = REORDER QUANTITY (4)
Q  = QUANTITY AVAILABLE (4)
C  = COST (6)
U  = UNIT SELLING PRICE (6)
```

If you wanted to change some data from product number 9827, you would have to search through the random access file records one at a time, until you found product number 9827. Alternatively you could add a sequential "pointer" file that contains the product numbers (in a string variable) followed by the record number where the proper dataset is located in the random access file. To change the cost and selling price data in the random access file, follow these steps:

1. Enter product number.
2. Quickly search the sequential pointer file for the product number and corresponding record location.
3. Access the correct random access record.
4. Make the changes in the random access file record.

It looks easy, but there are a few "tricks." Here is the first part of the program. Read it through carefully.

```
100   REM    SEQ.POINTER FILE USED WITH R-A FILE 'BUSINESS INVENTORY'
110   REM      THIS PROGRAM PERMITS THE USER TO CHANGE THE COST AND
120   REM      UNIT SELLING PRICE FOR AN EXISTING INVENTORY ITEM IN FILE
130   :
140   REM    VARIABLES USED
150   REM      R$ = DATA ENTRY STRING
160   REM      R1=RECORD COUNT
170   REM      N$=N1$=N2$=PROD.# (4 CHAR)
180   REM      P$=PROD.DESCRIPTION(20 CHAR)
190   REM      S$ = SUPPLIER (20)
200   REM      L = REORDER POINT (3)
210   REM      Y = REORDER QUANTITY (3)
220   REM      Q=QUANTITY IN STOCK (3 CHAR)
230   REM      C=C1=COST (6 CHAR)
240   REM      U=U1=UNIT SELLING PRICE (6 CHAR)
250   :
260   REM    FILES USED
270   REM      SEQ. FILE NAME: POINTER
280   REM      DATASET FORMAT: N$,R1
290   REM      R-A FILE NAME: BUSINESS INVENTORY
300   REM      FILE LENGTH: 75 BYTES
310   REM      DATASET FORMAT: N$,P$,S$,L,Y,Q,C,U
320   :
330   REM    INITIALIZE
340   :
350   LET D$ =  CHR$ (4)
360   REM    'POINTER' OPENED AT TIME OF FILE SEARCH
370   PRINT D$;"OPEN BUSINESS INVENTORY,L75"
380   :
390   REM    DATA ENTRY MODULE
400   :
410   INPUT "ENTER PRODUCT # (4 CHAR):";N2$
420   REM    DATA ENTRY TESTS
430   :
```

This segment provides for entry and testing of the product number. It is time to search the sequential file for the record location for this product number in the random access file. On chance that the operator made an entry error that escaped the error tests, include an error trap in case you read all the way to the end of the sequential file and find no matching product number. This error message routine is shown below in lines 560 through 610. You fill in lines 460, 480, 490, and 500.

(a)
```
440   REM       SEARCH POINTER FILE
450 :
460
470   ONERR   GOTO 560
480
490
500
510   IF N1$ = N2$ THEN  PRINT D$;"CLOSE POINTER": GOTO 650
520   GOTO 480
530 :
540   REM       ERROR TRAP
550 :
560   IF  PEEK (222) = 5 THEN 580
570   PRINT : PRINT  CHR$ (7);"UNUSUAL ERROR. PROGRAM TERMINATED.": PRINT :
      GOTO 940
580   PRINT D$;"CLOSE POINTER"
590   PRINT "THIS PRODUCT # IS NOT IN OUR FILE"
600   PRINT "CHECK YOUR NUMBERS AND REENTER"
610   GOTO 410
620 :
```

(b)   In which variable is the record number of the random access file located? _____

(c)   Under what conditions is the POINTER file closed? _____

_ _ _ _ _ _ _ _ _ _ _ _ _ _ _

(a)
```
440   REM       SEARCH POINTER FILE
450 :
460   PRINT D$;"OPEN POINTER"
470   ONERR   GOTO 560
480   PRINT D$;"READ POINTER"
490   INPUT N1$,R1
500   PRINT D$
510   IF N1$ = N2$ THEN  PRINT D$;"CLOSE POINTER": GOTO 650
520   GOTO 480
530 :
540   REM       ERROR TRAP
550 :
560   IF  PEEK (222) = 5 THEN 580
570   PRINT : PRINT  CHR$ (7);"UNUSUAL ERROR. PROGRAM TERMINATED.": PRINT :
      GOTO 940
580   PRINT D$;"CLOSE POINTER"
590   PRINT "THIS PRODUCT # IS NOT IN OUR FILE"
600   PRINT "CHECK YOUR NUMBERS AND REENTER"
610   GOTO 410
620 :
```

(b)   R1

(c)   If the account number entered by the user is found (line 510), or if the end of
      file is encountered (lines 500 to 610)

Next the correct dataset is accessed from the random access file. Fill in lines
650, 660, and 670.

(a)
```
630   REM       READ RECORD FROM R-A FILE
640 :
650
660
670
680 :
```

- - - - - - - - - - - - - - -

(a)
```
630  REM     READ RECORD FROM R-A FILE
640  :
650  PRINT D$;"READ BUSINESS INVENTORY,R"R1
660  INPUT N$,P$,S$,L,Y,Q,C1,U1
670  PRINT D$
680  :
```

Complete lines 820, 830, and 840 below.

(a)
```
690  REM    ENTER DATA CHANGES
700  :
710  PRINT : PRINT "OLD COST: ";C1
720  PRINT "OLD UNIT SELLING PRICE: ";U1
730  PRINT
740  INPUT "ENTER NEW COST:";C
750  REM    DATA ENTRY TESTS GO HERE
760  INPUT "ENTER NEW SELLING PRICE:";U
770  REM    DATA ENTRY TESTS GO HERE
780  :
790  :
800  : REM      REPLACE WITH NEW DATA
810  :
820
830
840
850  :
```

- - - - - - - - - - - - - - -

(a)
```
690  REM    ENTER DATA CHANGES
700  :
710  PRINT : PRINT "OLD COST: ";C1
720  PRINT "OLD UNIT SELLING PRICE: ";U1
730  PRINT
740  INPUT "ENTER NEW COST:";C
750  REM    DATA ENTRY TESTS GO HERE
760  INPUT "ENTER NEW SELLING PRICE:";U
770  REM    DATA ENTRY TESTS GO HERE
780  :
790  :
800  : REM      REPLACE WITH NEW DATA
810  :
820  PRINT D$;"WRITE BUSINESS INVENTORY,R"R1
830  PRINT N$: PRINT P$: PRINT S$: PRINT L: PRINT Y: PRINT Q: PRINT C:
     PRINT U
840  PRINT D$
850  :
```

The remainder of the program looks like this:

```
860  REM      MORE?
870  :
880  INPUT "MORE ENTRIES?";R$
890  REM    DATA ENTRY CHECK GOES HERE
900  IF LEFT$ (R$,1) = "Y" THEN 410
910  :
920  REM      CLOSE
930  :
940  PRINT D$;"CLOSE"
950  END
```

This completes the first random access file application—one part of an entire product inventory application. Now enter and RUN the program. After that, display the contents of BUSINESS INVENTORY to verify the changes.

```
100   REM     SEQ.POINTER FILE USED WITH R-A FILE 'BUSINESS INVENTORY'
110   REM       THIS PROGRAM PERMITS THE USER TO CHANGE THE COST AND
120   REM       UNIT SELLING PRICE FOR AN EXISTING INVENTORY ITEM IN FILE
130   :
140   REM       VARIABLES USED
150   REM       R$ = DATA ENTRY STRING
160   REM       R1=RECORD COUNT
170   REM       N$=N1$=N2$=PROD.# (4 CHAR)
180   REM       P$=PROD.DESCRIPTION(20 CHAR)
190   REM       S$ = SUPPLIER (20)
200   REM       L = REORDER POINT (3)
210   REM       Y = REORDER QUANTITY (3)
220   REM       Q=QUANTITY IN STOCK (3 CHAR)
230   REM       C=C1=COST (6 CHAR)
240   REM       U=U1=UNIT SELLING PRICE (6 CHAR)
250   :
260   REM       FILES USED
270   REM       SEQ. FILE NAME: POINTER
280   REM       DATASET FORMAT: N$,R1
290   REM       R-A FILE NAME: BUSINESS INVENTORY
300   REM       FILE LENGTH: 75 BYTES
310   REM       DATASET FORMAT: N$,P$,S$,L,Y,Q,C,U
320   :
330   REM       INITIALIZE
340   :
350   LET D$ =  CHR$ (4)
360   REM   'POINTER' OPENED AT TIME OF FILE SEARCH
370   PRINT D$;"OPEN BUSINESS INVENTORY,L75"
380   :
390   REM       DATA ENTRY MODULE
400   :
410   INPUT "ENTER PRODUCT # (4 CHAR):";N2$
420   REM       DATA ENTRY TESTS
430   :
440   REM       SEARCH POINTER FILE
450   :
460   PRINT D$;"OPEN POINTER"
470   ONERR  GOTO 560
480   PRINT D$;"READ POINTER"
490   INPUT N1$,R1
500   PRINT D$
510   IF N1$ = N2$ THEN  PRINT D$;"CLOSE POINTER": GOTO 650
520   GOTO 480
530   :
540   REM       ERROR TRAP
550   :
560   IF  PEEK (222) = 5 THEN 580
570   PRINT : PRINT  CHR$ (7);"UNUSUAL ERROR. PROGRAM TERMINATED.": PRINT :
      GOTO 940
580   PRINT D$;"CLOSE POINTER"
590   PRINT "THIS PRODUCT # IS NOT IN OUR FILE"
600   PRINT "CHECK YOUR NUMBERS AND REENTER"
610   GOTO 410
620   :
630   REM       READ RECORD FROM R-A FILE
640   :
650   PRINT D$;"READ BUSINESS INVENTORY,R"R1
660   INPUT N$,P$,S$,L,Y,Q,C1,U1
670   PRINT D$
680   :
690   REM       ENTER DATA CHANGES
700   :
710   PRINT : PRINT "OLD COST: ";C1
720   PRINT "OLD UNIT SELLING PRICE: ";U1
730   PRINT
740   INPUT "ENTER NEW COST:";C
750   REM   DATA ENTRY TESTS GO HERE
760   INPUT "ENTER NEW SELLING PRICE:";U
```

continued on next page

```
770   REM    DATA ENTRY TESTS GO HERE
780  :
790  :
800  : REM       REPLACE WITH NEW DATA
810  :
820   PRINT D$;"WRITE BUSINESS INVENTORY,R"R1
830   PRINT N$: PRINT P$: PRINT S$: PRINT L: PRINT Y: PRINT Q: PRINT C:
      PRINT U
840   PRINT D$
850  :
860   REM    MORE?
870  :
880   INPUT "MORE ENTRIES?";R$
890   REM    DATA ENTRY CHECK GOES HERE
900   IF LEFT$ (R$,1) = "Y" THEN 410
910  :
920   REM    CLOSE
930  :
940   PRINT D$;"CLOSE"
950   END
```

(a)   What other programs are needed to complete this series of application programs?

_____

_____

_____

– – – – – – – – – – – – – – – –

(a)   1) Add new inventory items. 2) Delete inventory items. 3) Change supplier and/
      or description. 4) Change reorder point, etc., to name a few.

PERSONAL MONEY MANAGEMENT APPLICATION

The second example program in this chapter could form part of a large home financial
management software package. The example gives some hints for setting up your own
home finance programs. The objectives of this application are to show you how to
process a "transaction" file and to demonstrate how account numbers can be used to
point out the file and record in a random access file.

The first step is to decide exactly what expenditures you want to computerize.
Record all income and all expenditures into particular accounts. Include the capability
to discern taxable from non-taxable items so these records can be used as data for your
income tax returns. To keep things simple, the following chart of accounts has been
prepared for this application:

1001	TAXABLE SALARIES
1002	TAXABLE INTEREST
1003	TAXABLE DIVIDENDS
1004	TAXABLE OTHER INCOME
1005	NON-TAXABLE INCOME
1006	MISC. NON-TAXABLE MONEYS
2001	GROCERIES
2002	NON FOOD STAPLES
2003	MORTGAGE
2004	GAS/ELECTRICITY
2005	WATER & GARBAGE
2006	TELEPHONE
2007	HOME INSURANCE
2008	PROPERTY TAXES
2009	FURNITURE
2010	AUTO PAYMENTS
2011	GAS AND OIL
2012	AUTO REPAIR
2013	PARKING/TOLLS
2014	AUTO INSURANCE
2015	FATHER'S CLOTHES
2016	MOTHER'S CLOTHES
2017	SON'S CLOTHES
2018	DAUGHTER'S CLOTHES
2019	CLOTHING REPAIR/CLEANING
2020	SPORTS FEES/TICKETS
2021	SPORTS EQUIPMENT
2022	MAGAZINES/BOOKS
2023	MOVIES/PLAYS
2024	ALCOHOL
2025	DINING OUT
2026	VACATION EXPENSES
2027	POSTAGE
2028	SCHOOL/HOUSEHOLD SUPPLIES
3001	LEGAL/ACCTG. FEES
3002	LIFE INSURANCE
3003	MEDICAL INSURANCE
3004	DENTAL INSURANCE
3005	UNREIMBURSED MEDICAL EXPENSES
3006	DRUG EXPENSES
3007	EDUCATIONAL FEES AND TUITIONS
3008	BOOKS AND SUPPLIES
3009	EXCESS SALES TAXES PAID
3010	CONTRIBUTIONS
3011	SAVINGS DEPOSITS
3012	INVESTMENTS

The account number has important significance. The first digit of the account number is the number of the random access file in which the account details can be found. All random access files are called BUDGET #. The details of the taxable salaries account are found in file BUDGET1 (account number 1001). The details of the telephone account are in file BUDGET2 (account number 2008).

(a)   Which file contains the details of the dining out account? _____

(a)   BUDGET2 (account number 2006)

The last three digits of the account number indicate the record number of the random access file containing the account details. The investment account (3010) will be found in the file BUDGET3, record number 10.

(a)   The legal/accounting account details are found in file _____

record number _____ .

— — — — — — — — — — — — — — —

(a)   BUDGET2, record 30

For convenience, the account number is always entered as a string variable so that you can use the LEFT$ and RIGHT$ functions to separate the file number and record number.

To demonstrate the file number concept, we use three separate files (BUDGET1, BUDGET2, and BUDGET3) for this small list of accounts. Of course, all these accounts could be placed in one file, but that will not be the case when your account list grows. At that point you may want to use this scheme.

The random access files (BUDGET#) contain the details of each account. Each record contains the following information in the order shown.

```
N$ = ACCOUNT # (4)
A$ = ACCOUNT NAME (20)
B$ = BUDGETED AMOUNT (8). ANNUAL BUDGET
E$ = EXPENDED/EARNED AMOUNT (8). YEAR-TO-DATE
```

Write one program that you can use to create three random access file named BUDGET1, BUDGET2, and BUDGET3, using the dataset shown above as the format in each record. Using the chart of accounts we have provided, enter the correct number of datasets (one per record) for each file; i.e., six records in BUDGET1, twenty-eight records in BUDGET2, and twelve records in BUDGET3. Use the value of the right-most three digits of the account chart number (N$) to determine the record number into which each dataset will be placed. You decide on the value for BUDGETED AMOUNT in each record, and enter zero (0) as the value for EXPENDED/EARNED amount in all records in all files (happy new fiscal year). Also write the companion program to display the contents of the file one dataset at a time.

(a)
```
100   REM      CREATE BUDGET# R-A FILES
110   :
120   REM      VARIABLES USED
130   REM        N$ = ACCOUNT CHART NUMBER (4)
140   REM        A$ = ACCOUNT NAME (20)
150   REM        B$ = BUDGETED AMOUNT (8)
160   REM        E$ = EXPENDED/EARNED AMOUNT (8)
170   REM        R1 = RECORD NUMBER (EXTRACTED FROM N$)
171   REM        N = USER ENTERED NUMBER FOR BUDGET# FILE NAME
172   REM        F1$ = BUDGET FILE NAME
180   REM        D$ = CONTROL D
190   REM        R$ = USER RESPONSE
200   REM      FILE USED
210   REM        R-A FILE NAMES: BUDGET1,2,3
220   REM        DATASET FORMAT:N$,A$,B$,E$
230   REM        RECORD LENGTH: 44
```

```
(a)   100   REM       CREATE BUDGET# R-A FILES
      110   :
      120   REM       VARIABLES USED
      130   REM          N$ = ACCOUNT CHART NUMBER (4)
      140   REM          A$ = ACCOUNT NAME (20)
      150   REM          B$ = BUDGETED AMOUNT (8)
      160   REM          E$ = EXPENDED/EARNED AMOUNT (8)
      170   :
      180   :
      190   :
      200   REM    FILE USED
      210   REM       R-A FILE NAMES: BUDGET1,2,3
      220   REM       DATASET FORMAT:N$,D1$,B,E
      230   REM       RECORD LENGTH: 44
      240   :
      250   REM       INITIALIZE
      260   :
      270   LET D$ =   CHR$ (4)
      280   LET R1 = 1
      290   INPUT "WHICH BUDGET FILE(1,2, OR 3)?";F2$
      300   REM   DATA ENTRY TESTS GO HERE
      310   LET F1$ = "BUDGET" + F2$
      320   PRINT D$;"OPEN"F1$",L44"
      330   :
      340   REM       READ FILE
      350   :
      360   ONERR  GOTO 470
      370   PRINT D$;"READ"F1$",R"R1
      380   INPUT N$,A$,B$,E$
      390   PRINT D$
      400   PRINT : PRINT N$: PRINT A$: PRINT B$: PRINT E$: PRINT
      410   PRINT : PRINT : INPUT "PRESS RETURN TO CONTINUE.";R$
      420   LET R1 = R1 + 1
      430   GOTO 370
      440   :
      450   REM    CLOSE FILE
      460   :
      470   PRINT D$;"CLOSE"
      480   PRINT : PRINT "FILE DISPLAYED AND CLOSED."
```

You have now created the budget files for the personal money management system of programs. A second set of files is needed to store data on all money transactions. Each month a new sequential transaction file is created containing the information found in your checking account check register. For the month of January, the file is called MONTH1. March is MONTH3, etc. You may keep "old" files on your disk for other analyses you may want to do. Each month you will create a transaction file, then process or "post" it to the BUDGET # file. Each sequential transaction file entry includes the following information in the order shown:

```
C  = CHECK #/DEPOSIT SLIP #
Y$ = DATE (6)
W$ = PARTY TO WHOM CHECK IS DRAWN/SOURCE OF FUNDS (20)
A$ = ACCOUNT # (4)
D  = DOLLAR AMOUNT
```

Notice that the format is set up to be used with deposits and payments and that the transaction file includes more information than you will actually be using. This file, however, can be used for other things as well, so all this information is included.

(a)   Using the dataset information above as a guide, write a program that allows you
to create the sequential monthly transaction file. Use your checkbook register or
your imagination for the monthly checks and deposits to enter in the file. Then
write the companion program to display MONTH#, using the "PRESS RETURN
TO CONTINUE" technique.

```
100    REM    CREATE A SEQ.FILE OF CHECKBOOK TRANSACTIONS FOR EACH MONTH OF Y
110    :
120    REM    VARIABLES USED
130    REM      D$=CONTROL D
140    REM      C=CHECK # OR DEPOSIT SLIP # (3 CHAR)
150    REM      Y$=DATE (XX-XX-XX) (8)
160    REM      W$=PARTY TO WHOM CHECK IS WRITTEN OR SOURCE OF FUNDS FOR
       DEPOSIT (20 CHAR.MAX.)
170    REM      N$=ACCOUNT NUMBER (4 CHAR)
180    REM      D=DOLLAR AMOUNT
190    REM      M = USER ENTERED MONTH NUMBER FOR FILE NAME
200    REM      F$=FILE NAME
210    REM      R$=USER RESPONSE VARIABLE
220    REM    SEQ.FILE NAME:MONTH#
230    REM    DATASET FORMAT: C,Y$,W$,N$,D
```

_____

_____

_____

_____

_____

_____

_____

_____

_____

_____

_____

_____

_____

_____

_____

_____

_____

_____

_____

_____

_____

(a)

```
100   REM     READ MONTHLY TRANSACTION FILES
110   :
120   REM     VARIABLES USED
130   REM       D$=CONTROL D
140   REM       C=CHECK # OR DEPOSIT SLIP # (3 CHAR)
150   REM       Y$=DATE (8 CHAR)
160   REM       W$=PARTY TO WHOM CHECK IS WRITTEN OR SOURCE OF FUNDS FOR
      DEPOSIT (20 CHAR.MAX.)
170   REM       A$=ACCOUNT # (4 CHAR)
180   REM       D=DOLLAR AMOUNT
190   REM       M=USER ENTERED MONTH NUMBER
200   REM       F$=FILE NAME
210   REM       R$=INPUT VARIABLE FOR PRESS RETURN TO CONTINUE
220   REM     SEQ.FILE NAME:MONTH#
230   REM     DATASET FORMAT:C,Y$,W$,A$,D
240   :
250   REM     INITIALIZE
260   :
270   LET D$ =  CHR$ (4)
280   INPUT "WHAT MONTH #(1=JAN,2=FEB,ETC)?";M
290   IF M ( 1 OR M ) 12 THEN  PRINT "ENTER 1 TO 12 ONLY.": GOTO 280
300   REM     OTHER DATA ENTRY TESTS GO HERE
310   LET F$ = "MONTH" + STR$ (M)
320   PRINT D$;"OPEN"F$
330   :
340   REM     READ AND DISPLAY
350   :
360   ONERR  GOTO 470
370   PRINT D$;"READ"F$
380   INPUT C,Y$,W$,A$,D
390   PRINT D$
400   PRINT C: PRINT Y$: PRINT W$: PRINT A$: PRINT D
410   PRINT : PRINT
420   INPUT "PRESS RETURN FOR NEXT DISPLAY";R$
430   HOME : GOTO 370
440   :
450   REM   CLOSE FILE
460   :
470   PRINT D$;"CLOSE"
480   PRINT : PRINT "ALL TRANSACTIONS DISPLAYED."
```

Let's review the application. Each year, create random access files (BUDGET#) that contain the beginning status of all your personal accounts. This status includes a yearly budget estimate. Each month create a sequential file (MONTH#) using the information found in your checkbook register. After the MONTH# file is completed, process or post it to the BUDGET# files. Periodically, you can print a status report of the BUDGET# files.

The task is to write the program that processes the monthly transaction file. Here is the introductory module with the file initialization module:

```
100   REM       PERSONAL MONEY MANAGEMENT
110   REM       SEQ/RA FILE APPLICATION
120   :
130   REM       VARIABLES USED
140   REM       N$=N1$=ACCOUNT CHART NUMBER(4)
150   REM       A$ = ACCOUNT NAME (20)
160   REM       Y$ = DATE (8)
170   REM       W$ = CHECK WRITTEN TO/SOURCE OF DEPOSIT (20)
180   REM       M = USER ENTERED MONTH NUMBER (USE 1 FOR JAN, 2 FOR FEB, ETC)
190   REM       N = BUDGET FILE NUMBER (EXTRACTED FROM N$)
200   REM       C = CHECK # OR DEPOSIT SLIP #
210   REM       D = DOLLAR AMT. OF CHECK OR DEPOSIT
220   REM       B$ = BUDGETED AMT. (8)
230   REM       E$ = AMT. EXPENDED OR EARNED TO DATE (8)
240   REM       F$ = SEQ FILE NAME
250   REM       F1$ = R-A FILE NAME
260   REM       R1 = RECORD NUMBER (EXTRACTED FROM N$)
270   REM       D$ = CONTROL D
280   :
290   REM       FILES USED
300   REM       MONTH# = SEQ/TRANSACTION FILE. # IS USER SELECTED
310   REM       DATASET FORMAT: C,Y$,W$,A$,D
320   REM       BUDGET# = R-A FILE. # IS EXTRACTED FROM N$
330   REM        AND CHANGES WITH EACH TRANSACTION
340   REM       DATASET FORMAT: N$,A$,B$,E$
350   REM       RECORD LENGTH: 44 BYTES
360   :
370   REM       FILE INITIALIZATION
380   :
390   LET D$ =  CHR$ (4)
400   INPUT "WHAT IS THE MONTH NUMBER TO BE PROCESSED?";M
410   REM      DATA ENTRY TESTS
420   LET F$ = "MONTH" +  STR$ (M)
430   PRINT : PRINT "WORKING"
440   :
```

(a)   In lines 400 through 420, if the user enters 3 for M, what is the file name F$ in

line 420? _____

_____

(a)   MONTH3.

```
450   REM       READ SEQ FILE TRANSACTIONS
460   :
470   PRINT D$;"OPEN"F$
480   ONERR  GOTO 920
490   PRINT D$;"READ"F$
500   INPUT C,Y$,W$,N$,D
510   PRINT D$
520   POKE 216,0: REM    TURN OFF ERROR TRAP
530   :
540   REM       EXTRACT FILE #/INITIALIZE R-A FILE
550   :
560
570   LET F1$ = "BUDGET" +  STR$ (N)
580   PRINT D$;"OPEN"F1$",L44"
590   :
```

Line 480 tests for the end of the transaction file. When all datasets in that file have been read, the program terminates. Line 500 reads an entire dataset from the transaction file. Then the file number is "extracted" from the account number, to be used in line 570 to make the complete BUDGET file name. Complete line 560, extracting the file number from the account number (it's the first digit of N$).

(a) 560 _____

— — — — — — — — — — — — — — — —

(a) ```560 LET N = VAL (LEFT$ (N$,1))```

The next operation extracts the record number from the account number (the last three digits of N$).
Fill in line 620.

(a)
```
600   REM       EXTRACT/CONVERT RECORD #
610   :
620
630   :
```

— — — — — — — — — — — — — — —

(a)
```
600   REM       EXTRACT/CONVERT RECORD #
610   :
620   LET R1 =  VAL ( RIGHT$ (N$,3))
630   :
```

(Warning: Don't forget the double closing parentheses.)

The remaining modules accesses the proper random access file and record, updates the amount expended/earned, and prints the new value back to the file.

Complete this module (lines 660, 670, 680, 720, 740, 780, 790, and 800.)

(a)
```
640   REM      READ R-A FILE RECORD
650 :
660
670
680
690 :
700   REM      MAKE CHANGES TO DATA
710 :
720
730   LET E = E + D
740
750 :
760   REM      UPDATE BUDGET# FILE
770 :
780
790
800
810 :
820   REM      CLOSE BUDGET FILE
830 :
840   PRINT D$;"CLOSE"F1$
850 :
860   REM      RETURN FOR NEXT TRANSACTION
870 :
880   GOTO 480
890 :
900   REM      CLOSE FILE
910 :
920   PRINT D$;"CLOSE"
930   PRINT : PRINT "TRANSACTIONS POSTED"
```

– – – – – – – – – – – – – – –

(a)
```
640   REM      READ R-A FILE RECORD
650 :
660   PRINT D$;"READ"F1$",R";R1
670   INPUT N1$,A$,B$,E$
680   PRINT D$
690 :
700   REM      MAKE CHANGES TO DATA
710 :
720   LET E =   VAL (E$)
730   LET E = E + D
740   LET E$ =  STR$ (E)
750 :
760   REM      UPDATE BUDGET# FILE
770 :
780   PRINT D$;"WRITE"F1$",R"R1
790   PRINT N1$: PRINT A$: PRINT B$: PRINT E$
800   PRINT D$
810 :
820   REM      CLOSE BUDGET FILE
830 :
840   PRINT D$;"CLOSE"F1$
850 :
860   REM      RETURN FOR NEXT TRANSACTION
870 :
880   GOTO 480
890 :
900   REM      CLOSE FILE
910 :
920   PRINT D$;"CLOSE"
930   PRINT : PRINT "TRANSACTIONS POSTED"
```

This completes the program. It will continue reading checking transactions and processing them until the end of the transaction file is reached, at which point files are closed and the program ends. This program keeps your disk drive working, but does nothing on your screen or printer.

Enter and RUN the program, then read and display the BUDGET# files to see the posted and updated accounts.

```
100  REM     PERSONAL MONEY MANAGEMENT
110  REM       SEQ/RA FILE APPLICATION
120  :
130  REM       VARIABLES USED
140  REM       N$=N1$=ACCOUNT CHART NUMBER(4)
150  REM       A$ = ACCOUNT NAME (20)
160  REM       Y$ = DATE (8)
170  REM       W$ = CHECK WRITTEN TO/SOURCE OF DEPOSIT (20)
180  REM       M = USER ENTERED MONTH NUMBER (USE 1 FOR JAN, 2 FOR FEB, ETC)
190  REM       N = BUDGET FILE NUMBER (EXTRACTED FROM N$)
200  REM       C = CHECK # OR DEPOSIT SLIP #
210  REM       D = DOLLAR AMT. OF CHECK OR DEPOSIT
220  REM       B$ = BUDGETED AMT. (8)
230  REM       E$ = AMT. EXPENDED OR EARNED TO DATE (8)
240  REM       F$ = SEQ FILE NAME
250  REM       F1$ = R-A FILE NAME
260  REM       R1 = RECORD NUMBER (EXTRACTED FROM N$)
270  REM       D$ = CONTROL D
280  :
290  REM       FILES USED
300  REM       MONTH# = SEQ/TRANSACTION FILE. # IS USER SELECTED
310  REM       DATASET FORMAT: C,Y$,W$,A$,D
320  REM       BUDGET# = R-A FILE. # IS EXTRACTED FROM N$
330  REM        AND CHANGES WITH EACH TRANSACTION
340  REM       DATASET FORMAT: N$,A$,B$,E$
350  REM       RECORD LENGTH: 44 BYTES
360  :
370  REM       FILE INITIALIZATION
380  :
390  LET D$ =  CHR$ (4)
400  INPUT "WHAT IS THE MONTH NUMBER TO BE PROCESSED?";M
410  REM       DATA ENTRY TESTS
420  LET F$ = "MONTH" +  STR$ (M)
430  PRINT : PRINT "WORKING"
440  :
450  REM       READ SEQ FILE TRANSACTIONS
460  :
470  PRINT D$;"OPEN"F$
480  ONERR  GOTO 920
490  PRINT D$;"READ"F$
500  INPUT C,Y$,W$,N$,D
510  PRINT D$
520  POKE 216,0: REM     TURN OFF ERROR TRAP
530  :
540  REM       EXTRACT FILE #/INITIALIZE R-A FILE
550  :
560  LET N =  VAL ( LEFT$ (N$,1))
570  LET F1$ = "BUDGET" +  STR$ (N)
580  PRINT D$;"OPEN"F1$",L44"
590  :
600  REM       EXTRACT/CONVERT RECORD #
610  :
620  LET R1 =  VAL ( RIGHT$ (N$,3))
630  :
640  REM       READ R-A FILE RECORD
650  :
660  PRINT D$;"READ"F1$",R";R1
670  INPUT N1$,A$,B$,E$
680  PRINT D$
690  :
```

continued on next page

```
700   REM      MAKE CHANGES TO DATA
710   :
720   LET E = VAL (E$)
730   LET E = E + D
740   LET E$ = STR$ (E)
750   :
760   REM      UPDATE BUDGET# FILE
770   :
780   PRINT D$;"WRITE"F1$",R"R1
790   PRINT N1$: PRINT A$: PRINT B$: PRINT E$
800   PRINT D$
810   :
820   REM      CLOSE BUDGET FILE
830   :
840   PRINT D$;"CLOSE"F1$
850   :
860   REM      RETURN FOR NEXT TRANSACTION
870   :
880   GOTO 480
890   :
900   REM      CLOSE FILE
910   :
920   PRINT D$;"CLOSE"
930   PRINT : PRINT "TRANSACTIONS POSTED"
```

(a) Only one small component of this application has been completed. List the other programs you would need to make a complete personal finance management system?

(a) Programs:
1. Edit MONTH# file for entry errors
2. Print BUDGET# file accounts
3. "Exception report" showing over budget accounts or projected over budget accounts

We have found random access files much easier to use than sequential files. But let's not forget that sequential files have their place in computing. With the knowledge gained from this book, you should now be able to read the reference manual for your computer with new understanding. You should also be able to write your own data file programs and read programs written by others.

CHAPTER 7 SELF-TEST

1.   The first application in this chapter was an inventory control system. Before you continue you may want to review the system description so you are familiar with the contents of BUSINESS INVENTORY and POINTER.

   To this system is added a third file; a sequential transaction file in which is placed the data regarding each transaction that affects the inventory. Two types of transactions will affect inventory:

   Type 1 – units are added to inventory.
   Type 2 – units are taken from inventory.

   Data is recorded in the sequential transaction file in this format.

   T = TRANSACTION TYPE (1 OR 2)
   Y$ = DATE
   I$ = INVOICE # OR RECEIPT #
   N$ = PROD # (4)
   Q1 = QUANTITY ADDED OR DEDUCTED

   Write a program to create the transaction file described above. Name this sequential file BUSINVTRANSACT.

```
100   REM     PROGRAM CREATES A SEQ FILE
110   REM     OF INVENTORY CHANGES FOR FILE
120   REM     NAMED 'BUSINESS IVENTORY'
130 :
140   REM       VARIABLE LIST
150   REM       T=TRANSACTION TYPE(1 OR 2)
160   REM       Y$=DATE (XX-XX-XX)
170   REM       I$=INVOICE OR RECEIPT NUMBER
180   REM       N$=PRODUCT # (4 CHAR)
190   REM       Q1=QUANTITY ADDED OR SUBTRACTED FROM INVENTORY (3 CHAR MAX)
200   REM       D$=CONTROL D
210   REM     FILES USED
220   REM       SEQ FILE NAME: BUSINVTRANSACT
230   REM       DATASET FORMAT: T,Y$,I$,N$,Q1
240 :
```

2. Write the companion program to display the contents of BUSINVTRANSACT.

```
100   REM   DISPLAY CONTENTS OF BUSINVTRANSACT
110   :
120   REM      VARIABLES USED
130   REM       T=TRANSACTION TYPE
140   REM       Y$=DATE
150   REM       I$=INVOICE OR RECEIPT #
160   REM       N$=ACCOUNT NUMBER
170   REM       Q1=QUANTITY ADDED OR SUBTRACTED
180   REM       D$=CONTROL D
190   REM       R$=USER RESPONSE VARIABLE
200   REM      SEQ FILE USED:BUSINVTRANSACT
210   REM        DATASET FORMAT:T,Y$,I$,N$,Q1
220   :
```

```
]RUN
TRANSACTION TYPE: 2
DATE: 2-22-83
INVOICE OR RECEIPT #: S73846
ACCOUNT #: 1234
QUANTITY ADDED OR SUBTRACTED: 10

PRESS RETURN TO CONTINUE
```

_____

_____

_____

_____

_____

_____

_____

_____

_____

_____

_____

_____

_____

_____

_____

_____

_____

3.   Write a program to post the inventory changes in BUSINVTRANSACT to
     BUSINESS INVENTORY.

```
100   REM   PROCESS BUSINVTRANSACT FILE TO BUSINESS INVENTORY FILE
110   :
120   REM   VARIABLE LIST
130   REM     D$=CONTROL D
140   REM     R$=USER RESPONSE VARIABLE
150   REM     N$=N1$=N2$=PRODUCT # (4 CHAR)
160   REM     P$=PROD.DESCRIPT. (20 CHAR MAX)
170   REM     S$=SUPPLIER NAME (20 CHAR MAX)
180   REM     L=REORDER POINT (3 CHAR)
190   REM     Y=REORDER QUANTITY (3 CHAR)
200   REM     Q=QUANITIY IN STOCK (3 CHAR)
210   REM     Q1=QUANTITY ADDED OR SUBTRACTED FROM STOCK (3 CHAR)
220   REM     C=COST (6 CHAR)
230   REM     U=UNIT SELLING PRICE (6 CHAR)
240   REM     R1=RECORD COUNT
250   REM     T=TRANSACTION TYPE
260   REM     Y$=TRANSACTION DATE (XX-XX-XX)
270   REM     I$=INVOICE OR RECEIPT NUMBER
280   :
290   REM   FILES USED
300   REM     SEQ FILE NAME:POINTER
310   REM       DATASET FORMAT:N$,R1
320   REM     R-A FILE NAME:BUSINESS INVENTORY
330   REM       DATASET FORMAT:N$,P$,S$,L,Y,Q,C,U
340   REM       FILE LENGTH:75 BYTES
350   REM     SEQ FILE NAME:BUSINVTRANSACT
360   REM       DATASET FORMAT:T,Y$,I$,N1$,Q1
370   :
```

_____

_____

_____

_____

_____

_____

_____

_____

_____

_____

_____

_____

_____

_____

_____

_____

4. Write a program that, after all the transactions have been processed, will search
    the entire BUSINESS INVENTORY file and display a report of products that
    have fallen below the reorder point and need reordering.

```
100  REM     SEARCH BUSINESS INVENTORY FILE FOR REORDERS AND DISPLAY REPORT
110  :
120  REM  VARIABLES USED
130  REM     N$=PRODUCT # (4 CHAR)
140  REM     P$=PROD.DESCRIPT.(20 CHAR MAX)
150  REM     S$=SUPPLIER (20 CHAR MAX)
160  REM     L=REORDER POINT (3 CHAR)
170  REM     Y=REORDER QUANITIY
180  REM     Q=QUANTITY IN STOCK
190  REM     C=COST
200  REM     U=UNIT SELLING PRICE
210  REM     D$=CONTROL D
220  REM     X=FOR NEXT LOOP CONTROL VARIABLE
230  REM     R1=RECORD COUNT
240  REM     R$=USER RESPONSE VARIABLE
250  REM  FILES USED
260  REM     R-A FILE NAME:BUSINESS INVENTORY
270  REM     DATASET FORMAT:N$,P$,S$,L,Y,Q,C,U
280  REM     FILE LENGTH:75 BYTES
290  :


]RUN

ACCOUNT #: 1234
SUPPLIER: COVEN INC
REORDER POINT: 35
REORDER QUANTITY: 50
QUANITIY NOW IN STOCK: 30
COST: .45
UNIT SELLING PRICE: 1.375

PRESS RETURN TO CONTINUE.
```


Answer Key

1.

```
100   REM      PROGRAM CREATES A SEQ FILE
110   REM      OF INVENTORY CHANGES FOR FILE
120   REM      NAMED 'BUSINESS IVENTORY'
130   :
140   REM       VARIABLE LIST
150   REM       T=TRANSACTION TYPE(1 OR 2)
160   REM       Y$=DATE (XX-XX-XX)
170   REM       I$=INVOICE OR RECEIPT NUMBER
180   REM       N$=PRODUCT # (4 CHAR)
190   REM       Q1=QUANTITY ADDED OR SUBTRACTED FROM INVENTORY (3 CHAR MAX)
200   REM       D$=CONTROL D
210   REM      FILES USED
220   REM       SEQ FILE NAME: BUSINVTRANSACT
230   REM       DATASET FORMAT: T,Y$,I$,N$,Q1
240   :
250   REM      INITIALIZE
260   :
270   LET D$ =  CHR$ (4)
280   PRINT D$;"OPEN BUSINVTRANSACT"
290   PRINT D$;"DELETE BUSINVTRANSACT"
300   PRINT D$;"OPEN BUSINVTRANSACT"
310   :
320   REM      DATA ENTRY
330   :
340   PRINT "TRANSACTION CODES:"
350   PRINT "   ENTER '1' FOR UNITS ADDED TO INVENTORY."
360   PRINT "   ENTER '2' FOR UNITS TAKEN FROM INVENTORY."
370   INPUT "ENTER TRANSACTION TYPE: ";T
380   IF T <  > 1 AND T <  > 2 THEN  PRINT : PRINT  CHR$ (7);"ENTER THE
      DIGITS 1 OR 2 ONLY.": PRINT : GOTO 370
390   INPUT "ENTER TRANSACTION DATE:";Y$
400   REM      DATA ENTRY TESTS GO HERE
410   INPUT "ENTER INVOICE OR RECEIPT #:";I$
420   REM      DATA ENTRY TESTS GO HERE
430   INPUT "ENTER PRODUCT # (4 CHAR):";N$
440   REM      DATA ENTRY TESTS GO HERE
450   INPUT "ENTER QUANTITY:";Q1
460   REM      DATA ENTRY TESTS GO HERE
470   :
480   REM      WRITE TO FILE
490   :
500   PRINT D$;"WRITE BUSINVTRANSACT"
510   PRINT T: PRINT Y$: PRINT I$: PRINT N$: PRINT Q1
520   PRINT D$
530   INPUT "MORE TRANSACTIONS(Y OR N)?";R$
540   IF R$ <  > "Y" AND R$ <  > "N" THEN  PRINT  CHR$ (7);"PLEASE ENTER 'Y'
      FOR YES OR 'N' FOR NO.": PRINT : GOTO 530
550   IF R$ = "Y" THEN  HOME : GOTO 340
560   :
570   REM   CLOSE FILES
580   :
590   PRINT D$;"CLOSE"
600   PRINT : PRINT "FILE CLOSED."
610   END
```

2.

```
100   REM   DISPLAY CONTENTS OF BUSINVTRANSACT
110   :
120   REM      VARIABLES USED
130   REM       T=TRANSACTION TYPE
140   REM       Y$=DATE
150   REM       I$=INVOICE OR RECEIPT #
160   REM       N$=ACCOUNT NUMBER
170   REM       Q1=QUANTITY ADDED OR SUBTRACTED
180   REM       D$=CONTROL D
190   REM       R$=USER RESPONSE VARIABLE
200   REM      SEQ FILE USED:BUSINVTRANSACT
210   REM        DATASET FORMAT:T,Y$,I$,N$,Q1
220   :
230   REM      INITIALIZE
240   :
250   LET D$ =  CHR$ (4)
260   PRINT D$;"OPEN BUSINVTRANSACT"
270   :
280   REM      READ & DISPLAY
290   :
300   ONERR  GOTO 440
310   PRINT D$;"READ BUSINVTRANSACT"
320   INPUT T,Y$,I$,N$,Q1
330   PRINT D$
340   PRINT "TRANSACTION TYPE: ";T
350   PRINT "DATE: ";Y$
360   PRINT "INVOICE OR RECEIPT #: ";I$
370   PRINT "ACCOUNT #: ";N$
380   PRINT "QUANTITY ADDED OR SUBTRACTED: ";Q1
390   PRINT : INPUT "PRESS RETURN TO CONTINUE";R$
400   PRINT : GOTO 310
410   :
420   REM      END OF FILE ERROR TRAP
430   :
440   IF  PEEK (222) = 5 THEN  PRINT : PRINT "CONTENTS DISPLAYED": GOTO 490
450   PRINT : PRINT "UNUSUAL ERROR. PROGRAM TERMINATED.": GOTO 490
460   :
470   REM      CLOSE FILE
480   :
490   PRINT D$;"CLOSE"
500   PRINT "FILE CLOSED"
510   END
```

```
3.  100   REM   PROCESS BUSINVTRANSACT FILE TO BUSINESS INVENTORY FILE
    110   :
    120   REM      VARIABLE LIST
    130   REM         D$=CONTROL D
    140   REM         R$=USER RESPONSE VARIABLE
    150   REM         N$=N1$=N2$=PRODUCT # (4 CHAR)
    160   REM         P$=PROD.DESCRIPT. (20 CHAR MAX)
    170   REM         S$=SUPPLIER NAME (20 CHAR MAX)
    180   REM         L=REORDER POINT (3 CHAR)
    190   REM         Y=REORDER QUANTITY (3 CHAR)
    200   REM         Q=QUANITIY IN STOCK (3 CHAR)
    210   REM         Q1=QUANTITY ADDED OR SUBTRACTED FROM STOCK (3 CHAR)
    220   REM         C=COST (6 CHAR)
    230   REM         U=UNIT SELLING PRICE (6 CHAR)
    240   REM         R1=RECORD COUNT
    250   REM         T=TRANSACTION TYPE
    260   REM         Y$=TRANSACTION DATE (XX-XX-XX)
    270   REM         I$=INVOICE OR RECEIPT NUMBER
    280   :
    290   REM      FILES USED
    300   REM         SEQ FILE NAME:POINTER
    310   REM            DATASET FORMAT:N$,R1
    320   REM         R-A FILE NAME:BUSINESS INVENTORY
    330   REM            DATASET FORMAT:N$,P$,S$,L,Y,Q,C,U
    340   REM            FILE LENGTH:75 BYTES
    350   REM         SEQ FILE NAME:BUSINVTRANSACT
    360   REM            DATASET FORMAT:T,Y$,I$,N1$,Q1
    370   :
    380   REM         INITIALIZE
    390   :
    400   HOME : PRINT "WORKING"
    410   LET D$ =  CHR$ (4)
    420   PRINT D$;"OPEN BUSINESS INVENTORY,L75"
    430   PRINT D$;"OPEN BUSINVTRANSACT"
    440   :
    450   REM    READ ONE BUSINVTRANSACT DATASET AND FIND CORRESPONDING RECORD #
          FROM POINTER
    460   :
    470   ONERR  GOTO 790
    480   PRINT D$;"READ BUSINVTRANSACT"
    490   INPUT T,Y$,I$,N1$,Q1
    500   PRINT D$
    510   ONERR  GOTO 770
    520   PRINT D$;"OPEN POINTER"
    530   PRINT D$;"READ POINTER"
    540   INPUT N$,R1
    550   PRINT D$
    560   IF N$ = N1$ THEN  PRINT D$;"CLOSE POINTER": GOTO 610
    570   GOTO 530
    580   :
    590   REM      FIND AND CHANGE Q IN R-A FILE
    600   :
    610   POKE 216,0: REM   TURN OFF ERROR TRAP
    620   PRINT D$;"READ BUSINESS INVENTORY,R"R1
    630   INPUT N2$,P$,S$,L,Y,Q,C,U
    640   PRINT D$
    650   IF T = 1 THEN  LET Q = Q + Q1: GOTO 700
    660   IF T = 2 THEN  LET Q = Q - Q1: GOTO 700
    670   :
    680   REM      WRITE UPDATED DATASET TO R-A FILE
    690   :
    700   PRINT D$;"WRITE BUSINESS INVENTORY,R"R1
    710   PRINT N2$: PRINT P$: PRINT S$: PRINT L: PRINT Y: PRINT Q: PRINT C:
          PRINT U
    720   PRINT D$
    730   GOTO 470
    740   :
    750   REM      ERROR TRAPS FOR SEQ FILES
    760   :
    770   IF  PEEK (222) = 5 THEN  PRINT : PRINT  CHR$ (7);"ACCOUNT # REFERENCED
          IN BUSINVTRANSACT FILE NOT FOUND IN POINTER FILE. PROGRAM TERMINATED.":
          PRINT : GOTO 830
    780   PRINT : PRINT  CHR$ (7);"UNUSUAL ERROR. PROGRAM TERMINATED.": GOTO 830
    790   IF  PEEK (222) = 5 THEN  PRINT : PRINT "ALL TRANSACTIONS POSTED.":
          GOTO 830
    800   :
    810   REM      CLOSE FILES
    820   :
    830   PRINT D$;"CLOSE"
    840   PRINT "FILES CLOSED"
    850   END
```

4.

```
100  REM     SEARCH BUSINESS INVENTORY FILE FOR REORDERS AND DISPLAY REPORT
110  :
120  REM   VARIABLES USED
130  REM      N$=PRODUCT # (4 CHAR)
140  REM      P$=PROD.DESCRIPT.(20 CHAR MAX)
150  REM      S$=SUPPLIER (20 CHAR MAX)
160  REM      L=REORDER POINT (3 CHAR)
170  REM      Y=REORDER QUANITIY
180  REM      Q=QUANTITY IN STOCK
190  REM      C=COST
200  REM      U=UNIT SELLING PRICE
210  REM      D$=CONTROL D
220  REM      X=FOR NEXT LOOP CONTROL VARIABLE
230  REM      R1=RECORD COUNT
240  REM      R$=USER RESPONSE VARIABLE
250  REM    FILES USED
260  REM      R-A FILE NAME:BUSINESS INVENTORY
270  REM      DATASET FORMAT:N$,P$,S$,L,Y,Q,C,U
280  REM      FILE LENGTH:75 BYTES
290  :
300  REM      INITIALIZE
310  :
320  LET D$ =  CHR$ (4)
330  PRINT D$;"OPEN BUSINESS INVENTORY,L75"
340  :
350  REM     READ ONE DATASET, DETERMINE IF INVENTORY IS BELOW REEORDER
          POINT
360  :
370  PRINT D$;"READ BUSINESS INVENTORY,R0"
380  INPUT R1
390  PRINT D$
400  FOR X = 1 TO R1
410  PRINT D$;"READ BUSINESS INVENTORY,R"X
420  INPUT N$,P$,S$,L,Y,Q,C,U
430  PRINT D$
440  IF Q < L THEN  GOSUB 500
450  NEXT X
460  GOTO 620
470  :
480  REM     SUBROTUINE TO PRINT REPORT
490  :
500  PRINT : PRINT "ACCOUNT #: ";N$
510  PRINT "SUPPLIER: ";S$
520  PRINT "REORDER POINT: ";L
530  PRINT "REORDER QUANTITY: ";Y
540  PRINT "QUANITIY NOW IN STOCK: ";Q
550  PRINT "COST: ";C
560  PRINT "UNIT SELLING PRICE: ";U
570  PRINT : INPUT "PRESS RETURN TO CONTINUE.";R$
580  HOME : RETURN
590  :
600  REM     CLOSE FILES
610  :
620  PRINT D$;"CLOSE"
630  PRINT : PRINT "REORDER DISPLAY COMPLETED AND FILE CLOSED."
640  END
```

Final Self-Test

1. Write a program to create a sequential disk file named PHONE1, containing the following data concatenated into one string in fields as indicated:

> Last name (fifteen character maximum)
> first name (fifteen character maximum)
> area code (three digits)
> phone number (eight characters, including hyphen between third and
> > fourth character)

```
100   REM    CREATE SEQ FILE PHONE1(NAME&# DIRECTORY)
110   :
120   REM    VARIABLES USED
130   REM      L$=LAST NAME (15 CHAR FIELD)
140   REM      F$=FIRST NAME (15 CHAR FIELD)
150   REM      A$=AREA CODE (3 CHAR FIELD)
160   REM      N$=PHONE # (8 CHAR CODE)
170   REM      C$=L$+F$+A$+N$ (CONCATENATED DATASET)
180   REM      D$=CONTROL D
190   REM      R$=USER RESPONSE VARIABLE
200   REM    FILE USED
210   REM      SEQ FILE NAME:PHONE1
220   REM      DATASET FORMAT:C$
230   :


]RUN
TYPE 'STOP' IF NO MORE ENTRIES.

ENTER LAST NAME:BROWNING
ENTER FIRST NAME:MAXWELL
ENTER AREA CODE:440
PHONE NUMBER FORMAT: 999-9999
WHAT IS THE NUMBER?123-4321
CHECK FOR MISTAKES!
LAST NAME: BROWNING
FIRST NAME: MAXWELL
PHONE NUMBER: (440) 123-4321

IS THE INFO CORRECT(Y OR N)?
```

2.   Write a program to display all the datasets in PHONE1, with the data items
     separated (undo concatenation) and displayed.

```
100   REM     DISPLAY PHONE1 FILE CONTENTS
110   :
120   REM     VARIABLES USED
130   REM       C$=DATASET
140   REM       R$=USER RESPONSE VARIABLE
150   REM       D$=CONTROL D
160   REM     SEQ FILE NAME: PHONE1
170   REM       DATASET FORMAT: C$
180   :
```

3. Write a program that will select and display all names and numbers in a user-selected area code from PHONE1, with the option to continue or STOP when the display is complete.

```
100  REM     SELECT PHONE1 NUMBERS BY AREA CODE AND DISPLAY
110  :
120  REM     VARIABLES USED
130  REM      C$=DATASET
140  REM      R$=USER RESPONSE VARIABLE
150  REM      A$=USER SELECTED AREA CODE
160  REM     SEQ FILE NAME: PHONE1
170  REM      DATASET FORMAT:C$ (FIELDED STRING 15+15+3+8 CHARACTERS)
180  :
```

_____

_____

_____

_____

_____

_____

_____

_____

_____

_____

_____

_____

_____

_____

_____

_____

_____

_____

_____

_____

_____

4. Write a program to change each dataset in BUSINESS INVENTORY by increasing the unit sales price of each item by 10 percent. The program should display the product number, the old price, and the new price.

```
100   REM    INCREASE UNIT SELLING PRICE IN BUSINESS INVENTORY FILE &
             DISPLAY OLD AND NEW PRICE
110   :
120   REM    VARIABLES USED
130   REM      N$=ACCOUNT NUMBER
140   REM      P$=PROD.DESCRIPT.
150   REM      S$=SUPPLIER NAME
160   REM      L=REORDER POINT
170   REM      Y=REORDER AMOUNT
180   REM      Q=QUANTITY IN STOCK
185   REM      C=COST
190   REM      U=OLD UNIT SELLING PRICE
200   REM      U1=NEW UNIT SELLING PRICE
210   REM      R$=USER RESPONSE VARIABLE
220   REM      D$=CONTROL D
230   REM      R1=RECORD COUNT
240   REM      X=FOR NEXT LOOP CONTROL VARIABLE
245   REM    R-A FILE NAME: BUSINESS INVENTORY
250   REM      DATASET FORMAT: N$,P$,S$,L,Y,Q,C,U
260   REM      FILE LENGTH: 75 BYTES
270   :
```

```
]RUN
PROD#              OLD $           NEW $
1234               1.5125          1.66375
1235                .9559          1.05149

CHANGES DISPLAYED AND FILE CLOSED
```

_____

_____

_____

_____

_____

_____

_____

_____

_____

_____

_____

_____

_____

_____

_____

Answer Key

1.

```
100   REM    CREATE SEQ FILE PHONE1(NAME&# DIRECTORY)
110   :
120   REM     VARIABLES USED
130   REM       L$=LAST NAME (15 CHAR FIELD)
140   REM       F$=FIRST NAME (15 CHAR FIELD)
150   REM       A$=AREA CODE (3 CHAR FIELD)
160   REM       N$=PHONE # (8 CHAR CODE)
170   REM         C$=L$+F$+A$+N$ (CONCATENATED DATASET)
180   REM       D$=CONTROL D
190   REM       R$=USER RESPONSE VARIABLE
200   REM     FILE USED
210   REM       SEQ FILE NAME:PHONE1
220   REM       DATASET FORMAT:C$
230   :
240   REM    INITIALIZE
250   :
260   LET D$ =  CHR$ (4)
270   PRINT D$;"OPEN PHONE1"
280   PRINT D$;"DELETE PHONE1"
290   PRINT D$;"OPEN PHONE1"
300   :
310   REM    DATA ENTRY
320   :
330   HOME : PRINT "TYPE 'STOP' IF NO MORE ENTRIES.": PRINT
340   INPUT "ENTER LAST NAME:";L$
350   IF L$ = "STOP" THEN 760
360   IF LEN (L$) = 0 THEN  PRINT  CHR$ (7);"NO ENTRY MADE. PLEASE ENTER AS
      INDICATED.": PRINT: GOTO 340
370   IF  LEN (L$) > 15 THEN  PRINT  CHR$ (7);"LIMIT NAME TO 15 CHAR. AND

      REENTER.": PRINT : GOTO 340
380   IF  LEN (L$) < 15 THEN  LET L$ = L$ + " ": GOTO 380
390   :
400   INPUT "ENTER FIRST NAME:";F$
410   IF  LEN (L$) = 0 THEN  PRINT  CHR$ (7);"NO ENTRY MADE. PLEASE ENTER AS
      REQUESTED.": PRINT : GOTO 400
420   IF  LEN (F$) > 15 THEN  PRINT  CHR$ (7);"LIMIT NAME TO 15 CHAR. AND

      REENTER.": PRINT : GOTO 400
430   IF  LEN (F$) < 15 THEN  LET F$ = F$ + " ": GOTO 430
440   :
450   INPUT "ENTER AREA CODE:";A$
460   IF  LEN (A$) <  > 3 THEN  PRINT  CHR$ (7);"PLEASE ENTER 3 DIGIT AREA
      CODE ONLY.": PRINT : GOTO 450
470   :
480   PRINT "PHONE NUMBER FORMAT: 999-9999"
490   INPUT "WHAT IS THE NUMBER?";N$
500   IF  LEN (N$) <  > 8 THEN  PRINT  CHR$ (7);"ENTRY ERROR.": PRINT : GOTO
      480
510   IF  ASC ( MID$ (N$,4,1)) <  > 45 THEN  PRINT  CHR$ (7);"ENTRY ERROR.
      USE HYPHEN AFTER FIRST 3 DIGITS.": PRINT : GOTO 480
520   :
530   REM    DISPLAY DATA FOR VERIFICATION BEFORE WRITING TO FILE
540   :
550   HOME : PRINT "CHECK FOR MISTAKES!"
560   PRINT "LAST NAME: ";L$
570   PRINT "FIRST NAME: ";F$
580   PRINT "PHONE NUMBER: (";A$;") ";N$
590   PRINT : INPUT "IS THE INFO CORRECT(Y OR N)?";R$
600   IF R$ <  > "Y" AND R$ <  > "N" THEN  PRINT  CHR$ (7);"PLEASE ENTER 'Y'
      FOR YES OR 'N' FOR NO.": PRINT : GOTO 590
610   IF R$ = "Y" THEN 680
620   IF R$ = "N" THEN  PRINT : PRINT "PLEASE REENTER THE ENTIRE DATASET."
630   INPUT "PRESS 'RETURN' WHEN READY.";R$
640   GOTO 330
650   :
```

```
660    REM    CONCATENATE & WRITE DATASET
670    :
680    LET C$ = L$ + F$ + A$ + N$
690    PRINT D$;"WRITE PHONE1"
700    PRINT C$
710    PRINT D$
720    GOTO 330
730    :
740    REM    CLOSE FILE
750    :
760    PRINT D$;"CLOSE"
770    PRINT : PRINT "FILE CLOSED"
780    END
```

2.

```
100    REM     DISPLAY PHONE1 FILE CONTENTS
110    :
120    REM     VARIABLES USED
130    REM       C$=DATASET
140    REM       R$=USER RESPONSE VARIABLE
150    REM       D$=CONTROL D
160    REM     SEQ FILE NAME: PHONE1
170    REM       DATASET FORMAT: C$
180    :
190    :
200    REM     INITIALIZE
210    :
220    LET D$ =  CHR$ (4)
230    PRINT D$;"OPEN PHONE1"
240    :
250    REM     READ AND DISPLAY
260    :
270    ONERR  GOTO 370
280    PRINT D$;"READ PHONE1"
290    INPUT C$
300    PRINT D$
305    PRINT "NAME: "; LEFT$ (C$,30)
310    PRINT "PHONE: ("; MID$ (C$,31,3);") "; RIGHT$ (C$,8)
320    PRINT : INPUT "PRESS RETURN FOR NEXT DISPLAY";R$
330    PRINT : GOTO 280
340    :
350    REM     ERROR TRAP
360    :
370    IF   PEEK (222) = 5 THEN  PRINT : PRINT "ALL NUMBERS DISPLAYED.": GOTO
       420
380    PRINT  CHR$ (7);"UNUSUAL ERROR. PROGRAM TERMINATED.": GOTO 420
390    :
400    REM     CLOSE FILE
410    :
420    PRINT D$;"CLOSE"
430    PRINT "FILE CLOSED"
440    END
```

3.

```
100   REM     SELECT PHONE1 NUMBERS BY AREA CODE AND DISPLAY
110   :
120   REM     VARIABLES USED
130   REM       C$=DATASET
140   REM       R$=USER RESPONSE VARIABLE
150   REM       A$=USER SELECTED AREA CODE
160   REM     SEQ FILE NAME: PHONE1
170   REM       DATASET FORMAT:C$ (FIELDED STRING 15+15+3+8 CHARACTERS)
180   :
190   :
200   REM     INITIALIZE
210   :
220   LET D$ =  CHR$ (4)
230   PRINT D$;"OPEN PHONE1"
240   :
250   REM     USER SELECTS AREA CODE
260   :
270   INPUT "ENTER AREA CODE FOR THIS DISPLAY:";A$
280   REM   DATA ENTRY TESTS GO HERE
290   :
300   HOME : PRINT "AREA CODE SELECTED: ";A$
310   PRINT : PRINT "PRESS RETURN FOR NEXT DISPLAY"
320   :
330   REM     READ AND DISPLAY SELECTED #'S
340   :
350   ONERR  GOTO 470
360   PRINT D$;"READ PHONE1"
370   INPUT C$
380   PRINT D$
390   IF A$ <  > MID$ (C$,31,3) THEN 360
400   PRINT LEFT$ (C$,30)
410   PRINT "("; MID$ (C$,31,3);") "; RIGHT$ (C$,8)
420   INPUT "";R$
430   GOTO 360
440   :
450   REM       ERROR TRAP
460   :
470   IF  PEEK (222) = 5 THEN  PRINT : PRINT "ALL DISPLAYED.": GOTO 520
480   PRINT : PRINT "UNUSUAL ERROR. PROGRAM TERMINATED.": GOTO 520
490   :
500   REM   CLOSE FILE
510   :
520   PRINT D$;"CLOSE"
530   PRINT "FILE CLOSED"
540   END
```

4.

```
100   REM     INCREASE UNIT SELLING PRICE IN BUSINESS INVENTORY FILE &
      DISPLAY OLD AND NEW PRICE
110   :
120   REM     VARIABLES USED
130   REM       N$=ACCOUNT NUMBER
140   REM       P$=PROD.DESCRIPT.
150   REM       S$=SUPPLIER NAME
160   REM       L=REORDER POINT
170   REM       Y=REORDER AMOUNT
180   REM       Q=QUANTITY IN STOCK
185   REM       C=COST
190   REM       U=OLD UNIT SELLING PRICE
200   REM       U1=NEW UNIT SELLING PRICE
210   REM       R$=USER RESPONSE VARIABLE
220   REM       D$=CONTROL D
230   REM       R1=RECORD COUNT
240   REM       X=FOR NEXT LOOP CONTROL VARIABLE
245   REM     R-A FILE NAME: BUSINESS INVENTORY
250   REM       DATASET FORMAT: N$,P$,S$,L,Y,Q,C,U
260   REM       FILE LENGTH: 75 BYTES
270   :
280   REM     INITIALIZE
290   :
300   LET D$ =  CHR$ (4)
310   PRINT D$;"OPEN BUSINESS INVENTORY,L75"
320   :
330   REM     READ DATA, INCREASE PRICE, DISPLAY PRICES, WRITE NEW DATA TO
      FILE
340   :
350   :
360   PRINT "PROD#","OLD $","NEW $"
370   PRINT D$;"READ BUSINESS INVENTORY,R0"
380   INPUT R1
390   PRINT D$
400   FOR X = 1 TO R1
410   PRINT D$;"READ BUSINESS INVENTORY,R"X
420   INPUT N$,P$,S$,L,Y,Q,C,U
430   PRINT D$
440   LET U1 = U + U * .1
450   PRINT N$,U,U1
460   PRINT D$;"WRITE BUSINESS INVENTORY,R"X
470   PRINT N$: PRINT P$: PRINT S$: PRINT L: PRINT Y: PRINT Q: PRINT C:
      PRINT U1
475   PRINT D$
480   NEXT X
490   :
500   REM     CLOSE FILE
510   :
610   PRINT D$;"CLOSE"
620   PRINT : PRINT "CHANGES DISPLAYED AND FILE CLOSED"
630   END
```

APPENDIX A
ASCII CHARACTER CODES

DEC = ASCII decimal code
CHAR = ASCII character name
n/a = not accessible directly from the APPLE II keyboard

DEC	CHAR	WHAT TO TYPE	DEC	CHAR	WHAT TO TYPE
Ø	NULL	ctrl @			
1	SOH	ctrl A	26	SUB	ctrl Z
2	STX	ctrl B	27	ESCAPE	ESC
3	ETX	ctrl C	28	FS	n/a
4	ET	ctrl D	29	GS	ctrl shift–M
5	ENQ	ctrl E	3Ø	RS	ctrl ^
6	ACK	ctrl F	31	US	n/a
7	BEL	ctrl G	32	SPACE	space
8	BS	ctrl H *or* ←	33	!	!
9	HT	ctrl I	34	"	"
1Ø	LF	ctrl J	35	#	#
11	VT	ctrl K	36	$	$
12	FF	ctrl L	37	%	%
13	CR	ctrl M *or* RETURN	38	&	&
14	SO	ctrl N	39	'	'
15	SI	ctrl O	4Ø	(	(
16	DLE	ctrl P	41	)	)
17	DC1	ctrl Q	42	*	*
18	DC2	ctrl R	43	+	+
19	DC3	ctrl S	44	,	,
2Ø	DC4	ctrl T	45	–	–
21	NAK	ctrl U *or* →	46	.	.
22	SYN	ctrl V	47	/	/
23	ETB	ctrl W	48	Ø	Ø
24	CAN	ctrl X	49	1	1
25	EM	ctrl Y	5Ø	2	2

DEC	CHAR	WHAT TO TYPE
51	3	3
52	4	4
53	5	5
54	6	6
55	7	7
56	8	8
57	9	9
58	:	:
59	;	;
6Ø	<	<
61	=	=
62	>	>
63	?	?
64	@	@
65	A	A
66	B	B
67	C	C
68	D	D
69	E	E
7Ø	F	F
71	G	G
72	H	H
73	I	I

DEC	CHAR	WHAT TO TYPE
74	J	J
75	K	K
76	L	L
77	M	M
78	N	N
79	O	O
8Ø	P	P
81	Q	Q
82	R	R
83	S	S
84	T	T
85	U	U
86	V	V
87	W	W
88	X	X
89	Y	Y
9Ø	Z	Z
91	[	n/a
92	\	n/a
93	]	] (shift-M)
94	^	^
95	_	n/a

APPENDIX B

LIST OF PROGRAMS

Pages 158-159   Credit File Editor (Version 2)
SEQ source file name: CREDIT (from page 127)
SEQ temporary file name: TEMPFIL, renamed CREDIT
dataset format: C$, N$, r

Pages 161-162   Credit File Editor (Version 3) allows user to delete complete datasets, change any data item in a dataset, or insert a new dataset.
SEQ source file name: CREDIT (from page 127)
SEQ temporary file name: TEMPFIL, renamed CREDIT

Pages 173-174   Program called Merge which merges the contents of two separate files into one, maintaining numeric order of account numbers.
SEQ source files: TRANSACTION1 and TRANSACTION2 (from page 129)
SEQ merged file name: TRANSACTIONMERGE
dataset format: A$, T$, C$

Pages 183-184   This program writes (prints) form letters (each was stored as a sequential data file), personalized with names and address information from ADDRESS.
SEQ source file names: LETTER1, LETTER2, LETTER3 (from page 132)
dataset format: T$ (one string)
SEQ source file name: ADDRESS (from page S4—5A
dataset format: A$ (one fielded string)

Chapter 5 Self-Test

Page 193, prob. 1   Program to make a copy of ADDRESS.
SEQ source file name: ADDRESS (from page 131)
SEQ copy file name: ADDRESSCOPY
dataset format: T$ (one fielded string)

Page 194, prob. 2a   Program to create files of magazine titles. Two alphabetized lists of titles are provided for the creation of two files.
SEQ file names: MAGLIST1 and MAGLIST2
dataset format: T$

Page 194, prob. 2b   Read/display files with MAGLIST# format.

Page 195, prob. 2c   Program to merge MAGLIST1 and MAGLIST2, maintaining alphabetized order in merged file.

Page 197, prob. 3   Program to create or add to or delete from a file of reminders for household or office tasks.
SEQ original or source file name: WORK REMINDER
SEQ temporary file name: TEMPFILE, renamed WORK REMINDER
dataset format: one string (255 characters maximum)

Chapter 6

Page 204   First demonstration program to create a random access file whose data is simplified business inventory information.

R—A (Random Access) file name: INVEN
dataset format: N$, P$, Q
record length: 32 bytes

Pages 204–207   Same as above, except the number of records existing in the file is
written in record number zero.
R—A file name: INVEN

Page 208   Reads/displays INVEN using a FOR NEXT loop and the record count
stored in record zero.

Page 211   This program creates a file of customer phone numbers, using a customer
ID number, name, and phone number as data.
R—A file name: PHONE
dataset format: C$, N$, P$
record length: 36 bytes

Page 213   Reads/displays PHONE.

Page 216   Program that allows user to add datasets to PHONE.

Pages 217–219   Program to create a "master" file for user-determined data.
R—A file name: MASTER
dataset format: G$, S, Q, M$
record length: 66 bytes

Pages 220–222   Reads/displays MASTER.

Page 230   Program to make a random access file copy of MASTER.
R—A source file name: MASTER
R—A copy file name: STORE1
dataset format: G$, S, Q, M$
record length: 66 bytes

Page 224   This program uses INVEN in an example of how to change data in a random access file.
R—A source file name: INVEN (from pages 204–207)
dataset format: N$, P$, Q
record length: 32 bytes

Page 231   Program to convert (copy) a sequential file to a random access file.
SEQ file name: CREDIT (from page 127)
R—A converted file name: R—A CREDIT
dataset formats: N$, C$, R
record length: 29 bytes

Pages 232–234   Reads/displays random access file R—A CREDIT (but not the sequential source file from which it was copied or converted).
R—A file name: R—A CREDIT

Chapter 6 Self-Test

Page 247, prob. 1a   Program to create a somewhat realistic file of business inventory data.
R–A file name: BUSINESS INVENTORY
dataset format: N$, P$, S$, L, Y, Q, C, U
record length: 75 bytes

Page 248, prob. 1b   Read/display BUSINESS INVENTORY.

Page 249, prob. 1c   Program to create a sequential pointer file using data from a random access file. Pointer file's two data items are the customer number and the record in which that customer number appears in the random access file.
SEQ. pointer file namer: POINTER
dataset format: N$, R
R–A source file name: BUSINESS INVENTORY
dataset format: N$, P$, S$, L, Y, Q, C, U
record length: 75 bytes

Page 249, prob. 1d   Read/display POINTER.
SEQ file name: POINTER
dataset format: N$, R

Page 250, prob. 2   Program to make a copy of a random access file.
R–A source file name: R–A CREDIT (from page 231)
R–A copy file name: R–A CREDIT COPY
dataset formats: N$, C$, R
record lengths: 29 bytes

Page 251, prob. 3   Program to read/display the contents of both R–A CREDIT and R–A CREDIT COPY to verify a correct copy.

Chapter 7

Pages 256–257   This program permits the user to change the cost and unit selling price for an existing dataset in BUSINESS INVENTORY, using POINTER to identify the record for the dataset to be modified.
SEQ file name: POINTER (from page 249)
dataset format: N$, R1
R–A file name: BUSINESS INVENTORY (from page 247)
dataset format: N$, P$, S$, L, Y, Q, C, U
record length: 75 bytes

Page 261   This program is used to create three random access files of year to date budget information, based on the categories in the Chart of Accounts (page 258).
R–A file name: BUDGET# (where # is 1, 2, or 3)
dataset format: N$, A$, B$, E$
record length: 44 bytes

Page 261   Read/display BUDGET# files.

Chapter 7 Self-Test

Final Self-Test

Index

NOTES

NOTES

NOTES

NOTES

NOTES

NOTES